Microsoft®Press

Grown-Up's Guide to Computing

Mary Furlong and Stefan B. Lipson
Craig Spiezle, Consulting Editor

PUBLISHED BY
Microsoft Press
A Division of Microsoft Corporation
One Microsoft Way
Redmond, Washington 98052-6399

Library of Congress Cataloging-in-Publication Data
Furlong, Mary S.
    Grown-Up's Guide to Computing / Mary Furlong, Stefan B. Lipson.
        p. cm.
    ISBN 0-7356-0637-4
    1. Microcomputers.   I. Lipson, Stefan B.   II. Title.
QA76.5.F867   1999
004.16--dc21   99-27357
                                                       CIP

Printed and bound in the United States of America.

1 2 3 4 5 6 7 8 9   QMQM   4 3 2 1 0 9

Distributed in Canada by Penguin Books Canada Limited.

A CIP catalogue record for this book is available from the British Library.

Microsoft Press books are available through booksellers and distributors worldwide. For further information about international editions, contact your local Microsoft Corporation office or contact Microsoft Press International directly at fax (425) 936-7329. Visit our Web site at mspress.microsoft.com.

Acquisitions Editor: Susanne M. Forderer
Project Editor: Sandra Haynes
Manuscript and Technical Editing: ProImage

from Mary
This book is dedicated to all the people who gathered around
to make ThirdAge a reality—our founders, our Board,
our investors, our wonderful team and our dedicated
community members and volunteers. What an inspiration it
has been to collaborate with you. And, to my family, my love
and appreciation for you grows each day.

from Steve
Pure and simple: this book is lovingly dedicated to my wife,
Jane, for all that she does in and for our family.
Thanks to my babe of babes.

Contents

Acknowledgments

This book couldn't have happened without the help and support of a whole lot of good people.

Special thanks to:

Dr. Arthur Bakal, Dave Block, Jane Breyer —who gets the William Safire In-house Reference Award, Pat Christen at SFAF for "vocational flexibility", Priscilla Corona, Bill Glenn and Scott Hafner for great cheer, John "Goinsy" Goins, , Junior Hansen Jr., Alvin Henry and Keith Bupp, Derrell Ireton, Mrs. Janet Johnson (Madera) for TinoWorks 2.0, Melanie Kaplan at NS Research for marvelous email support, Lance Kolding for great coaching, Manny Lenter, Larry Levitt and Regina Aragon, Greta and William Lipson, Arthur Martin (better late than never!), Anita Mascoli and Nancy Werthan, David Mash for his understanding during TED and listening to the "author rant", Jack and Diane Pearce for kids and Italian Gardens, Kitty Reeve for mentoring and good counseling, Steven Shepard @ Thermal Wave Imaging, Dr. Steven Stein (Oakwood Hospital), Lori Bennett Stein, Mickey Stein, Raymond "Not Very Biggie" Walker for his upcoming Web work (!), Kelli Wiseth, , and Joe Zakaria, a true Prince .Thanks so much to all of the folks who were kind enough to share their stories with hundreds of thousands of Third Age community members who inspire us each day with their forum posts, home pages and chat conversations.

Special thanks to the team at ThirdAge Media with extra praise to Rick Bowers for great news, Leslie Goldman for editorial fire fighting, Mike Herring for taking care of business, Gary Hromadko for calling the shots, Sarah Johnson for being the Producer Deadline Goddess, Jane Lerner for her great artist impersonation— and artistic contribution, Beth Rhodes for her great grass roots links, Judy Schneider for so many links, and Joe Szeucs for technical assistance and constant good nature.

To Larry Levitsky for his vision and ongoing support. To Craig Spiezle for his valuable council and his continued efforts to connect seniors with technology. To Susanne Forderer, Amy Roberts, and Sandra Haynes for keeping the book on track and on Internet time. To the great team at ProImage for the attractive pages you see before you. And, a special thanks for Barb Ellsworth for insisting on the great "projects" idea!

Introduction

Why This Book?

Chances are good that, as an older adult reading this book, you are new to computing. Like tens of millions of other older adults, you sense that the world of computing must hold enormous promise but jumping on so late in the game is more than a bit daunting. Like boarding a moving train, the longer you wait, the harder it seems to get on.

The solution is simple—jump!

The metaphor ends there. Unlike a train, you won't get hurt when you leap on the PC band wagon, and the truth is, you really can't miss. The sooner you get on board, the sooner you'll be able to explore new vistas, make new discoveries, and enhance and improve your life.

Is There a Sacrifice?

So just when, in the course of a full day, are you supposed to find the time to learn about computing?

Between volunteer work, part-time work, community organizations, family and friends, most grown-ups are now busier than ever. That means that if you want to learn about computing, you have to sacrifice a substantial block of time—precious time, right?

Nope! What you'll quickly learn from this book is that the time you spend learning about your PC is not a sacrifice, it's an investment. Your computer will give you back whatever you put in—with interest! The time you give over to learning computing will pay off handsomely. With a little effort, you can easily learn to track your personal finances, follow the stock market, learn about genealogy, meet new people, subscribe (at no additional charge) to magazines and newspapers, shop from home, and immerse yourself in any and every pursuit imaginable. If you have family members who are also "wired," you can knit brothers, sisters, kids, and grandkids closer together with this extraordinary new technology. That's a pretty wise investment for you to make.

The time you spend learning about your PC is not a sacrifice, it's an investment.

How This Book is Organized

The book is organized into three different parts. You don't have to read the parts in order, but if you're a neophyte, you'll be glad you did. The following sections describe what awaits you.

Part I   A Look At the Extraordinary Lives of Ordinary People—Who Compute!

In Part I of the *Grown-Up's Guide to Computing*, we provide a glimpse of the kind of people who use computers and how they have made computing a part of their lives. We suspect you'll see bits of yourself in these stories, and that's as it should be. People from all walks of life and all ages have come to embrace computer technology, make it work for them, and benefit from it. You can, too!

People from all walks of life and all ages have come to embrace computer technology, make it work for them, and benefit from it.

You don't need a degree in computer or software engineering to use a computer. You'll learn from the people who appear in these pages how they have successfully challenged themselves to learn about computers for different reasons, and in the process found the time to make computing a part of their lives. From reading the stories here, you'll also see that your age is a benefit to learning and using computers, *not* a hurdle or an obstacle to overcome.

So take a quick read and see how diverse the community of computer users is and know that by learning about computers, you will become a contributor to that diversity and community!

Part II   The Digital Leap—Welcome Aboard

In Part II we offer an introduction to the areas of computing most important to you. We present those subjects that you'll find most rewarding and most beneficial so that you can become productive *fast*. Part II includes chapters on:

- Buying a computer
- Getting around your PC with Windows 98
- Using your computer to write
- Understanding the Internet
- Getting online
- Managing your e-mail
- Connecting with a community
- Searching the Internet to find anything—and everything!

Part III   PC Recipes

Part III is our own special cook book, filled with easy-to-follow recipes that will have you creating digital treats with your PC like Julia Child does with an oven!

Like any good cookbook, the recipes here are result *and* time driven. We aren't interested in complicated creations that you have to spend hours preparing; computing, like time in the kitchen can—should—be a joyous experience!

You can think of these recipes as themes. As you become more comfortable in your digital kitchen, you'll quite naturally come up with lots of variations. You may find that an alternate way of mixing the ingredients is easier or more logical for you or maybe you'd just like to add a splash of color to your garage sale announcements. That's perfect! Consider the recipes here as a collection of great starting points for you; they show some of the most practical options available to you and still offer plenty of room for embellishment and exploration.

We Make An Assumption

This book offers information, explanations and recipes based on computers running Windows 98. If you have an older computer and you don't have Windows 98, some of the settings may vary.

Young vs. Old

Is the content in this book somehow different than what you would get in a book intended for younger readers? The kernel of information is the same, but we have worked with older adults and computing for a long time. Mary is the Founder of SeniorNet and the Founder and CEO of Thirdage.com; Stefan worked with Mary at SeniorNet and was the founding community producer for Third Age.com; and Craig Spiezle is the Director of the Microsoft Senior Initative. Over the past years, we have come to clearly understand the PC needs of older users and how best to communicate that information. That's what's different about this book: it's for you.

We aren't interested in complicated creations that you have to spend hours preparing; computing, like time in the kitchen can—should—be a joyous experience!

Without Further Ado…

In the famous words of Hillel: "If not now, when?"

Enough stalling! We invite you to jump aboard and learn about this remarkable 20th century phenomenon known as personal computing and the Internet. We know you're ready, and we're confident that you will be happily overwhelmed by the PC experience and how it can and will change your life.

Happy computing!

In our world of big names, curiously, our true heroes tend to be anonymous.
In this life of illusion and quasi-illusion, the person of solid virtues
who can be admired for something more substantial
than his well-knownness often proves to be the unsung hero:
the teacher, the nurse, the mother, the honest cop, the hard worker
at lonely, underpaid, unglamorous, unpublicized jobs.

Daniel Boorstin, Historian

Part One

Our PC Pioneers:

Ordinary People. Extraordinary Lives.

Chapter One

Coming Back from "The Wreck"

Lowell Rase is an inspiration to people with special physical needs. He overcame many more physical challenges than most of us will face in a lifetime, and discovered firsthand how computers would enrich—and even save—his life!

He had a choice: either kill the two kids or take his chances with the ditch.

Lowell Rase took the ditch. He swerved his pickup truck off the road and just barely avoided the passenger sedan that had unexpectedly pulled in front of him. He saved the two moppy-headed passengers in the car that cut him off; but it cost him. Dearly. His truck, hurtling through the air, had enough momentum to roll side over side *and* end over end. When the nose of the truck met the earth on one of the rolls, Rase crashed through the windshield, face first, changing his life forever. That was February, 1990.

The Wreck

Lowell Rase refers to that catastrophic accident simply as "The Wreck."

Since coming home from Vietnam in 1967 after being stationed in Lai Khe with the 1st Squadron, 4th United States Cavalry, First Infantry Division, he had been a carpenter, contractor, and homebuilder in the area around his hometown of Van Wert, Ohio. On that fateful day, he was on his way to a job site about four miles outside nearby Lakeview with a single passenger, a fellow carpenter. Neither man was wearing a seat belt for the short ride, but when their truck went off the road, Lowell's buddy was able to brace for the impact by putting his feet on the dash and his hands on the roof. His passenger walked away slightly bruised, but largely unscathed. Lowell Rase did not.

As fire and emergency personnel administered aid and cut away his shredded clothing, Lowell regained consciousness. He was aware enough of the events taking place around him to know he couldn't feel his arms or legs. He recognized a friend from the fire department who was helping in the operation and said, "Hey, Pat, I can't be no paraplegic...I've got houses to build." But it was too late. The cards had been dealt.

Lowell Rase wound up at Ohio State University's Dodd Center for Spinal Cord Injury Rehabilitation. There he underwent two major surgeries, one for the spinal cord injury and the other to remove his teeth, which had been badly damaged when he went through the windshield. The prognosis: the spinal cord damage was irreversible. Lowell Rase would have to adapt to an entirely new way of life—as a quadriplegic.

Lowell Rase Meets the Computer

Lowell was 44 years old in 1991 when he left the rehabilitation centers and nursing homes. He met his new wife, Rebecca, a nurse's aid, at the Roselawn Nursing Home in Spencerville. After he settled in with Becky, he was back in touch with the rehab

"Hey, Pat, I can't be no paraplegic...I've got houses to build."

H*e had opportunities in computing if he could retrain himself in the field of computer-aided drafting.*

center. Lowell had absolutely no experience with computers, so imagine his surprise when the experts gave him their recom—mendation: he had opportunities in computing if he could retrain himself in the field of computer-aided drafting. Lowell says today that their recommendation "scared him to death" because he knew he would have so much to learn. He had some experience with drafting and mechanical drawing as a housing contractor, but that experience had been with pencil and paper!

They got him started by generously providing a custom-built PC. It was not much by today's standards, but the desktop machine had what he would need to get started: a 33-megahertz Intel 486DX microprocessor, 16 megabytes of RAM , a 120-megabyte hard drive, and a "co-processor"—the circuitry required to do the complex math calculations associated with the drafting and blue-print work he would be learning.

Just Turn It On. . .

The people at the rehabilitation staff were right in their assessment of Lowell Rase's career options. But without the use of his limbs, an off-the-shelf computer would never work. Every task, every switch, every key had to be accessible by some alternate means. To accommodate his kind of disability, the customized computer included a special headset fitted with three infrared pointers, two mounted on the sides and one on top. (When Lowell saw it, it reminded him of a civilian version of the headset used by Apache Attack Helicopter Pilots.) Wearing the headset, he could aim the infrared beams at a point on the screen, and the cursor would go to the point at which the three beams focused. When he wanted to write, he used WiViK, a word processing program that includes an on-screen keyboard (see Figure 1-1). Lowell could aim the infrared pointers at the appropriate letter on the keyboard and select a letter with a puff controller, an air hose into which he blows a burst of air. With this system, Lowell has learned to type about 20–25 words a minute. What kept him motivated? Wanting to learn.

W*hat kept him motivated? Wanting to learn.*

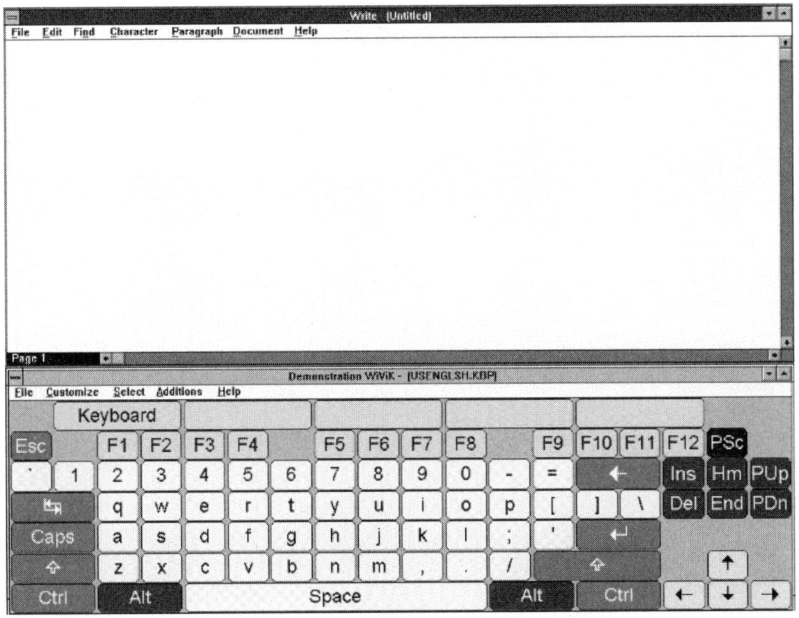

Figure 1-1
The WiViK keyboard lets a person type without the use of hands or arms

Lowell has had plenty of motivation. Along with trying to learn how to operate a computer without the use of his limbs, he needed to learn a lot about software. With about 20 hours of one-on-one tutoring, he began to study the ins and outs of Microsoft Windows. Learning to use online Help to obtain information helped a lot because searching for something on the computer was easier than setting up a way to turn book pages. But for his career path, he

N*o one could have predicted that his interest in online communities and meeting new people would soon save his life.*

needed to delve into the inner workings of AutoCAD(from AutoDesk, Inc.), a sophisticated CAD—computer-aided design—program used by architects, designers, and draftspeople all over the world (see Figure 1-2). The computing side of things was learned "by the seat of my pants," says Lowell, sometimes working 14 hours at a stretch. It took some getting used to, but he went through a couple of tutorials, and now he's comfortable with his AutoCAD drafting skills. His next challenge is to extend his range and professional toolbox to include another CAD program called Solid Builder, from Eagle Point Software.

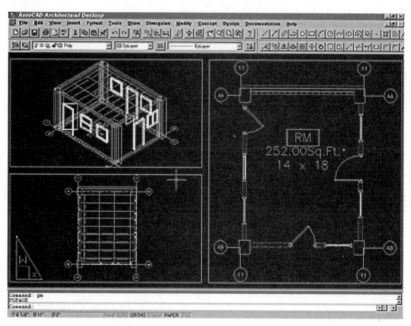

Figure 1-2
Lowell Rase is able to use AutoCAD, a sophisticated architecture and design program, to create blueprints and building plans

Saved—By a Chat

Since The Wreck, Lowell's overall computer experience has been remarkable, but no one could have predicted that his interest in online communities and meeting new people would soon save his life.

After spending a few years learning his way around the computer, Lowell discovered the Internet and began to explore what it had to offer. He put up his own Web site, at *http://www.angelfire.com/ok/bluprnts*, and used the Internet to help build up his business. In 1997, he read an article on Thirdage.com and, eager to be a part of an online community of grown-ups, joined the next day. He was glad he did. A few short weeks after joining, his wife, Becky—who rarely leaves him unattended—left the house for a couple of hours. During her absence, Lowell was participating in a chat on Thirdage.com when spasms of pain overcame him. He was unable to act except to let about 20 other Thirdage.com chat members know he was in serious trouble. While fellow chat participants stayed on the line and offered encouragement, one of his chat compatriots in Florida contacted a 911 number in Mr. Rase's county. Help was on the way. When the emergency medical team finally arrived, the EMT crew typed a thank you message to all the chat room participants and let them know everything was under control. Relieved that Lowell was being tended to, many of his chat room rescuers broke down in tears.

It's been about a year since his online rescue, but in that time, Lowell Rase has discovered immense potential and support on the Web. "When I first started chatting, I got a new Pentium 166 computer with 64 megs of RAM. I named it 'Frankenstein 2000,' but it just wasn't working. I couldn't even get on the Web." That's when a fellow Thirdage.com member whom Lowell calls a guardian angel, Don47, called. After hearing of Lowell's plight

After spending a few years learning his way around the computer, Lowell discovered the Internet and began to explore what it had to offer.

while chatting with other Thirdage.com members, Don47 decided to lend him a helping hand. He drove nearly 150 miles to troubleshoot Lowell's new machine and get him back online. For that kindness, Lowell is forever grateful. "I had never even met him," says Lowell. "I hadn't even met him online, and he really helped me out."

That wasn't the last time Lowell received help from online friends. In fact, when the engine blew in his 1977 Chevy Van that's fitted with a wheelchair lift, his online comrades banded together and raised about $4,000 to help him get it fixed. With their support, he was then able to replace the engine and badly worn brakes, ensuring that his only means of transportation remained available.

The Virtual Mayor

About the same time, a group of his online chat room acquaintances held an informal "virtual" election and voted unanimously to make Lowell the Honorary Mayor of Thirdage.com. "I was shoe-horned in," he says, chuckling. "And if you have complaints, don't send them to me! I just like talking to folks and helping when I can." In October of 1997, Lowell also became a chat manager, sort of a den father position to help keep everyone ruly, while running and monitoring various chat sessions on the Thirdage.com site.

Some Sound Advice

Ten years ago, Lowell Rase knew nothing about computers. Ten years ago, he never expected to be confined to a wheelchair. Yet,

"I just like talking to folks and helping when I can."

in one sudden twist of fate, he became a quadriplegic, and his future was inexorably linked to what he could learn about computers. "I'm no scientist," he says. "I'd never been near [a computer] before the accident, but I learned about 'em. . .just about anybody can." His advice to new computer users? "Don't think that you can't do it. You're never too old to learn, and you're never too young to teach. I learn a lot about computers and stuff online constantly." For those who face physical challenges and want to learn computing, Lowell says, "I don't think there's a disability that can't be overcome."

And how does he feel about helping others? "I'm happy to help whenever I can. I've been using a PC 'by the seat of my pants' for four years, and I have people ask me questions that I can't answer. But I'll flat-out tell you if I don't know the answers. You just keep going. Even when it seems hard to find the answers, I tell anybody and everybody: Don't give up."

Good advice from a man who came back from "The Wreck."

For information about accessibility options available for computer users, see the section entitled, "Special Needs," in Chapter 8 and visit *http: // www.microsoft.com/enable.*

> "*Don't think that you can't do it. You're never too old to learn and you're never too young to teach.*"

Chapter Two

An Insider's View:
The History of Computing

Here you will see how one physician's career has been influenced by computing, and how his experience has in turn affected family, friends, and students. In the process, you'll get an inside look at the history of computers and see how quickly this technology has evolved.

It's Thanksgiving and everybody is stuffed and happy. Family members have gathered in Michigan for this turkey celebration, and the head count of 24 loud and opinionated people doesn't explain why the noise level just went way up. The cause becomes apparent. Fifty-eight-year-old Dr. Mel Barclay, chief turkey carver and PC convert for many years, has started some friendly banter with family members who are strong Apple computer fans. Both of his kids have Apple computers, as do each of his three nephews and *both* of his sisters. Even his wife, Rosalyn, had a Mac until recently becoming a PC convert. Today's excitement is his 73-year-old sister's new Apple computer, an Apple Macintosh G3.

Dr. Barclay, an obstetrician and professor at the University of Michigan Medical Center, puts on a pretty good show in the good-natured bantering. For a physician who has spent an enormous amount of time learning about and teaching others about computing, he may like to tease people about their computers of choice, but he's gratified to know that so many people—including family members—have discovered this technology. Mel made the same discovery more than 20 years ago, when the first microprocessors became commercially available. As a result, he's had a chance to see firsthand the evolution of the PC industry.

The Gizmo Kid

Okay, Mel's not your standard obstetrician. His house and garage are scattered with all sorts of technologies: two-way radios, police scanners, pagers, cell phones, a ham radio (he got his operator's license many years ago), a meticulously restored Model A (see Figure 2-1), and a Chevrolet Suburban converted to run on natural gas (it's non-polluting). Throw in his gas welding gear and a basement carpentry shop, and you've got a touch of Dr. Frankenstein in the year 2000!

He's gratified to know that so many people—including family members—have discovered this technology.

Figure 2-1
Mel Barclay's technological pride and joy: An immaculately restored Model A Ford

66 **I**t *was obvious to me even then that this technology held so much promise as a tool for research and discovery. It was just a matter of time."*

Mel has always had a penchant for technology and problem solving, so it came as no surprise to those around him that he was drawn to computing. In 1973, an associate told him about microprocessors, the brains of what would become today's personal computers, and he ran out and got his first one that week. It was a KIM II, one of the first microcomputers. It had a 6502 microprocessor in it, the precursor to the microprocessors used in Apple's earliest Macintosh. "It was state-of-the art stuff by 1973 standards," Mel recalls fondly. "It had a whopping 4 KB of RAM (whereas a typical new computer today has 16,000 times that much), no monitor, no keyboard, and if you wanted software, you had to write it yourself." How did he learn to use a computer in the days that had few teachers and little documentation? The only option was asking the engineers themselves lots of questions. But warts and all, the computer world definitely had Mel hooked. "I wanted it to do everything," he says matter-of-factly. "Seriously, it was obvious to me even then that this technology held so much promise as a tool for research and discovery. It was just a matter of time."

Mel wouldn't have to wait that long. Learning all about newer computers as they appeared and relying on the University of Michigan mainframe for research, Mel finally got his hands on a just-released IBM PC/XT in the early 1980s. The IBM PC/XT was *the* machine that spawned "clones"—machines from competing manufacturers that were functionally identical to the IBM model but lower in price. This computer was a quantum leap forward. No Microsoft Windows existed yet, but the IBM computer ran MS-DOS, a disk operating system developed by Microsoft. When you wanted your computer to do something, you had to type in the appropriate, and often arcane, DOS commands. The PC/XT had a hard drive capable of storing what was then an impressive 10 megabytes of information (compared to standard computers today, which come with 6.4-gigabyte hard disks, 640 times the capacity!). It had a monochrome monitor (no color yet), no mouse, and no modem. The CPU, or central processing unit, was an Intel 8086 running at 4.77 megahertz, about 1/100th the speed of current microprocessors. The PC/XT had 64 kilobytes of RAM to start, about 1/1000th of what you typically get on a computer today! At the time, it was clearly a milestone in personal computing, and Mel was happy to have one.

The last 15 years have been witness to a host of astonishing developments in the computer industry. Mel has owned and used about 20 different computers over the years, ending up with his current machine, a 450-megahertz Pentium II. "That's more power on my desktop than the mainframe I used to access at the university!" he exclaims. He was right. It was only a matter of time.

What Does an Obstetrician Do with a Computer?

Mel accepts the joyful mysteries of life but wanted to shed light on the mysteries of the birthing process with Sherlock Holmes-like sleuthing. What if he could set up a computer to help monitor and alert doctors to things they couldn't see and previously could not detect?

To start, Mel wanted to use the computer to collect information on the basic physiology of the birth process. (See Figure 2-2 on

The last fifteen years have been witness to a host of astonishing developments in the computer industry.

page 15 for a picture of the doctor with a couple of his deliveries.) Mel and an associate built a computer system to detect and record pressure changes in the uterus during labor.

Collecting the data was one thing; analyzing it was another. So they designed the system to take advantage of the computer's ability to "crunch numbers," to do mathematical calculations with incredible speed. With that in place, they were able to do extensive data analysis, gain a better understanding of the fundamentals of uterine physiology, and understand what really happens in the delivery room.

Getting the Picture

Mel's work required that the data he was analyzing be represented *visually*. To facilitate this, he began exploring the world of "computer graphics," using a computer to create images. Computer graphics technology and the techniques for using it are now commonly employed in many areas, from architecture and automotive design to flight simulation and movies such as *Antz*, *Toy Story*, and *A Bug's Life*. Mel's purpose, however, was more specific. He needed computer graphics for "real-time imaging," the act of creating an image based on instantaneous data. The computer system he and his associate designed, therefore, was capable of recording the medical data, analyzing it, and producing three-dimensional pictures that could be more easily understood by the medical staff.

Can Your Doctor Keep a Secret?

Besides his research, Dr. Barclay has also been concerned with the issues of confidentiality and privacy and the impact that computer

H*e needed computer graphics for "real-time imaging," the act of creating an image based on instantaneous data.*

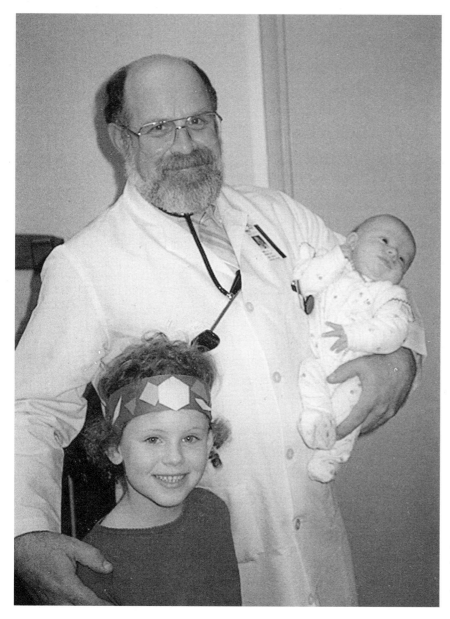

Figure 2-2
Dr. Mel L. Barclay, a practicing obstetrician and professor at the University of Michigan Medical Center, Ann Arbor, Michigan—with a couple of his deliveries

technology has had in these areas. To address these thorny topics, he has actively explored cryptography, the process of communicating information in secret codes.

As patients and as citizens, we all have a right to privacy, which means that our medical records must be kept secure, away from the prying eyes of others. When medical records are in electronic form, additional precautions must be taken to prevent them from being viewed or transmitted. To prevent such an invasion of privacy, Mel, with his son Josh (now a high school physics teacher), wrote an encryption program that could scramble—"encode"—a patient's medical records. The program required a special code to unscramble, or "decode," it. If any unauthorized individual opened the patient records, he or she would be met with an unreadable string of letters and symbols.

The Not-So-Nutty Professor: Learning and Teaching Computing

Medicine is Mel Barclay's profession, but he sees the importance of computing in the medical profession, in everyday life, and in teaching. "My students, my kids, my wife, my sisters, everybody benefits from learning about and using computers," he says. Mel notes that attitudes were very different just eight years ago, and he sees enormous changes in the last several years. "Nobody computed in the medical school. Everybody thought it was just for the engineering students," he remembers. "They all had to be dragged, kicking and screaming and objecting." Objections are rare now, and with Dr. Barclay present, the students assigned to obstetrics and gynecology must participate

"My students, my kids, my wife, my sisters, everybody benefits from learning about and using computers."

in a teaching conference—online—replete with pathologic data, images, and discussions. The students *must* learn the fundamentals of computing in order to get the information and get through the conference. "Faculty and students now recognize that computers are great tools for communication, and they're great for learning. They really help you learn on your own," he says. "I love the University of Michigan Web site (*http://www.umich.edu*) [shown in Figure 2-3]. There's an enormous amount of information and resources for students and faculty there for the taking."

> "*Faculty and students now recognize that computers are great tools for communication, and they're great for learning.*"

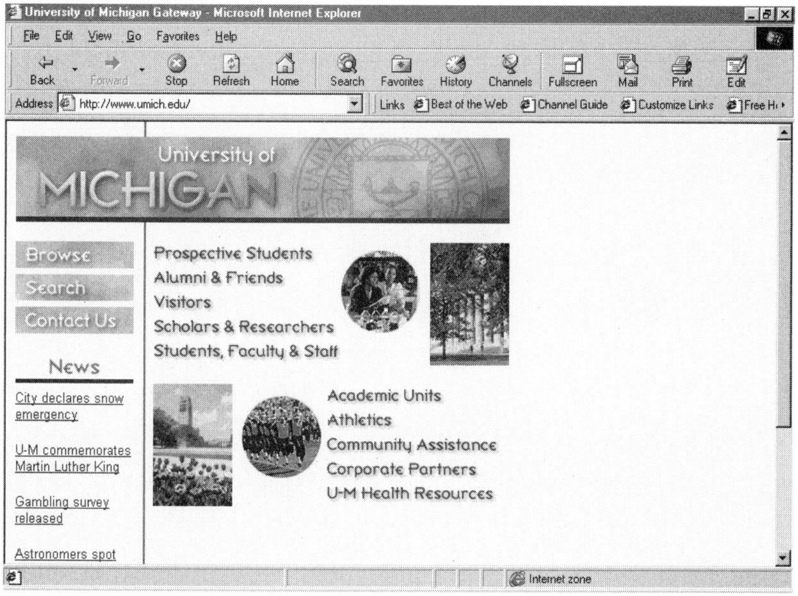

Figure 2-3
The University of Michigan Web site offers an enormous amount of information for the academically inclined

Medical Advice

Mel is very supportive of getting medical information via the Internet, but he draws a distinction between information and advice, recommending caution when looking for the latter. "There's a lot of chaff out there," he says. "It's not peer reviewed, it's not scientific, and much of it is anecdotal. You know, a friend of a friend of a friend says he was cured by eating Slim Jims and Circus Peanuts. You need to know the source of advice, and that can be very difficult on the Web."

Mel is quick to recommend, however, various sources of medical information on the Web. "The Web is an excellent way for patients to get more information," he says. He offers up the National Institutes of Health (*http://www.nih.gov*), The Library of Medicine (*http://www.nlm.nih.gov/*), and the National Center for Health Statistics (*http://www.cdc.gov/nchswww/*) as excellent Web resources. "You know your own body better than *anybody*, so doing your own research on what ails you can be enormously rewarding."

> *"The Web is an excellent way for patients to get more information."*

Some Sound Advice

Does Mel Barclay think computers are good for older adults? "Definitely," he says emphatically. "Computers are excellent tools for communication. For e-mail alone, a computer is worth having and, as a research tool, it's phenomenal." Mel's 73-year-old sister, an author with the new Apple computer, got hooked five or six years ago when she saw the power of doing word processing on a computer.

Mel has been learning about computers and teaching people about them for a long time, and his advice is straightforward. "It is hard and there are a lot of potholes, but it's a lot easier now than it used to be. Everybody learns differently and it's really important

> *"For e-mail alone, a computer is worth having and, as a research tool, it's phenomenal."*

that you know how you learn best, because computing can really be a head banger. I needed good human teachers, and I didn't have good human teachers, so I learned everything the hard way." Today many opportunities are available to find a class or computing center to learn from good teachers, and even Mel occasionally takes classes when he wants to learn about something new. He thinks classes "get you going and help you begin to explore. Otherwise, you don't always know where to start. Seeing someone do it once can make a big difference." Mel thinks it "doesn't take much to get a few successes under their belt" as people new to computers develop their confidence.

To learn more about what computer might work best for you, see Chapter 8, "The Secret to Buying Your Computer."

Mel thinks it "doesn't take much to get a few successes under their belt" as people new to computers develop their confidence.

≈ Chapter Three ≈

The Art of Living—On the Edge

Computers have had a significant impact on people involved in journalism and photography. Here is one example. At the same time, you'll learn how the computer and Internet community make a difference in people's lives, and how one woman is encouraging other women interested in computing.

The Time: 4:00 a.m.
The Place: A hotel room in downtown Peshawar, Pakistan
The Year: 1988
The Event: The Soviet pullout from Afghanistan
The Reporter: Catharine "Kitty" Reeve

Catharine (Kitty) Reeve was on assignment halfway around the world to watch history unfold. The Soviet Union had been defeated; Kitty was there on assignment and had to get the story to her editors at the *Dallas Times-Herald*, but the logistical obstacles were formidable. How did she expect to communicate with her editors and audience? Fast global communication back then just wasn't what it is today. In 1988 in Pakistan, Kitty had no working cellular phone, no laptop computer, and no satellite linkup; no fax machine was available to her. Most of the resources she had sat on a small desk before her in her hotel room: a pencil, a notepad, and a bad phone connection to her news desk in the U. S. But besides those meager tools, she had her well-honed reporting skills and the resourcefulness of a seasoned traveler. She filed the story by writing it on her notepad, phoning her editor, and reading it over the phone.

Photo by Catharine Reeve

Figure 3-1
Kitty Reeve captured the moment with this image of Afgahanistan refugee children

Ready for Anything

It's been awhile since Kitty Reeve has been back to that part of the world, but she is still always on assignment these days. This 58-year-old writer/photographer/artist who moved to Berkeley, California, in 1996 is right at home in the city forever associated with social dissent and cultural unrest. After talking to Kitty for even the briefest time, you realize that here she is truly in her element.

Call her on any given night and, although she's happy to talk with friends old and new, you'll typically hear the faint chatter of her computer keyboard as she works away intently, either meeting a newspaper deadline or researching a story on the Internet.

Because she has freelanced as both a writer and photographer for several newspapers and magazines, including the *Chicago Tribune*, and has authored a landmark book in experimental photography, you would think she'd slow down, maybe a little. Maybe her assignment in Afghanistan would have mellowed her a bit. Nope. Kitty just keeps on going.

Adventures in Silicon Valley

"I've made a vow to cut off the work at five so I can start to learn some new computer programs and do some exploring again, but I'm always against the wall with one deadline or another. And then there's life. . . ." she says. At this moment, the "life" is the arrival of her first grandson, Alexander. In spite of deadlines, Kitty is obviously savoring the joy that comes with being a new grandmother.

For a woman with such drive and passion, her introduction to and subsequent exploration of computer technologies have only added another dimension to her career. This is one woman whose energy seems boundless and, contrary to what she says, Kitty's days rarely end at five.

In this part of Northern California, much of the creative energy comes from the computer titans of Silicon Valley and the companies that have sprung up from Berkeley to San Francisco to San Jose—all of which are a stone's throw from Kitty's home. "I love being in the middle of things when so much is happening."

A Little History

Kitty did not have the typical upbringing of a pioneer. Born in Pensacola, Florida, and raised in Mobile, Alabama, Kitty didn't

> "*I've made a vow to cut off the work at five so I can start to learn some new computer programs and do some exploring again, but I'm always against the wall with one deadline or another.*"

challenge the ways of the South. "Drinking fountains were labeled when I was a kid," she remembers. Kitty is characteristically honest about the environment in which she was raised. "Many of the people I knew were prejudiced, and if all the people you're around think one way, it's hard to think another."

Prejudice didn't remain an issue for her for long. When she received a scholarship to Vanderbilt University in Nashville, Tennessee, it was, for Kitty, the beginning of her age of discovery.

Turning Points

She graduated from Vanderbilt in three years with a teaching certificate and a major in Latin. After she married, Kitty went to teach Latin in North Haven, Conn—that was the first time anyone in her family had crossed the Mason-Dixon line. The couple then moved to Washington, D.C., so that her physician husband could do his residency at the National Institutes of Health. It was in Washington, D.C., that they had three boys. When her first baby, Stephen, was born, Kitty's priorities changed: "I looked at my son and thought, "Who needs Latin?" The family moved to Chicago, where they lived for several years and then spent a year abroad in London. Upon their return, the marriage began to unravel and the couple divorced.

None from Column A and None from Column B

Alone with the three boys and faced with the harsh reality of being on her own, Kitty assessed her new status. Before she divorced, she made some lists. List A included everything she thought she *could* do based on education, experience, and talent. List B included

When she received a scholarship to Vanderbilt University, it was for Kitty, the beginning of her age of discovery.

what everybody, herself included, thought she *should* do based on the same criteria.

But she had a third list, a private one, and the words "should" or "could" didn't appear anywhere on it. That list consisted solely of things that Kitty would regret if she didn't pursue them, including writing, photography, and dance. Making her choices didn't take her long: she would choose from the last list and follow her passions of writing and photography. She was to have no regrets.

Pedal to the Metal

Wasting no time, Kitty enrolled in a photography course at The Chicago Art Institute and was fortunate to have Barbara Crane, winner of The Society of Photographic Educators' "Educator of the Year" award, as her teacher. "I thought I knew a lot," says Kitty. "I couldn't have been more naïve. I didn't even know photography was an art form. I barely crawled out of that class, but it was a wonderful experience with alternative and experimental approaches to photographic imaging. I never thought of myself as an artist, and suddenly I was one."

In 1977, Kitty began working as a photographer, and her willingness to experiment and try new techniques led her to a full fellowship at the Alden Dow Creativity Center in Midland, Michigan. That in turn led to a book contract with Prentice-Hall and her co-authored book on alternative photographic methods, *The New Photography*. That landmark title—still in print now, some 15 years later—is frequently used as a textbook in art schools and universities. Kitty had also begun to freelance for the *Chicago*

> "**M**aking her choices didn't take her long: she would choose from the last list and follow her passions of writing and photography. She was to have no regrets."

"**M**y editor gave me the opportunity to do feature stories for the Sunday Magazine *section, which was very exciting yet terrifying for me.*"

Figure 3-2
Kitty Reeve: photographer, journalist, artist

Tribune at about the same time. "My editor gave me the opportunity to do feature stories for the *Sunday Magazine* section, which was very exciting yet terrifying for me. She was the most demanding —the hardest person to work for—*and* she was my mentor. She just turned me on to writing!"

T*he motivation of being able to make her living doing the things she loved kept her going.*

K*itty was referred to* http://www.thirdage.com *and became a Web producer, forum host, content developer, feature writer, and Internet Chat Host for the site.*

The Computer Challenge

At the *Tribune* in 1988, Kitty was introduced to a PC. At that time, she used a PC to write and file her feature stories. Although she does not consider herself a technical person, the technology piqued her curiosity. The motivation of being able to make her living doing the things she loved kept her going. Says Kitty: "In economic terms, it's fun to earn one's living—or a good part of one's living—through work that is so enjoyable, which is what working on the Internet is for me." Her son David, a computer programmer who has helped her learn many things about computers, recently helped set her up with a 300-megahertz desktop PC.

After much freelancing, Kitty's adventurous side and her passion for new intellectual vistas led her to San Francisco and neighboring Berkeley. There she has been able to immerse herself in the culture and community of computing.

To document her explorations and to continue on her experimental photographic forays, Kitty recently obtained an Olympus Digital camera. The camera includes a serial interface so that she can transfer pictures from the filmless camera right to her PC. Although she denies having any innate technical prowess, her determination gets her where she wants to go.

Internet Chat Visionary

Shortly after arriving in California, Kitty was referred to *http://www.thirdage.com* and became a Web producer, forum host, content developer, feature writer, and Internet Chat Host for the site. Internet chats, the computer equivalent of the old telephone party lines, allow a number of people to communicate "live" by typing messages to one another. In a chat, there *should* be more order than chaos, but with the wrong chat host, it can quickly degenerate into a less-than-valuable experience. Kitty was the right host and developed a loyal following.

Kitty carefully set out to define her weekly chat hour to capture the imagination of other participants. She brought in vital guests and transformed her chat into a virtual Bauhaus, a place where men and women from all walks of life could come and share their ideas and views. It was a smashing success.

When asked what made her online chat successful, she deflects credit and instead describes the ingredients she used in her recipe. "A common purpose. If the chat doesn't have a purpose, it's banal. If it's the weather, it's no good. If it's what you did this morning, forget it. We always had great topics and great special guests. The fact that participants expressed very different opinions was expected and welcomed."

Kitty loves chats, but what are chats really good for? "Chats are a fabulous vehicle for forming community, and informing and expanding the horizons of participants, and having a lot of fun," she says. "Topic-centered chats are a wonderful way to get to know other people. We even had as guests a couple who had met online and wound up getting married."

She is quick to recommend those chats that engage and stimulate all the participants. She also raises a couple of flags. "Be careful of people you meet online," she says. "The virtual nature of the medium makes it easy for people to be dishonest, so you have to watch what you say and how much you are willing to reveal—

> "*Chats are a fabulous vehicle for forming community, and informing and expanding the horizons of participants, and having a lot of fun.*"

Older women need to know that there's a place for them to contribute, especially in computing and on the Internet, and that they stand to benefit by getting out there and grabbing the reins.

and to whom. When you find a good community, though, it can be magical. I can honestly say I have met some extraordinary people and new friends through the Internet. It's a remarkable experience."

Empowerment

Whether Kitty is out on assignment, at a speaking engagement, or on her daily bike ride up the hills of Berkeley, her mission and her goal are single minded: empowerment. "Older women need to know that there's a place for them to contribute, especially in computing and on the Internet, and that they stand to benefit by getting out there and grabbing the reins." Kitty Reeve is a wonderful role model. She has grabbed the reins on the Internet and everything else in her life, and wants other older women to know that they can do it, too.

Kitty always comes back to the theme of empowerment and how women can benefit from the Web, and so she's very excited about her work with the women's group Women in Multimedia (*http://www.wim.org*). At wim.org, Kitty co-founded and co-chairs a new group, WIM 40+, aimed at women 40 and over who either want to work in the computer field or are already in the industry and want to stay abreast of career opportunities and industry developments. The first meeting to get women with this common interest together attracted 44 women, several of whom are in their 60s.

Each One Teach One

Kitty is always willing to share what she has learned, and she encourages the approach of "Each one teach one" to help share information and get new people into computing. As she upgrades to new computers, she gives her previous one to a friend and helps get that person started. She knows many women in their 60s and 70s who are enjoying the opportunities their computers give them, such as e-mail, chats, and even developing their own Web sites! Kitty also encourages older adults to consider the idea of signing up as an employee of a temporary agency. The agencies will train new workers for free, and the experience can help build confidence and even put more spending money in your pocket.

Some Sound Advice

Kitty has a lot to say about the key challenge that she sees others face related to computers: their own fear. "People feel a lot of fear about destroying their PC," she says. Her son hammered it into her head over and over again that she really couldn't hurt her computer, and even if something did go wrong, there always was a way to fix it.

She also encourages adults to understand not just what keys to use but also what is really happening when they are using the computer. She says that context is important and was something she struggled with when she tried to learn by trial and error. She has a large collection of books on computing and uses them to help her learn new software.

To learn more about Internet chats, see Chapter 16, and for more information about books that help users learn not just how to do something but what is happening, see the Microsoft Press Web site at *http://mspress.microsoft.com* (click Find A Book) or *http:// shop.microsoft.com*.

She also encourages adults to understand not just what keys to use but also what is really happening when they are using the computer.

≈ Chapter Four ≈

Resistance Was Futile

Computers help make businesses operate more easily. Read how one business owner overcame his reluctance to let computers help him be successful and now recommends them to everyone.

A modest man of 66, Al Young has his own business, a solid family, a commitment to his church, and a lifelong dedication to helping others. Helping his community has been the theme of his life; when friends, family, or community members ask for support, Al is there. For a man to raise six children, maintain a marriage, volunteer for numerous organizations, be active in his church, *and* run a business that employs some 300 workers—as Al Young's does—he needs to be of exceptional character. And he needs to be exceptionally organized! For the character part, Al finds support in his family and church. For the organizational part, he has come to rely on his computer, a technology that he resisted until he saw what impact it could have on his business and his personal life.

Some History

Al grew up in Apex, North Carolina, a small town just outside Raleigh. After high school and two years of community work, Al returned to Apex, where he remained only briefly before joining the U.S. Army to be assigned to the Military Police Corps in Augusta,

Georgia. His three-year enlistment started at the end of the Korean conflict and was an exciting time for him. He would have stayed in, too, having qualified for the Officer's program, but his ambition had always been to go to college. So when he was accepted at Brigham Young University in Utah, he jumped at the chance. He moved to Utah and worked hard in his studies in the College of Business Administration. While in Utah, he had the good fortune to meet Rose, the woman who would become his wife. After college, they moved to Los Angeles, California, where he went to work for a major theater chain right in the heart of Hollywood. After about 15 years, Al began to look around a bit and found—or more accurately, made—a niche for himself in the airline industry. His new business afforded him the opportunity to learn about computers.

A New Business Is Born

In 1982, Al identified an accounting problem that cost the airlines millions of dollars, and he had a solution. He saw that airlines weren't being reimbursed by other airlines for certain kinds of transferred ("off-line") tickets. He approached one airline and proposed that they outsource the task to him. "It's very difficult to go to a company and tell them they are making some mistakes and that you can solve their problem in that area," Al says. "But that's what we did, and they listened and we got a contract with our first airline."

Although that contract was a successful start, Al knew he would have to win over more airlines in order to make the business grow. That's when a computer entered the picture. "I resisted," he says matter-of-factly. "I figured the process was already complicated enough, and a computer would only make it more complicated. I was terribly wrong about that."

Al soon saw that a computer would be a pivotal part of the company's success. He knew how important it was to produce high-quality, professional-looking letters and proposals if he was to secure more contracts, and the computer promised to do that and more. Now 67, he bought that first computer when he was 52 years old. He admits that he felt rather intimidated by how much he had to learn, but his need for an efficient accounting system was his motivation. His reward was the fun of seeing that accounting system take shape without a dozen different paper-based ledgers.

With a personal computer, a copy of Microsoft Works, and a good printer, Al's proposals took on an air of professionalism to which the airlines responded well. "The companies took us seriously because of the service we offered and what we could do with the computer. As a result, our business expanded nicely," Al says.

Accounting for Growth

How much has the company grown? The business now employs about 250–300 part-time employees with approximately 50 people waiting for a position. The waiting list exists because Al's business offers a unique form of employment: part-time work with employees operating from home for only a few hours a day. The stay-at-home staff does not require any computers. Workers examine literally millions of tickets, by hand, to find those that need to be cashed in by one airline from another airline.

Employees get paid with a combination of cash and travel vouchers, and many of Al's workers have saved between $5,000

> *" I resisted," he says matter-of-factly. "I figured the process was already complicated enough and a computer would only make it more complicated. I was terribly wrong about that."*

and $10,000 in travel credits by the end of a year. It's a great deal for his employees, but it means that Al has a number of typical accounting tasks that he must perform, tasks that would require a staff of accountants—or one good computer—to complete. It was fortuitous that Al accepted the computer when he did, because doing so not only helped him bring in new business but also track and maintain his increasingly complex in-house accounting needs.

How Did He Do It?

Al started early with a Microsoft Works spreadsheet, graduated to Microsoft Excel, and then incorporated other programs for tasks that performed peripheral accounting tasks. What was his strategy for learning about computers? "More clicking," he says. He likes the trial-and-error method and chose that over classes, books, online help, or calling someone with related experience. He does encourage people to take classes, however, believing that he might be more proficient or have become proficient more quickly if he had done that himself. But he sees no substitute for "hands on, do-it-yourself" learning at the keyboard.

On the Personal Side

Al knows the impact computing has had on his business, and because his office is in his home, that's where he uses his computers—three of them, no less. He admits to taking some time for fun with a computer, too, with Microsoft Flight Simulator, an occasional game of Solitaire, e-mail to all his family, and, of course, some surfing to investigate investing or favorite topics.

Al doesn't hesitate to extol the virtues of computing in his personal life. " I couldn't do without it. It's so practical for writing

The companies took us seriously because of the service we offered and what we could do with the computer. As a result, our business expanded nicely".

alone. Every adult should take the time to develop enough skill to leave [his or her] life history, to write it down, so that the kids can tell their kids, and the grandchildren, about their mom and dad, grandma and grandpa." To that end, Al, using Microsoft Word, has been working on his own life story and the family genealogy. He's also thinking about trying out voice-activated software to be able to record his memories.

Giving Back

Since his days in Apex, Al has always been a giver and a helper and, when possible, he has helped others to learn about computers as well. Recently, he gave a Pentium PC to an official in his church and provided assistance in bringing everyone using it up to speed. With his involvement in volunteer opportunities, Al isn't looking for applause or recognition, he's just looking to make a difference. Being a devoted father and grandfather, he spent years working with kids ages 11 to 18 in both the church and the Boy Scouts of America. He reminisces about some great trips, including an awesome 83-mile canoe trip on the Colorado River. Although canoeing gets his adrenaline pumping, the yearly summer vacations with two to four of his grandkids offer this proud grandparent another kind of high.

Some Sound Advice

Al Young is a practical man. He's not one to adopt technology for appearance's sake, and he's interested in something only if it helps him get the job done. It should come as no surprise, then, that Al highly recommends upgrading to Windows 98. "I'm thoroughly

"I couldn't do without it [computing]."

sold on it, and I absolutely love it over Windows 95," he says. "And I'm happy with MSN (Microsoft Network). I send e-mail to all the kids and grandchildren all over the country."

A*l isn't looking for applause or recognition, he's just looking to make a difference.*

Figure 4-1
Al Young supports numerous causes as well as his family and church

Al's other advice is a reflection of his dedication to family: "You owe it to your children and grandchildren to get a computer. If I did nothing else in my retirement than my genealogy, that would be enough. Kids don't know enough about their parents, and it's not the kids' fault," he continues. "Kids can't do that themselves. If all you do is write about yourself for your kids, it makes the computer worth it. Every grandparent *owes* that to their kids."

To learn more about how to get started writing with your computer, don't miss Chapters 10 and 11.

> Y*ou owe it to your children and grandchildren to get a computer. If I did nothing else in my retirement than my genealogy, that would be enough.*

Chapter Five

Computers? Who Needs One?

Even if you're starting late in life with "no previous experience," computers can add value and efficiency to your work, hobbies, and your ability to keep in touch, as you will see here.

Iowa. The Heartland of America. Rhapsodized by folk and country singers alike is Jones County, eight miles outside the town of Monticello and the location of Beal Farms. The Beal home looks out over a 509-acre spread of rolling fields with a creek running right through the property. Eileen and Bill Beal, along with their son, John, preside over a farm that gives every appearance of an Andrew Wyeth painting. (See Figure 5-1 for a view of the farm.)

But look a little closer, and you can see that something in this bucolic landscape is slightly askew. The 75-year-old homestead, the barn, the farm implements, the cattle and hogs all are right for this canvas, but there are some signs that point to a different image, signs of a creeping digital influence. Outside, near the house, an oversized satellite dish points skyward to bring in entertainment and cultural events from all over the country. And if you look in the front window, right next to the television set, you see the glow of a Pentium PC loaded with the necessary software to do the farm's bookkeeping.

Figure 5-1
*An aerial view of a portion
of Beal Farms*

The computer's arrival was inevitable, really. The satellite dish was installed about five years ago and, at the urging of the Beal's computer-savvy daughter, Barbara, the PC finally showed up in May of 1997. Eileen Beal, then 74, wasn't convinced she needed it or wanted it, but one day, daughter Barbara called to say she was sending one. Eileen thought she didn't need a computer just to do the farm books, but she grew comfortable quickly with the computer and abandoned the old tools of her trade: an adding machine and a handwritten, double-entry ledger system. Eileen has grown to enjoy doing the farm's bookkeeping with the computer, so she's glad she made the leap. What's more, she's found lots of other things to do with her computer, such as playing a miniature golf program she received for Christmas.

Eileen has grown to enjoy doing the farm's bookkeeping with the computer, so she's glad she made the leap.

Down on the Farm

The Beals established the Beal Family Corporation almost 20 years ago. Creating a farm corporation allows them to run the business efficiently with each member of the family as a shareholder. John Beal is now the President and runs the farm, with Bill as acting CEO and Eileen as the Secretary Treasurer. (See Figure 5-2.) The corporation can include up to 10 family members, so their daughters, who live all across the country, are also a part of the business. Regardless of titles, though, this is very much a family farm.

T*his is very much a family farm.*

Figure 5-2
Farmers Bill and Eileen Beal—without their Pentium II PC!

The Beals have been in Jones County for 25 years, moving there when their previous farm in Ohio was in the path of the ever-creeping city and fell victim to urban sprawl. The current farm is divided so that 325 acres of the land are given over to grain (corn, hay, and soybeans), and the remaining land is for the real cash crop, namely beef cattle and hogs. The work continues year 'round, including the bookkeeping chores. As the farm's Secretary Treasurer, Eileen must keep things accurate and current. That's where the Pentium II PC and the spreadsheets she creates in Microsoft Works really shine. She likes Microsoft Works because it is easy to use and has just what she needs, but not "too much."

Chores—For the PC

Bookkeeping for the farm wasn't always so easy. Before Eileen had the PC, her double-ledger system of bookkeeping was time-consuming and prone to simple math errors. The double ledger system allowed her to cross-reference expenses to ensure accuracy because two different tallies should have always come out equal, but in order to do the tallies, Eileen relied on an adding machine.

With Microsoft Works and the spreadsheet module it includes, her bookkeeping has been tremendously simplified. The tallies she once did on her adding machine can be executed instantly with the AutoSum feature. "When you select the AutoSum option and drag your mouse over the numbers in the column, the spreadsheet *automatically* totals them for you and puts that sum in the cell you designate to be the Total cell." The other efficiency she appreciates is being able to make a change or to fix a mistake in a column, and see the new total automatically recalculated to reflect the correction.

With Microsoft Works and the spreadsheet module it includes, her bookkeeping has been tremendously simplified.

L*earning to use the spreadsheet in Microsoft Works was relatively easy for Eileen, and she figured out how to accomplish many actions on her own.*

"You can make as many changes as you want, and the sum will adjust accurately, automatically, and instantaneously every time."

Learning to use the spreadsheet in Microsoft Works (see Figure 5-3) was relatively easy for Eileen, and she figured out how to accomplish many actions on her own. Some problems were more challenging. With warnings from her daughters to make sure she "backed up" all that work on the computer, she tried to figure out how to do it, but somehow it just didn't make sense. She wasn't sure she was doing it right until she read about the process in *The Way Microsoft Windows 95 Works*, an illustrated guide from Microsoft Press. She has also learned to use online help and usually finds it helpful.

When All the Chores Are Done

Although she doesn't like to push herself, Eileen has really begun to enjoy working on her PC. To add to her growing repertoire of computer skills, she took a course in Window 95 at the nearby

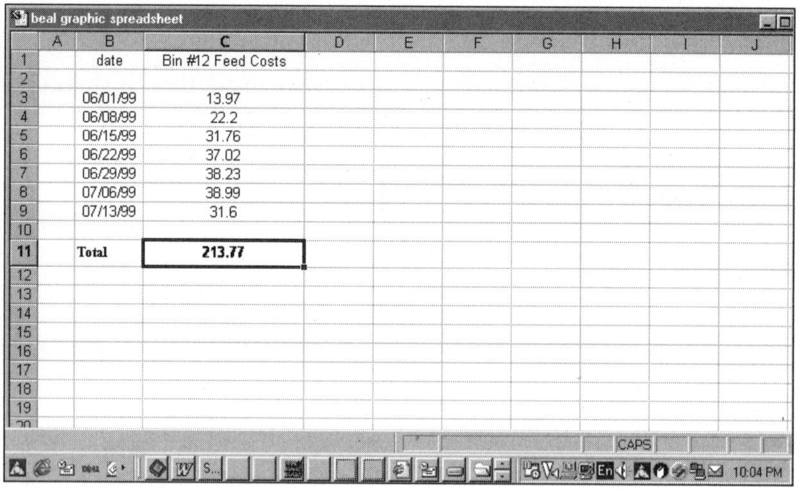

Figure 5-3
Eileen Beal uses her Microsoft Works spreadsheet and the AutoSum feature to speed up the farm's bookkeeping tasks

community college and also completed a course on the Internet sponsored by the Iowa League of Women Voters. The Internet course gave her a better sense of how to navigate on the Web. She and her husband are devotees of harness horse racing, so Eileen has enjoyed searching out Web sites featuring their favorite pastime.

In addition, Eileen has found the computer and Microsoft Works beneficial in the way they have helped her create a genealogical chart of her husband's family. She also used Microsoft Works to transcribe her mom's diary so that she could pass the memory of her mother on to her children.

In the last year or so, she has had to make room for another dedicated PC user, namely her five-year-old grandson, Joshua. "Joshua has some Winnie the Pooh CD-ROMs that he loves to play," says Eileen. "It's amazing to me how he catches on to it so quick!" She was the one who got Joshua started with the computer. How did she do it? "Oh, I just did it the first time or two while he watched, and then he said he could do it, and he has been playing with it ever since." Joshua even knows how to install a new CD program he receives—thanks to those "just put it in" installation instructions.

She's finding that more of the women in the area are going online and making use of computers to keep in touch with their kids.

Some Sound Advice

Eileen's computer experience hasn't been very extensive, but she enjoys what her PC has allowed her to do. Although she's not interested in immersing herself in the intricacies of computing, she still wants to learn and explore—and share her own experience. She's finding that more of the women in the area are going online and making use of computers to keep in touch with their kids.

L*ike so many others, Eileen has discovered the power of e-mail and recommends it highly.*

Like so many others, Eileen has discovered the power of e-mail and recommends it highly. "My kids are in Nebraska, Minnesota, and Washington, and my brothers and sisters are in Ohio, Tennessee, and Oklahoma. E-mail really helps us to stay in touch no matter how spread out we are."

She did find many of the options vexing at first. "It can be confusing, like a roadmap," she observes. "There are a lot of ways to get to where you're going, but if you take a wrong turn, you can get all messed up. Nowadays, though, when something comes up, I just figure it out, and now that I have used it for a while, time goes by real fast when I'm working on it." If she had it to do over again, Eileen says she would have taken the class at the community college earlier. By the time she took it, she didn't learn that much, but it helped to build her confidence so that she felt that she really did know what she was doing with her computer. What does she suggest to others? "For one thing," she says, "I keep a notebook with my questions in it, divided into different sections for different subjects, like printers and spread-sheets. Keeping a notebook really helps."

Eileen offers up one last bit of advice to folks who don't live close to a major metropolis: "Make sure you find a service provider (the companies that give you access to the Internet) that has a local access number, or your phone bills will shock you!"

You'll read more about service providers and getting on the Internet in Chapter 13 of this book.

44

Part One Our PC Pioneers: Ordinary People. Extraordinary Lives.

Chapter Six

Bond's the Name. James Bond...Johnson

Not everyone has 10 hours a day to spend on the Internet, but James Johnson demonstrates how engaging it can be to be able to research your favorite interests and share them with friends and acquaintances around the world through the mediums of e-mail and the Internet.

Talk on the telephone to retired U.S. Army Colonel James Bond Johnson (see Figure 6-1) and, between his incredible stories, the booming resonance of his voice, and the John Wayne-like drawl, you get the distinct impression that 1) he's at least 6' 4" and 2) he could easily throw your Toyota off a cliff.

Okay, we were only half-right: Mr. Johnson is 5' 10" .

His name—to get that out of the way—has nothing to do with Ian Fleming's fictional secret agent. Colonel Johnson's father, a Methodist minister for 50 years, named his son to honor the preacher who was his mentor and guide to the ministry.

But make no mistake about it, Texas-born James Bond Johnson is the kind of guy who has a million great stories. And when you hear his background, you'll understand that those stories come from a life rich with amazing experiences. In fact, if you do a simple Internet search on his name, you'll come up with more than 100 sites that provide information about him and his hobby! For someone who "didn't have time" for the Internet, how did that happen?

Is This Guy for Real!?

Growing up in Texas, James finished high school at the age of 15 when World War II was just beginning. He was hired as a full-time police reporter at age 16 by the *Fort Worth Star-Telegram* and received his degree in journalism in just three years. He later received master's and doctorate degrees in clinical psychology, along with a divinity degree. In World War II, he was in the Army Air Corps. In 1948, he was commissioned in the Marine Corps Reserve and received officer's basic training at Quantico in Virginia. He served as a Marine Corps Technical Advisor on three Hollywood films: *Retreat Hell* with Russ Tamblyn, *The Sands of Iwo Jima*, and *Flying Leathernecks*, the latter two starring John Wayne.

During the Korean War, James served as a public information officer with the United States Marines. Receiving yet another commission in the Army during Vietnam, he was a psychological-political officer working under General Alexander Haig. Four churches exist today because he was their pastor, and in 1970, he founded a youth home for emotionally disturbed teenagers in Long Beach, California. He has been a board-certified and state-licensed clinical psychologist since 1960. Up until two years ago, he was Senior Pastor of the First United Methodist Church of San Pedro, California.

Ian Fleming could never have imagined James Bond Johnson.

The Colonel Gets Bit—By the Computer Bug

As spellbinding as his stories are, we wanted to talk to James about his computing experience, and we got an earful.

James, age 72, has been a computer enthusiast for a very long time, having obtained his first PC back in the early eighties. It

Figure 6-1
Colonel James Bond Johnson, Retired, United States Army

What was his motivation? He "hated White Out," the standard necessity for correcting typing mistakes in the days of typewriters.

had little memory and two floppy drives, and the daisy wheel printer was definitely slow. What was his motivation? He "hated White Out," the standard necessity for correcting typing mistakes in the days of typewriters. As word processing software added more features and more functionality, he was motivated to learn how to take advantage of them and enjoyed seeing how each new upgrade allowed him to add more fonts and features to his word processing. His second machine was an Intel 386[1]-based computer that gave him the opportunity to learn Microsoft Windows. He didn't have any formal computer classes, and he didn't read technical books very often, but he did spend a lot of time learning by trial and error.

Since the acquisition of his 386, he has yet to purchase a new desktop computer! Taking advantage of his son Jerry's computer expertise (Jerry has a Microsoft certification as a Microsoft Windows NT systems administrator), he has continued to upgrade the machine over the years so that the machine now has a Pentium II microprocessor and runs Windows 98. He denies being technically savvy, but *nobody* we know has upgraded a machine in this way— even with the help of a computer-whiz son. To put this in perspec-tive, upgrading a single computer over so many years of new technological advances is like transforming your Model T Ford into a new Lincoln Continental. Theoretically, it's possible, but in the case of a computer, you would have to replace every part, including the power supply, the fan, and even the case! That sort of undertaking requires the skills of a technician, a magician, and an alchemist. But that, apparently, describes James—and his son.

[1] The Intel 386 was an early predecessor of the Pentium, introduced about 10 years ago.

Keeping *Away* from the Internet

James knew years ago that the Internet was the place to be. That's why he refused to get anywhere near it until a couple of years ago when he retired from the ministry. "I deliberately *didn't* get online before then because I knew how much time it was going to take," he says, "and I didn't want to get into it until I knew I'd have the time." Enough time to satisfy Mr. Johnson's interest is only about 10 hours a day! "It's a great tool for communicating, and I get to meet people from all around the world," he says enthusiastically. "We are sharing information and discussing important issues, even though we are all over the globe."

Mr. Johnson gets at least a hundred e-mail messages a day from his global network of friends, so it's no wonder that he's online so much. When we last spoke to him, he was responding to a message from an associate at a university in Manchester, England. His circle of friends and contacts now includes a professor in Khazakstan in the former Soviet Union, as well as a computer engineer in Sydney, Australia. Taking into account that James's primary interest is extraterrestrial life and UFO research, and that these topics are among the most popular topics of research on the Internet, James has plenty to keep him busy. It still amazes him that he can chat with his friends and research team over the Internet in real time, even though they are located all over the world. He thinks most people would enjoy real-time chats with others who have related interests, without having to travel across the state or country to meet with those people in person.

> "*It's a great tool for communicating, and I get to meet people from all around the world.*"

James sees that the Internet has completely revolutionized organizations and the way people communicate.

The Officers Club—Online

As much as James likes to meet people from around the world, he also likes to stay in touch with his fellow retired officers through their area chapter of The Retired Officers Association (TROA). He encourages other retired officers to get on the Internet and helps them find useful information after they do. With James's help, that Association is beginning to offer a variety of options via the Internet, including a chapter Web site (*http://www.execpc.com/alph/troa/*). Mr. Johnson, as President of the Los Alamitos, California, chapter, is in charge of the Web page for the site.

"I lucked out because I don't know HTML (HyperText Markup Language), but through the Internet, I met a 12-year-old kid named Joey Horne, Jr. from Wisconsin," says James. "He's so computer literate, he put the page together just while we were talking. Originally, the flag that appears on the site didn't move, and I said, 'Joey, the flag has to wave'—he changed it right away and now it's waving!"

James sees that the Internet has completely revolutionized organizations and the way people communicate, and he definitely sees those changes in The Retired Officers Association. For instance, TROA in California is abandoning its monthly printed newsletter and changing it to an e-mail newsletter. Mr. Johnson describes how else the focus is beginning to shift. "All these older folks are getting computers," he says with obvious satisfaction. "In my chapter, we have a lot of engineers, technologists, and scientists, and they lead computer groups. It's like a mutual aid society. Some know hardware, some know software, so you trade information. It's great!"

Some Sound Advice

James Johnson is a wellspring of information and experience, and he's very accommodating of others and genuinely excited to see "other old folks" jumping on the computer bandwagon. "They're having a ball," he says with obvious satisfaction. "In the last year, it has really taken off. There are a lot of white-haired folks in the college computer classes my son takes," he says. "It's a good thing because old folks who have the time can be the pioneers in implementing all this technology." Being a member of what he calls the "crank phone and crystal radio" generation, he can definitely relate.

He encourages seniors to "stretch themselves," to go beyond the fear of not knowing how to use a computer or the Internet so that they can take advantage of all the wonderful things the Internet has to offer. For James, that also includes checking out real-time information on topics such as viewing what the weather is like at the moment at Niagara Falls, or which wild game is currently migrating past the waterholes in Africa. Where is a good place to start to find out about all the wonderful information online? James recommends an Internet directory.

Although he has established a presence online and has been able to continue his favorite research, James sees the Internet as being an important vehicle for expressing political views and making our votes count. For that, he believes all older adults should become savvy about computers and get on the Internet.

"Computers and the Internet are changing the whole lobbying effort," James says emphatically. "We don't have to write our congressmen, we can just e-mail them without licking a stamp, and

Some know hardware, some know software, so you trade information. It's great!

James sees the Internet as being an important vehicle for expressing political views and making our votes count. For that, he believes all older adults should become savvy about computers and get on the Internet.

the older folks are right on top of that. These people are starting to rise up on their hind legs; the senators are now hearing from home from these folks!" James urges everyone to get online and e-mail his or her congressperson (*http://www.congress.org*).

Any warnings about the Internet? From experience, James knows that viruses are a risk. "Sure, there are viruses and the like out there," he says, "but it's not a reason to *not* get online. You need to be aware and alert. You *can* get a virus by downloading, so don't download from sources you don't know, and use reasonable protection, but don't stay home all winter. You can't be a hermit!" You'll learn more about avoiding computer viruses in Chapter 12 of this book.

Chapter Seven

Finding a Job—After Sixty

Computers have opened the doors to employment opportunities for seniors. Jacqui Fulton's story shows how one senior successfully avoided an unhappy path to welfare by learning computer skills.

At 61 years of age, Jacqui Fulton's future looked grim. Her husband of 40 years had passed away and her savings had dwindled. She could see the possibility of ending up on welfare. That's when Mrs. Fulton realized that she would need to find a job. Unfortunately, her job search wasn't immediately successful. "When I began to interview and search for jobs," Jacqui explains, "I quickly learned I did not have the skills required to work in a job that earned more than minimum wage. Employers asked me what word processor I used, or whether I used a PC or a Mac. I felt like I was being asked to speak a foreign language." Jacqui began to realize that learning about computers would be her chance for employment.

Today, Jacqui Fulton isn't just employed, she actually runs her own business, Direction and Exposure, a company specializing in providing hard-to-find people, particularly seniors, for the film and commercial community. Becoming computer literate has enabled her to be financially independent and has even led to another very memorable experience that recognizes her success. Recently, Jacqui

Figure 7-1
*Jacqui Fulton is
now running her
own show*

had the honor of meeting with Vice President Gore and sharing her inspiring story with him.

Growing Up Backstage

Her current career in the talent placement business has roots back as far as Jacqui's childhood. Jacqui tells us that she was "raised backstage." Her father made his living doing behind-the-scenes work in the motion picture industry as a spotlight man and motion picture operator, so Jacqui grew up seeing great movies and watching great entertainers perform, including Duke Ellington and Ella Fitzgerald. Knowing the motion picture industry from the inside gave her the contacts that would eventually lead her to start the business she has today.

But much was to happen in the meantime. Jacqui spent about 30 years in the working world as an executive secretary. She did plenty of typing, but never once came in contact with a computer. So when she needed a job at age 61, she had no idea that a computer with a word processing program would make such a difference in her life.

Creating Magnificent Documents

She found that she loved having an instructor to explain how to do the new things she was learning at her computer.

Jacqui's quest to learn about computers led to a church that taught computer classes in her neighborhood in Philadelphia. The church's computer center had originally been developed as a lab for children, but those who ran the center realized quickly that seniors needed it just as much. Learning computer basics from classes taught by a nun helped Jacqui progress toward her goal of finding a job. She found that she loved having an instructor to explain how to do the new things she was learning at her computer. She started by learning how to create letters, and the wonders of creating great documents with word processing quickly became exciting and motivating.

As she progressed along the path to starting her own business, she also had the opportunity to work with the Small Business Administration (SBA). With assistance from the SBA, she wrote a business plan and obtained her business license. But just as important was the opportunity the SBA gave her to learn more about how to use a computer to create letters and documents. Young people at the Small Business Administration were available to answer her questions, and her computer skills continued to expand.

Jacqui now belongs to the Philadelphian Computer Club and likes being able to learn from other members and help others, too. She now uses the Internet to "visit" places around the world and to visit with friends. "Being computer literate has opened a whole new window onto the world," she explains.

Getting Others into the Movies

The path to self-employment started for Jacqui when she saw an ad about an organization called WORC (Women's Opportunities Resource Center *http//:www.worc.pa-com/*), that helps people who feel they are under-employed or displaced but have the desire to work and to learn how to be entrepreneurs. Instead of finding a job, Jacqui decided to create her own. Jacqui explains that "in the past, I had gained experience helping others find jobs in the talent industry, so I decided to turn my hobby and experience into a full-time job by creating my own talent and casting agency. W.O.R.C. helped to make my dream a reality." Her agency specializes in placing hard-to-find talent and seniors. "Recently, I placed a 99-year-old actor on the television show "Unsolved Mysteries," Jacqui says. She's been involved with every film that has been produced in Philadelphia, including *Twelve Monkeys*, *Philadelphia*, *Beloved*, and *Rocky V*. She also was responsible for providing half of the extras who appear in the movie *Fallen*. She's even appeared in a few movies herself, including *Philadelphia*, *Snake Eyes*, and *Rocky V*.

Now that she's running her own business, she also has a new task: managing her investments. The Internet helps her with this task as well. And Jacqui's computer use doesn't stop there. "After

> "**B**eing computer literate has opened a whole new window onto the world."

> "**I**t's really amazing how far I've come in such a short time."

> "**T**he results of my efforts definitely prove that if there's a will, there's a way!"

recently regaining my credit rating, I purchased a new computer and am creating a database that tracks my clients and my presentations, and manages my business financials. It's really amazing how far I've come in such a short time." Her next goal? Turning her company into an international business.

Some Sound Advice

Today, at 65, Jacqui has a passion for empowering seniors, and her energy and enthusiasm for helping others come through in everything she says about her experience. The great advice she has for other seniors appears in an article about her for Microsoft's Seniors and Technology site: "The results of my efforts definitely prove that if there's a will, there's a way! But I also realize that I am not alone in having to overcome the challenges I faced. Many seniors are not computer literate and, therefore, are unable to continue to actively participate in the new information age. In the past, most jobs required that you be able to read, write, and do arithmetic. Now and in the new millennium, computer literacy is essential for almost any job, from working as a receptionist to starting your own business or obtaining an exciting career in information technology.

"My experience has taught me a wonderful lesson: Always believe in yourself and have an attitude of gratitude. I grew up in a generation that believed one should contribute to society, not draw from it. By becoming computer literate and taking a chance on something I believed in, I'm able to work, pay taxes, and help others. At the same time, I'm setting a positive example for my family and others to follow."

Microsoft's Seniors and Technology Web site is located at *http://www.microsoft.com/seniors* and provides a wealth of information useful to seniors who are interested in the world of computers. To investigate employment options, see *http://www.microsoft.com/seniors/employability.asp*.

"By becoming computer literate and taking a chance on something I believed in, I'm able to work, pay taxes, and help others."

*There will always be a frontier where there is
an open mind and a willing hand*
CHARLES F. KETTERING

Part Two

—◦•◦—

Taking the Digital Leap—

Welcome Aboard

Chapter Eight

The Secret to Buying Your First Computer

If you think you'd like to own a computer, but you aren't sure which one would be best for you, this chapter can help you decide.

The first part of this chapter provides you with a tool to help you get behind the "silicon curtain" and find the computer that meets your wants and needs. The second part of this chapter offers you a guide to the different components of a computer, what they do for you, and how important or unimportant they are in the scheme of things.

Selecting the PC That Is Right for You

Many books, clever ad campaigns, and other resources stand ready to help you decide which computer to buy. The books and magazines sometimes expect you to have the ability to understand technical information or various computing concepts, but that's a pretty tall order if you're new to computing. The endless amount of information available may not be at all helpful if you're overwhelmed with the seemingly infinite number of choices. Therefore, we have developed a questionaire designed to help you choose a computer by looking at your needs and interests, rather than at processor speeds and RAM size. The expertise and ability to understand the important-sounding terms associated with computers will come after you have used a computer, but for right now, narrowing down your choices is as easy as thinking about your interests and preferences.

The results of your responses in the questionaire will create a profile of your computing needs. With that profile, you can look up the computer that best suits your needs. The first set of questions helps to narrow down your choices of computers. The second set of questions helps to rank how important certain computer components might be to you. Don't worry that you wouldn't recognize a computer component if it were sitting on your desk. Instead, just read each question and check the box indicated.

If you don't want to record your answers in this book, record the letters indicated on a separate piece of paper. This questionaire will take only about 15 minutes, but you'll be surprised by how well it helps to prioritize your wants and needs.

Just grab a pen or pencil, and turn the page to get started.

Narrowing down your choices is as easy as thinking about your interests and preferences

Narrowing Down the Choices

If a statement reflects your thinking, place a check mark in the column indicated in each statement.

	A	B	C	D	E	F	G
I'm waiting until the price of the machines comes down. Check F.							
This is my first computer, but I don't mind shelling out for a great one. Check A or B.							
This is my first machine, and it doesn't need to be great. It just needs to work. Check C.							
I don't want to have to pay for stuff afterward. Check B (or A).							
I want it working right out of the box. Check B (or A).							
I travel a lot and I want my computer with me. Check D.							
My neighbor is selling a computer for cheap. The price sounds right to me. Check C.							
Can't I just get a cheap machine to test the waters? Check C.							
Spare no expense. I'm loaded and I just want the flashiest thing in town! Check A.							
I want a really good machine that won't break the bank and won't be obsolete in two years. Check B (or A).							
I want something that fits in my pocket. Check E.							
Several members of my family have a Mac, and they want me to get one, too. Check F.							
I'm not really sure what I want to do with a computer. Check G.							
I just need a personal organizer. Check E.							
I want to work at the beach. Check D.							
One of my kids wants to get rid of his/her old machine. Check C.							
I have grandkids in school who use Apple computers. Check F.							
I'm not buying anything without a great warranty. Check all.							

Scoring Your Results   To find out what your preferences say about your computer needs, add up the number of checks you have in each column here:

If you have two or more checks in . . .

Column A _____ turn to box A on page 66

Column B _____ turn to box B on page 66

Column C _____ turn to box C on page 66

Column D _____ turn to box D on page 67

Column E _____ turn to box E on page 67

Column F _____ turn to box F on page 67

Column G _____ turn to "Try Before You Buy" on page 82

To learn about the best places to buy a computer, turn to "Where to Get Your Dream Machine" on page 78.

Needs, Wants, and Interests Important to Me

Because computers come with various features, add-ons, or bells and whistles, buying a computer with what you need means figuring out what is most important to you.

If a statement reflects your thinking, place a check mark in the column indicated.

	A	B	C	D	E	F	G	H
I have numerous hobbies or interests such as sports, current affairs, travel, genealogy, investing, arts and crafts. Check B.								
I've got a bad back and can't sit comfortably at a desk. Check A.								
I'm interested in flying, and I want to learn to play Microsoft Flight Simulator. Check E.								
I enjoy music. Check C.								
I want to make sure I don't lose important information on my computer. Check G.								
I like to watch movies. Check F.								
I want to write to friends who don't have computers. Check D.								
I want to use photographs I have taken in cards and letters to friends. Check H.								
My friends and family are all across the country. Check B.								
I want to create neat cards to send for holidays and special occasions. Check D.								
My grandkids have educational CDs they like to use. Check C.								
I'm a game nut. The more exciting, the better! Check E.								
My eyes aren't (or my hearing isn't) that great. I'm afraid I won't be able to use a PC. Check A.								
My kids say DVD will replace videos and CDs. Check F.								
I've got a million photos I want to preserve. Check G or H.								

Scoring Your Results

To find out what your preferences say about features you want on your computer, add up the number of checks you have in each column here:

If you have two checks in . . .	Then a high priority for you is . . .
Column A _____	Getting special equipment to work with your computer that supports your special needs. To learn about these, turn to "Special Needs" on page 76
Column B _____	Getting a modem for your computer. Turn to "Modems" on page 72
Column C _____	Getting a CD-ROM drive for your computer. Turn to "CD_ROM Drive" on page 71
Column D _____	Getting a printer for your computer. Turn to "Printers" on page 74
Column E _____	Getting a joystick for your computer. Turn to "Joysticks" on page 74
Column F _____	Getting a DVD drive for your computer. Turn to "Now Playing" on page 75
Column G _____	Getting a Zip drive for your computer. Turn to "Zip drives" on page 73
Column H _____	Getting a scanner for your computer. Turn to "Scanners" on page 75

A   The Donald Trump Special: An Unbelievably Great Computer—for about $ 2500*

Typical components:

500 MHz Pentium (II or III) or equivalent preferred
256 megabytes of RAM / 16 or 17-gigabyte hard drive
19" monitor
Internal (built-in) DVD Drive / Internal Zip drive
High-quality scanner/High-quality laser printer
Also great speakers, great sound card, 56 K modem, graphics card with 16 megabytes of VRAM, Keyboard, Mouse, Floppy disk drive, Great software (Microsoft Office with Word + Excel + more), Windows 98, preconfigured (software already installed)

This computer is the top of the line. It's fast, it has lots of storage, and at this price, it often includes an excellent printer and perhaps even a scanner. It's great if you have no budgetary constraints. Check any current computer magazine for articles and ads that provide information on manufacturers and their toll-free phone numbers. For information on each of the typical components listed, see the related section later in this chapter.

B   The Best "Under $1,000*" Buy at the Local Computer Outlet Store or Web Store

Typical components:

333 MHz Intel Celeron or equivalent
64 megabytes of RAM /6.4-gigabyte hard drive
17" monitor / 56 Kbps modem
40x CD-ROM drive / Inexpensive ink jet printer (may or may not be included)
Mouse, Floppy disk drive, Standard keyboard, Good speakers / Good sound card, Graphics card with 8 megabytes of VRAM / Microsoft Windows 98 and software including Microsoft Works / Preconfigured (software already installed)

A Perfect First Computer. The price is low for the value, and these computers can easily meet the needs of new computer users. Check any current computer magazine for articles and ads that provide information on manufacturers and their toll-free phone numbers. For information on each of the typical components listed, see the related section later in this chapter.

C   A Used Computer—from the Kids — $0–$500

Typical components:

Pentium or Pentium II or equivalent microprocessor
15" monitor
16–32 megabytes of RAM
1-gigabyte hard drive
Sound card
Speakers
28.8 K modem
Windows 95
Keyboard, Mouse, CD-ROM drive, Floppy disk drive, Software

If this is a hand-me-down from one of your kids or from a friend or relative, that's good. As in buying a used car, knowing that the previous owner is someone you trust can make this decision easier. As savvy computer users choose to upgrade, computers that match this configuration are often available and certainly won't be as "worn out" as some of those cars on the used car lots. For information on each of the typical components listed, see the related section later in this chapter. If you don't know the seller, try getting guidance from someone well versed in the used computer market.

*All prices are estimates at the time of printing and can change drastically.

D | A Portable, Hard-Working Laptop — $2,400*

Typical components:

300–350 MHz processor
32–64 megabytes of RAM
3–4-gigabyte hard drive
1.44-megabyte floppy disk drive
Internal modem
24x speed CD-ROM
Nav-pad (instead of a mouse)
Built-in keyboard, Windows 98, Microsoft Works or Office

Laptop prices can vary widely, so $2,400 can be seen as a mid-range. For people on the go, nothing is more convenient. You can get a laptop every bit as capable as a desktop computer. If you are concerned about reading the built-in monitor clearly, plug a regular monitor into your laptop when you're using it at home. A good point to keep in mind is that a laptop can make you a target for thieves. A laptop is a tempting package: small, lightweight, and worth more than a couple of thousand dollars. Make sure that you don't leave it unattended when traveling. Check any current computer magazine for articles and ads that provide information on manufacturers and their toll-free phone numbers. For information on each of the typical components listed, see the related section later in this chapter.

E | Handheld PC— $200–$800*

Typical components:

Small built-in LCD display
On-screen keyboard or small keyboard
1–16 megabytes of RAM
Up to 2 megabytes of storage / IR data transfer port
Built-in modem / Windows CE operating system with applications such as
Address book, Datebook, Memo pad, To-do lists, Calculator

These gizmos are great, especially if you have trouble keeping track of phone numbers, appointments, addresses, and to-do lists! They don't have all the features of a desktop or laptop computer, but some actually do fit in your pocket or purse. Organizers and handheld PCs are usually most effective when used in tandem with a computer. This way, you can enter your address book and date book information on your computer (where you have a big keyboard), and then transfer that information to the organizer via a connecting cable with the push of a button. Check any current computer magazine for articles and ads that provide information on manufacturers and their toll-free phone numbers.

F | A PowerBook, PowerMac, or iMac computer from Apple — $1,200–4,300*

Typical components:

266–400 MHz processor
32–128 megabytes of RAM
6–12-gigabyte hard disk
24x CD-ROM / DVD-ROM drive (with some configurations)
Modem, Keyboard,
Mouse, Monitor

Desktop computers, laptops, and colorful new iMac computers give computer purchasers lots of options. And it's easy to track down information. Find a friend with Internet access and check out *http://www.apple.com*, or go to your local bookstore for current magazines that describe Apple's latest computers. For information on each of the typical components listed, see the related section later in this chapter.

*All prices are estimates at the time of printing and can change drastically.

The Bells and Whistles That You've Decided Are Important

Now that you have completed the questionaire and examined the computer choices listed on the previous pages, you'll note that, for the most part, all the computers except the handheld PCs include many of the same basic components. They all have a processor, RAM, monitors, hard drives, keyboards, a mouse, a CD-ROM drive, a sound card, and a modem. The questionnaire may have indicated that some components that are important to you may or may not come as part of the computer package you want. Examples include a DVD drive, Zip drive, printer, or scanner. The rest of this chapter explains what these components, usually called peripherals, are and how they are used. A "peripheral" is any piece of hardware connected to your computer.

A Mouse

Most computers come with a mouse. A mouse is just a pointing device for selecting items on the screen. Some designs are different, including the mouse with a small wheel with which you can do some added tricks. An alternative to the mouse is a "track ball," a stationary cradle containing a ball that you roll with your fingertips. Laptop computers offer another alternative, the "touchpad"—a pressure-sensitive surface built into the keyboard console. It lets you move your cursor by tracing your finger on the touchpad itself.

Floppy Disk Drive

This comes as standard with most computers. For many years, the floppy disk was *the* way to give someone a document from your machine. You copied the information to the floppy and passed the floppy on. Then came the Internet and networking, which are new and convenient ways to exchange information. Floppy drives are still included on nearly every computer, and they are a common way of backing up files. For more information on backing up, see Chapter 10.

Sound Cards—Music to Your Ears

A "sound card" is like your stereo amplifier at home, although it does considerably more than that! Unless you open your computer, you won't see your computer's sound card, and if you don't have one, you won't be able to hear any of the sounds a computer is capable of generating.

A description of a sound card can be confusing because it has so many incomprehensible-sounding features: MIDI libraries, MIDI interface, sampling capabilities, and audio playback rates. Despite the confusing jargon, you want a sound card that supports the latest standards and features if possible. When a PC is described as a multimedia PC, it will include a soundcard. PCs intended for business use, however, don't always come with sound cards, so be sure to check for this before you buy. If you're not buying a new computer or are simply upgrading your existing sound card, look for the most common features across the different brands.

Speakers

With a sound card, CD-ROM drive, and speakers, you can play regular audio CDs on your computer and enjoy many of the other audio features of the applications on your computer. But as with

A *"sound card" is like your stereo amplifier at home, although it does considerably more than that!*

your stereo, you can't hear anything unless you have speakers! If the computer you are considering has a CD-ROM drive and a sound card, it will probably come with speakers. Speakers come in all price ranges, but even the less expensive ones work well. The speakers plug into the back of your computer.

Keyboards

The computer keyboard is the basic way of entering information into the computer, so most computers have one except certain types of handheld devices. If you've used a typewriter, you can use a computer keyboard. Keyboards come in a variety of styles. The Microsoft keyboard shown in Figure 8-1 has an ergonomic design that reduces the muscle and tendon strain in the wrists, arms, and elbows.

Figure 8-1
The optimized keyboard helps reduce the stress on wrists, arms, and elbows.

RAM: Short-Term Memory You Can Buy

All computers come with internal memory, called RAM (pronounced like the animal), which is short for "random access memory." RAM is sometimes confused with hard disk storage, which is completely different (see "Hard Disk Drives," later in this chapter). Your computer needs RAM to run programs. You don't need to know the ins and outs right now, but if you are picking out a new PC, look for one that provides at least 64 megabytes of RAM to work effectively on the Internet. If your computer has less, it won't operate as quickly, but as long as it has enough memory to run current software, your computer will still operate correctly. The minimum for current software is usually 32 megabytes.

CD-ROM Drive

New computers today have CD-ROM drives as standard equipment. Most software today is shipped on CD-ROMs, as are all the essential learning programs, games, and reference tools such as Microsoft Encarta, an encyclopedia. A CD-ROM drive also allows you to use CDs (short for "compact disc") with your computer. CD-ROM drives are rated by the speed at which they can access information on the CD, indicated with a number like 12x, 20x, 32x, or 40x, which is read as "40 speed."

The one catch with a CD-ROM: you can't save or store any of your own information on a normal CD. A CD-ROM is the computer equivalent of a stereo record that can also hold text and graphics. Recently, recordable CD-ROMs that allow you to copy information to them as you would to floppy disks have become available for consumers, but they are not especially useful to the vast majority of beginner PC users.

Monitors

Monitors are a requirement, so they are often included as standard equipment, but not always. Today, monitors are available in all price ranges. Most people think the bigger the monitor, the better,

TIP

A computer equipped with a CD-ROM drive, sound card, and speakers can act as a stereo. The CD-ROM drive will play your favorite audio CDs.

as long as it fits within their allotted budget range. Granted, bigger is more expensive, but today a 17-inch monitor costs only about $100 more than a 15-inch monitor and the difference is more than worth it. The more "screen real estate," or screen space, you have, the easier it is to work with your applications on the computer. Remember, however, that the bigger the display, the larger the tube. A larger tube takes up more room on your desk. (Many manufactuers do offer "short-tube" monitors that don't eat up a lot of desktop real estate.)

The latest development in monitor technology is the flat-panel display, or LCD monitor. An LCD is a tubeless monitor that uses a liquid crystal technology. These monitors require much less desk space, and the absence of a picture tube means lower power consumption and less heat thrown off in your room. (They also look very "high tech.") You can get one of these cutting edge displays, but you'll pay quite a bit for it: a 15-inch LCD monitor in lieu of a standard monitor (with a tube) will add about $600 to the cost of your new PC!

Hard Disk Drives—Closet Space for Your Computer Creations

Today, a computer without a hard disk is practically unknown. The hard disk drive is a physical part of your computer where you save all your work for access at another time. For new users, the multi-gigabyte drives of today are more than adequate, but some users run out of disk space and need to expand their digital closet space with higher-capacity hard drives. Graphic artists and photographers, for example, can easily gobble up 40 megabytes of disk space just for one image, and some programs require several

The hard disk drive is a physical part of your computer where you save all your work for access at another time.

hundred megabytes of free space to run. If you are going to be working with photos extensively, you may want to check out Zip drives, which are described in a later section.

Modems

Modems are now as ubiquitous as computers and, more often than not, they come built into computers. You must have a modem to connect to the Internet, so make sure that your computer has one. The current standard speed for a home modem is 56 K. Modem speeds have typically doubled every other year, and the prices have continued to drop. A modem speed of 28.8 K will still let you surf the Internet, but if you have a modem slower than 56 Kbps, and you expect to spend much time on the Internet, you might want a faster one. If your computer doesn't have one already installed internally, you can obtain an external modem, which sits near your computer rather than inside it. External modems are widely available and require minimum installation.

Zip Drives

An Iomega Zip drive is the newer version of a floppy disk drive. Zip drives, commonly built into new computers, use a Zip disk that is about twice as thick as a 3.5" inch disk and holds 100 megabytes of information (250 megabytes for the newest model)—about 80 times more than a standard floppy disk. A Zip drive is something to consider if you will be working with many photographs that take up a lot of disk space for each image. These drives also provide a convenient way to make backup copies of all the important files you want to keep.

These drives also provide a convenient way to make backup copies of all the important files you want to keep.

Printers: Gutenberg in the Year 2000

Hundreds of different printers are on the market, ranging in price from $100 to several thousand dollars. Printer technology has advanced dramatically in the last 10 years, so even a $100 printer can produce impressive results. Some new computer packages include a printer. Printers are easy to buy and easy to install if the computer you obtain doesn't have one.

Printers are distinguished by printing features, output quality, and speed—that is, how many pages they can print in a minute. The most popular printers for home use are ink jet printers. Ink jets print pages by spraying a fine ink mist onto the page and are the type of printers most often used for color printing. Laser printers, although more expensive, are faster, high quality, and primarily intended only for black-and-white printing. There are color laser printers, but they can be quite expensive. You can also find multipurpose machines that print, fax, copy, and scan. If you have a need for all these features, check with a local computer store or current magazines to learn more about features and trade-offs.

Laser Printers Laser printers, long the standard for professional and corporate users, are fast and efficient, and typically are much faster than ink jet printers. Some laser printers can print 32 ppm (pages per minute), which is blazingly fast. They also offer multiple trays for different paper sizes and a host of other features. If you have a small business that requires a good deal of printing or invoicing, or if you expect to use your printer for a community publishing system for a club or group, this type of printer will give

TIP

Ink jet printers take a special kind of cartridge that costs about $30. If you're printing many pages dense with color, cartridges do run out fast.

you very fast results. However, unless you buy an expensive color laser, you are signing up for black-and-white printing only.

Ink Jet Printers Ink jet printers are the home standard. They provide color capabilities as well as crisp black and white, but their speed doesn't match that of laser printers. The cheaper models can take more than a minute to print a full page of text. But for most people, the benefits outweigh the inconvenience.

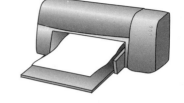

Joysticks for the NASCAR Racer and Future Pilot

Computers have become phenomenal game stations, and certain hardware additions can make your play time wildly enjoyable. You can find several different types of game controllers, including joysticks. As with all computer peripherals, prices vary widely, but a standard joystick is relatively inexpensive. Simple joysticks consist of a single post fixed at the base like a stick shift that can move in all directions. You have probably seen one on a motorized wheelchair to allow the driver to steer with minimal movement. If you are planning to "learn to fly" with Microsoft Flight Simulator, a joystick is required.

Besides joysticks, you can even find steering wheels with dashboard consoles if you want to try your hand at a race car game. The newest controllers include vibration; when something happens on-screen, the controller vibrates and you feel the jolts and motions of the game you are playing.

Now Playing: A Movie on Your DVD Drive

Never mind the technical details: a DVD drive lets you watch full-length movies on your computer, and you don't even have to rewind!

TIP
DVD drives still accept standard CD-ROM disks and audio CDs, so you don't need a CD-ROM drive if you get a DVD drive.

If you are interested and if your computer is set up in a room to allow easy viewing, you can rent videos, not on videotape, but on the newest form of CD-ROM, the DVD. The DVD is the most recent generation of CD-ROM drives; a DVD disk can hold about six times as much information as a regular CD-ROM, however.

Scanners for Transferring Photos onto Your Computer

A scanner is used to copy an image or page for storage and display on the computer. Scanners typically look like little copying machines, with a glass platen (the plate you put the copy on) and a heavy rubberized mat that lies on top of that. A popular scanner is shown in Figure 8-2.

Figure 8-2
A good, high-resolution, flatbed color scanner costs approximately $150, but prices vary considerably

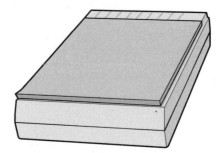

Scanners are great if you have many pictures that you want to preserve or share with others. Scanners are also great if you have a lot of typed text that you want to store on the computer. Scanners now come with OCR (optical character recognition) software that actually reads the text on the page and turns it into a text file. This doesn't work very well with handwritten text, however, so if your intention is to use a scanner to translate your brother's badly written letters into something legible, don't count on it.

Special Needs

What happens when someone can't use a standard keyboard or mouse? Or what if someone can't read the screen well or hear the computer's audio cues? Smaller companies have created a whole class of hardware for special needs. If you're visually or hearing impaired, or suffer from arthritis or partial paralysis, some useful and well-conceived alternatives are available for you. Some special needs options are built into Windows, and there is a universe of hardware and software options available as well.

The range of options is almost as diverse as the range of special needs. To find the best software and hardware solution, ask your specialist or local gerontologist for more information. When you get on the Web, you'll find a huge number of resources to choose from as well. For example, *http://www.closing thegap.com* provides a special resource directory of hardware and software products available for people with special needs. They also publish a guide to regional and national organizations that are active in promoting this technology.

Attachments

Besides all the things commonly attached to a computer, an impressive array of gadgets and gizmos exists. Here are some of the things that might catch your eye. If it's an electrical appliance, there's a good chance that one model or another can connect to your computer:

- Some types of musical keyboards referred to as MIDI keyboards or MIDI compatible keyboards (rhymes with "city") can be connected to your computer so that you can record a performance, edit it, and play it back.

NOTE

Windows 98 comes with Accessibility Options, which address many special computing needs. Visit http://www. microsoft.com/enable/products/ *for details on how to access these features and for more information on other accessibility products.*

If it's an electrical appliance, there's a good chance that one model or another can connect to your computer:

- Robotics toys allow you to build a robot, program it on your PC, and then let it roam around your home executing your instructions.

- Certain video cameras can be attached to your computer, and you can transfer images to or from your computer.

- Digital cameras, which are cameras that take instant, filmless pictures, allow you to snap away and then transfer the pictures directly to your PC.

- Sewing machines connect to a personal computer and do extraordinary, multicolored stitchwork based on the orders you give it.

Hey, What's a PCI Local Bus?[1] No matter what you're interested in, and no matter how much you try to learn, you will always encounter a host of products and peripherals whose purpose escapes you. For instance, when you look at any computer magazine, you'll find advertisements for items such as routers, Ethernet hubs, NICs, UPSs, servers, RAID arrays, network operating systems, CPU accelerators, and LCD projectors. That's the nature of technology. You can derive many years of enjoyment and benefit from your computer without knowing about many aspects of the technology, but if you ever get curious, a visit to the computer section of your local bookstore will help you supplement your know, how. In addition, the magazine racks in those same bookstores serve up computer magazines specific to every subject and level of expertise you could hope for.

---

[1] Peripheral Component Interconnect local bus, a specification for fast communication between components in the computer and the processor.

Where to Get Your Dream Machine

What you really want from a computer isn't much different from what you want and expect from anything else that you buy: you want it to be sturdy, dependable, and require low maintenance. You don't need to understand the inner workings of a computer before you have one and, when you do get one, don't worry about learning the inner workings if you don't want to! Not many people know what size engine they have in their cars or how to change the oil, for that matter. And you already know why not. After you've purchased a car, you're satisfied as long as it does what you want it to do, and there are plenty of ways to get your oil changed if you don't want to learn to do so yourself.

After all is said and done, the only thing standing between you and learning about computing is having a computer to use every day. So, where do you go to get one?

You have the choice of many sources from which to obtain a computer: computer stores, electronics stores, appliance stores, department stores. You can also buy computers directly from the manufacturers, either via the Internet (if you're connected at work, perhaps) or with a toll-free number. And prices have never been better. A lot of computer power can be packed into computers that cost less than a thousand dollars today. Some of the sources are described in the next sections to help you decide on the best way to buy.

Buying Direct

One option is to buy your computer by ordering over the Internet or by phone directly from a manufacturer or reseller. The manufacturer has a vested interest in seeing that you are happy in order

What you really want from a computer isn't much different from what you want and expect from anything else that you buy: you want it to be sturdy, dependable, and require low maintenance.

to protect its reputation and to vie for your return business. Other advantages of buying direct are as follows:

- The computer is often custom built for you. That means you get exactly what you want. If you want a bigger monitor, you specify the size. If you want more RAM, you specify how much.
- As with features on a car, you don't pay for things you don't want or need.
- The manufacturers have this process down to a science, so the response is very quick. You should have your new computer within a week.
- Manufacturer-direct computers come preloaded with the software you need. Your computer is ready to go when you receive it.
- The manufacturer might include great warranties, including on-site service, and it usually offers excellent extended warranties.
- Your computer can be shipped by air or some other means chosen by you, and then it arrives at your door.

*P*ick up any computer magazine in your local grocery store, and you will find the toll-free phone numbers and Web sites for all the major computer manufacturers.

Pick up any computer magazine in your local grocery store, and you will find the toll-free phone numbers and Web sites for all the major computer manufacturers. Plenty of "disinterested" third parties review the latest offerings from the manufacturers and write up their advice in magazines to help educate readers on which computers have the best value or demonstrate the most reliability.

Buying from a Store

If you want to talk to someone in person about what you need, you'll find no shortage of stores with inventory on hand and a knowledgeable sales staff. This can be a distinct advantage because you can take your computer in for repair if necessary. Other advantages include

- You can see what you're buying before you buy it. For example, if you're buying a laptop, you can test drive the keyboard to see whether it accommodates your typing style and feels right.
- You can test similar models side by side. Sometimes, small things that make a difference to you can be assessed when you actually try out the PC.
- You can see the newest add-ons and how they work.
- You can take advantage of limited-time discount offers.
- Computer stores may offer training and support nearby.
- Some computer stores will custom build the computer you want, just like the manufacturers who sell by phone or over the Internet.

Specific items to check if you work with a store:

- What support do they provide? Get it in writing.
- Are there any hidden costs? An advertised price may be exceptionally low to get you in the door, but the fine print might read, "Monitor not included."
- Does the computer come with the software you want preinstalled? Is the software included in the price?

Those Pre-Owned PCs

A used machine can be a great deal, but there are important things to look out for if you are considering a used computer. If it comes from a trusted source who can provide some support and guidance,

TIP

Be certain that a used machine can effectively connect to the Internet. Do this by trying it yourself, if possible, before you take it home. Also, check the RAM to be sure you can use it with the software you'll be using. All software packages specify the minimum amount of RAM needed to run them.

Software and computers always become easier to use as new versions are released.

a used PC can be a great way to learn about computers without investing any hard-earned savings. Normally, these computers, however, are "earlier models"—the ones someone used before upgrading to the latest and greatest. Software and computers always become easier to use as new versions are released. Nevertheless, used might be the way to go at first, especially if a friend or relative is offering some help to get you started.

A number of potential problems can crop up with a used machine from anyone but a friend or family member. Here are a few:

- Unless you find a trusted pro to help you check out the potential buy, you don't know what's really "under the hood."
- Diagnosing or isolating problems with the machine before you buy it is difficult.
- Unless you are a pro, it's tough to know what price is the right price. You might pay too much.
- You have little or no recourse in the event the machine fails.

Try Before You Buy?

If you turned right to this section from the questionnaire on page 64, then perhaps you are still undecided about whether a computer is for you. Check any of the statements below that apply to you.

____I'm still doing research. I want to gather more information about a good computer.

So, has it been two months or two years that you've been gathering information? New information continually becomes available. If you find yourself falling into the trap of feeling that you'll never know enough to make the right decision, set a realistic time limit for yourself, and declare that you will get a computer when you reach your deadline. In the meantime, search out a computer club or community computing center to talk to others about how they got their computers and how best to make a successful purchase.

_____I'm waiting until the prices drop.

The prices have been dropping for 15 years, and the downward trend continues. But the big secret is, the price of a computer really doesn't drop. You can always find good computers in about the same price range as computers were 15 years ago. The difference is that you get a lot more for your money now, and you'll get more for your money 10 years from now, but if you keep waiting, you'll never have a computer!

_____I'm afraid of looking dumb!

This is the toughest one. Everybody has to learn how to drive before safely getting behind the wheel of a car, and nobody wants to look dumb. Kids learn the way they do because they aren't self-conscious about how they look to others. You're not dumb and computing isn't beyond you. The personal portraits in this book describe how other people moved beyond their fears and learned about computing. No one ever knows it all. But even beginners can be successful and derive much enjoyment from their computers. A good strategy is to find a local computer club or community computing center to talk to others about how they got their computers and how they moved from "feeling dumb" to having confidence.

If you want to "try before you buy," here are some options to investigate:

- Take a class at a local community college or community center.

No one ever knows it all. But even beginners can be successful and derive much enjoyment from their computers.

- Ask friends (or your grandkids!) to show you how they use their computer.
- If you are highly motivated to earn some money, sign up at a temporary employment agency. They will train you in the latest computer programs and help to find you a job to practice your new skills.

Read more books. Many excellent books are available that explain what you can do with a computer and how it works. Start by checking out the books at your local bookstore, or see the Microsoft Press Web site at *http://mspress.microsoft.com*. Books and training materials of interest to new computer users can be accessed from *http://mspress.microsoft.com/findabook/list/series.htm*. Here's a partial list of Microsoft Press series:

Many excellent books are available that explain what you can do with a computer and how it works

At A Glance	Quick visual guides for task-oriented instruction
Starts Here™	Interactive instruction on CD-ROM that helps students learn by doing
Quick Course®	Fast, to-the-point instructions for new users
Running	A comprehensive curriculum alternative to standard documentation books
* Field Guides	Concise, task-oriented A–Z references for quick, easy answers

Check with your library. You may find computers available for public use.

---

* For Microsoft Office 2000 titles and later, these are now known as Pocket Guides

Remember, you can always find many very good choices and a few bad choices, just as you can in purchases of other appliances or automobiles. After you have a computer, everything described in the rest of this book is available for you to learn about and enjoy. If you are ready to learn more, turn to the next chapter.

Chapter Nine

Gentlefolk, Start Your Engines!

Congratulations, you've made the leap! You've probably made a few excuses along the way to avoid the inevitable moment of having to unwrap this enigma, but now your machine's unpacked and ready to go. You're sitting in front of your PC, and you probably aren't sure what to do first.

This chapter is designed to familiarize you with the basics of your computer, including how to turn it on, what the pictures and buttons and menus mean, and how to turn it off when you're done. After you get through this chapter, you'll be a lot more comfortable using this new contraption, and you'll discover that, short of pushing it off your desk, you can't do any real damage to your PC by using it.

Preparing to Drive One of These Things

Consider what you do as a driver when you get into a new car. To get oriented, you acquaint yourself with all the necessary displays and controls that will let you drive safely and comfortably. You look at the dashboard controls to get a sense of what is available to you and how things work. You may not use everything on that first voyage in your new car, but you want to know where things are so that you can get to them easily when you need to. You'll be well served if you approach your computer in the same way: look at the screen and investigate different options. Find the areas that look intriguing, and make a mental note that you want to explore those things. You don't need to know what *everything* does right away, but learning by trying is a valuable approach to computing.

It Really Is Safe for You to Drive

Almost everyone is reluctant to approach a computer for the first time. Don't sweat it. Like the dashboard controls of your car, the options that appear on your computer screen invite experimentation and exploration. The sooner you get your hands on the wheel—or the mouse, in this case—the better off you'll be.

Don't Forget a Travel Log/Journal

Here's some good up-front advice: buy a spiral notebook and keep a log of your computing travels and adventures, being sure to include the following information as it arises:

- Questions you can't answer
- The answers to your questions—when you get them!
- The steps you took to do that new cool thing
- The name of a program you are interested in learning about
- That Internet address that a friend referred you to
- The cryptic on-screen message that appeared when something went wrong
- The name of the computer guru who helped you with a computer problem
- The phone number for technical support (for your computer)
- The e-mail address for a potential computer pen pal

We recommend a real notebook, not a document on your computer, to serve as your journal because you never know when you'll think

You don't need to know what everything does right away, but learning by trying is a valuable approach to computing.

TIP

Use a pad of sticky notes, and post the most important notes on the edge of your monitor or nearby where you can read them quickly.

of something, and you don't want to have to turn on the machine just to make a note to yourself. Also, you'll want to write down "error messages," those irritating computer dispatches that pop up on your screen when something goes wrong. A notebook is especially useful because the message is often the only clue in helping diagnose the problem, and the appearance of the message may prevent you from getting to your journal!

Getting to Know All Those Switches and Buttons

Your new computer has no shortage of buttons. You'll find an on/off switch, a button on the floppy disk drive, and another on the CD-ROM drive. Your printer has another set of buttons, your speakers probably have at least one button, and your monitor has an additional set. For now, you just need to know the power switches on your PC and on your monitor.

Start the Ignition

One of the buttons on your computer is the power or on/off switch, sometimes designated with the symbol "0/1." Find the power switches on your computer and on your monitor, and press them (or flip, as the case may be) to turn them on. Don't be flustered if you can't find the switches immediately.

Not Everything Starts When You Turn on the Computer

Not everything is going to start when you turn on your computer. Some things, such as your monitor, may start automatically. Other

NOTE

Laptops commonly don't have a conventional power switch on them. If no power switch is visible, that means you turn it on by pressing a key on the keyboard. Check your laptop user guide for more information.

components, such as your printer and speakers, might have to be turned on separately.

Becoming Acquainted with Your Digital Dashboard

After your machine performs a few start-up tasks (as we all do when we just get up), you'll see a screen similar to Figure 9-1. Don't worry if your screen doesn't look exactly the same. The screen's appearance depends on what programs you have installed and how the machine was set up. The entire image you see on your screen is called the "desktop," and you can get to everything you need from here. If you ever get lost or confused, you'll want to get back to the desktop. You find out how to do that a little later in this chapter.

Don't worry if your screen doesn't look exactly the same. The screen's appearance depends on what programs you have installed and how the machine was set up

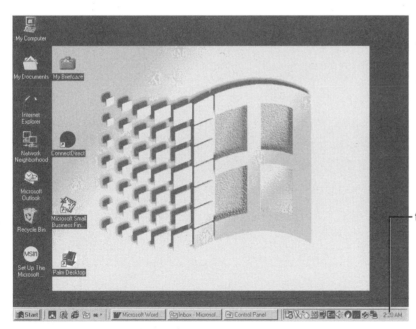

taskbar

Figure 9-1
The starting screen: the Windows 98 desktop

TIP

Click the right mouse button on an icon, and choose Properties to get more information about the icon.

The initial screen has a background color, image, pattern, or perhaps the computer manufacturer's logo emblazoned on it. That image, color, or pattern is called the "background screen." The background screen, shown in Figure 9-1, displays the Microsoft Windows logo.

Understanding the Pictures on the Screen

After your computer starts up and finishes checking everything, you'll see several small pictures, called "icons," sprinkled along the left edge of the screen. Clicking the icons with the left mouse button gives you access to a plethora of options or information (or both) related to the icon. The icon itself conveys some information about what you'll get when you click it. A folder icon, for instance, indicates that it's a container for documents, pictures, and other computer files. An icon showing a small video camera represents a video clip. Double-clicking a folder icon reveals all the document and picture names within that folder. Double-clicking a video icon allows you to watch the associated video segment.

Using the Strip at the Bottom of the Screen

The band that runs across the bottom of the screen is called the "taskbar." It gives you fast access to any single activity or task that you are working on. Chapter 10 goes into more detail to explain how helpful the taskbar is when you have several tasks going simultaneously.

Your PC Chauffeur: The Mouse

When you begin to move your mouse around on your desk, you'll see a small arrow come to life on the screen, its movement corresponding to the movement of your hand. You use the mouse to select options, start programs, open folders, and move items around. The buttons on the mouse allow you to perform all these tasks. Not all mice are created equal, however; some have just two buttons, some have two buttons and a small wheel, along with other variations on this basic theme. For this book, we do everything using the standard two-button mouse.

Teaching Your Mouse Some Tricks

Without clicking either mouse button, move the mouse around and get a feel for how your hand movement corresponds to the arrow's movement. If you have a problem with the mouse because you reach the edge of your work surface, lift the mouse *off* the table and move it to a better spot so that it doesn't roll off the edge.

When you're comfortable moving the mouse around, position it so that it points the cursor to the icon that reads "My Computer" on the left side of your desktop. With the tip of the pointer on the My Computer icon, click the left mouse button once. When you do, the icon is highlighted, as indicated by a change in color. If you move the mouse to another icon and click it once, that icon becomes highlighted. For now, work under the assumption that you can select only one of these icons on your desktop at a time (remember, that's the desktop on your computer screen, not the one that your mouse sits on).

Rearrange Your Desktop

Just as you adjust the seat and mirrors in your new car, you'll probably want to move the icons on your desktop. To start, you need to know what's required to move an icon. To move the My Computer

TIP

The mouse must be on a smooth, stationary surface, such as a mouse pad. A "mouse pad" is a non-skid, rubberized pad made specifically for mouse use. If you don't have a mouse pad, you can get one at any computer store for a few dollars.

icon, for example, move your mouse to the icon, and then click once and *hold the button down*. With the mouse button pressed down, move your mouse to a new location on the desktop. A shadow of the icon follows your arrow. When you're happy with the new location, let go of the mouse button to release the icon, and the icon snaps to the new location. Congratulations! You've just begun customizing your desktop.

Open a Window

It's not too early to do a little cruising on your computer, and you can do it with your mouse. To begin, move the arrow to the "My Computer" folder, and double-click the left mouse button; that is, click twice in rapid succession. When you do, a window appears, similar to the one shown in Figure 9-2.

NOTE

The items shown for your computer may be different.

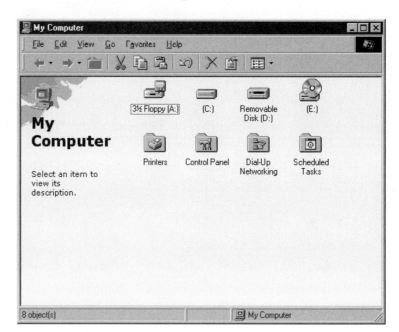

Figure 9-2
Double-clicking an icon—in this case, My Computer—opens a window showing what that icon offers

Move a Window

When you double-click an icon, a window opens on your desktop (in this case, it's a window for My Computer). Sometimes you'll need or want several windows open on your desktop simultaneously, and you'll have to move them around to work effectively. Here's how to do it.

1. Move the mouse to the "title bar," the colored bar at the top of the window that you want to move. The title bar always includes the name of the window, which in this case is My Computer.

2. Click once in the title bar and, while holding the mouse button down, drag the mouse. When you do this, the entire window and everything in it travels with your mouse.

3. Let go of the mouse button when you're satisfied with the new location for the window.

TIP

If you don't like the way the mouse responds to your hand movement or to double-clicking, you can adjust it from the Control Panel, discussed later in this chapter.

Making Progress: A Window of Opportunity

Every window you open gives you a unique view onto something stored or some feature available on your computer. Every window also includes an identical set of features that you'll need to familiarize yourself with in order to get around. Figure 9-3 shows some of the features common to all windows.

Using the Title Bar

You just saw that the title bar appears at the top of every window. The title bar provides the name of the window (in this case, My

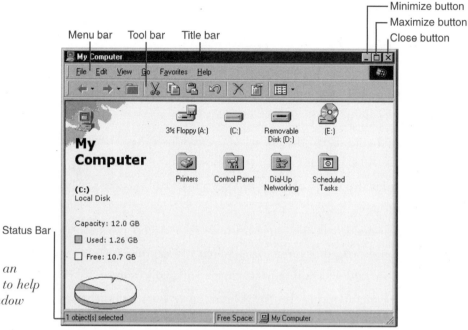

Menu bar   Tool bar   Title bar

Minimize button
Maximize button
Close button

Status Bar

Figure 9-3
Every window offers an identical set of tools to help you manage the window and its contents

TIP

If you double-click the title bar, it will expand the window to fill the entire screen. To reduce the window back to its previous size, double-click the title bar again.

Computer, the icon you double-clicked) and also includes three buttons in the right corner for resizing.

Opening a Window with the Maximize Button

The Maximize button is functionally equivalent to double-clicking the title bar. Click the Maximize button once, and it automatically opens the window to occupy your entire screen. When the window is maximized, click the Restore button to restore the window to its previous size.

Maintaining Easy Access with the Minimize Button

The Minimize button allows you to close the window so that it appears at the bottom of the screen as a button for quick access. To reopen the window, click the button in the taskbar, and the window reappears.

Closing a Window with the Close Button

The Close button allows you to close the window completely, as if you are putting it away. To re-access a window after clicking its Close button, you must return to the icon and double-click it.

Sizing a Window and Seeing What's Inside

When you open a window, you may want it partially opened, but not so much as to obscure your view of other windows or icons. In addition, when a window is partially opened, you may not be able to see everything that it contains. Here are two important features (available in every window) that address these situations.

Resizing a Window Aside from using the buttons available on the title bar, you can resize a window to any dimensions you want manually. To do so, follow these steps:

1. Move the arrow to edge or corner of the My Computer window. The arrow changes into a double-headed arrow.

2. When the double-headed arrow appears, click and hold the left mouse button, and drag to enlarge or reduce the size of the window. If you drag on the corner, you resize the window in two directions.

Scrolling Through a Window   Scroll bars appear alongside a window if the window is too small to display all its contents at one time. Scroll bars also appear when you are writing a document or painting a picture, for example, and the letter or image flows "off" your screen. Scroll bars let you see what's not currently displayed.

To better understand scroll bars, use the sizing options to make the My Computer window very small. Notice that when you make the window smaller, you lose sight of some of the icons within the window, and the scroll bars appear, as shown in Figure 9-4. Scroll bars let you see things that are in the window but "off camera." As soon as an item can't be seen in a window, the necessary scroll bars appear to give you access again. Each window can have two separate scroll bars: one for moving left and right, the other for scrolling up and down, when either of these becomes necessary.

Scroll bars let you see things that are in the window but "off camera."

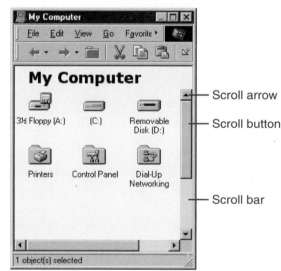

Figure 9-4
Scroll bars let you get to everything in a window, even if the window is quite small

You can work with scroll bars in three different ways:

- Move the mouse to the small triangular arrow—the "scroll arrow"—at either end of the scroll bar, and click it. This action allows you to move through the window or document in small increments.

- Move the mouse to the small block that appears on the path between the triangles. Click and hold your mouse on the little box, the "scroll box," and slowly glide it along the track. This action allows you to move through the window at the pace you determine.

- Move the mouse to the track above or below (or to the right or left of) the scroll bar, and click it. This action allows you to move through the window quickly.

Choosing the Special of the Day: The Menu Bar

The indispensable menu bar appears directly below the title bar, and you'll discover its importance in a short time. Every window has a menu bar, but the menu bars aren't always the same. For example, Microsoft Word uses a different menu bar than the My Computer window. Most words on a menu bar have an associated "secondary menu," a list of options that opens beneath the word you chose from the menu bar. You can see an example of a menu by following these steps:

1. Click the word "File" on the menu bar for the My Computer window.

2. The File menu appears.

3. Move the mouse down within the File menu, and notice how each item is highlighted as you pass over it.

NOTE

Some of the entries in the menu appear dimmed, which means that they are unavailable. These options become available only after you have done something that tells the PC you need them.

Finding Menus Within Menus

Some menus offer more than just a single column of options, offering instead a tree of possibilities. In programmer speak, these are called "submenus." To see an example of one of these and to learn how to select options from it, follow these steps:

1. Click the word "View" in the menu bar, and the menu appears. Notice that some of the entries have a small, triangular arrowhead in their right margins.

2. Move the mouse down through the menu options, and stop on the Arrange Icons entry. After a moment, another menu, or submenu, appears to the right of the first one.

3. Move the mouse over the new menu to get a feel for selecting from a submenu.

4. To escape without selecting, move the mouse outside the frame of the menu before releasing the button.

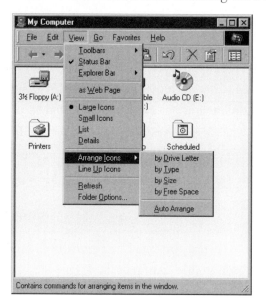

Using the Start Button on Your Desktop

There, sitting not so inconspicuously in the lower left corner of your screen, is the Start button. Your computer is already on, you've already opened windows, so what *exactly* does it start? Pretty much whatever you want it to start—whatever is on your PC, anyway. The Start button enables you to initiate any program that is on your computer. Think of it as Control Central.

To explore the Start menu, click the Start button and the Start menu appears, as shown in Figure 9-5.

Figure 9-5
The Start menu gives you access to just about everything on your computer, from one easy place

As you do with the drop-down menus, you select an option by gliding your mouse to the Start menu and clicking. You should also note that several of the entries have the right-pointing arrowheads, indicating that they are hierarchical menus.

The two entries on the Start menu that will prove to be the most useful for you, at least initially, are Programs and Settings. To view the Programs menu now, move the mouse pointer to (or point to) Programs. When you do, a submenu appears, showing the programs that exist on your computer. Figure 9-6 shows one example of a Programs menu.

Figure 9-6
The Program listing on the Start menu gives you access to all your programs

Several of the entries in this menu may also have submenus, as evidenced by the triangular arrowheads.

Each of these menu entries is a program on your PC that you can run. The list of programs is in alphabetical order to help you find them faster. As you obtain more programs, the list grows until an arrow pointer appears at the bottom to allow you to scroll to entries that can't fit on the screen. You'll see how to start a few different programs in Chapter 10, so for now, just quickly view what you have in your list of programs.

Personalizing Your PC

Your computer is very much like a home in Levittown, New York, the famous postwar subdivision. On the outside, your computer looks like everybody else's cookie-cutter computer, but on the inside—on the screen, anyway—it can be transformed to make a very personal statement or to make it more efficient and comfortable for your individual use. Just about everything on your computer can be adjusted. The following sections show you how to start making your computer your own.

*J*ust about everything on your computer can be adjusted

Working with the Control Panel

Does the color of your desktop give you the blahs? Are the sounds too loud? Are you unhappy with the sensitivity of your mouse or the speed at which you have to double-click? Are you having some difficulty reading the screen, given the size of the fonts? You can adjust all these things and more, whenever and as often as you want.

To make these adjustments easy, Microsoft Windows has centralized the options in one place called the "Control Panel." To access Control Panel, click the Start menu, move the mouse to the Settings entry, and select Control Panel from the submenu. The Control Panel window opens, as shown in Figure 9-7.

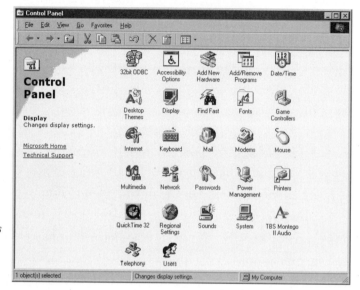

Figure 9-7
Control Panel is brimming with options that enable your computer to better reflect the real you

Each icon that appears in this window represents some feature of your computer that you can adjust. Several of these items represent mundane, technical aspects of your computer that you won't necessarily want to tinker with, but many offer fundamental and useful control. Here are a few that you might find immediately useful:

- **Accessibility Options:** Offers a set of controls to help individuals with visual impairment or limited dexterity with the mouse or keyboard (or both).

- **Date/Time:** Allows you to reset your computer's clock and specify your time zone.

- **Desktop Themes (only in Windows 98):** Gives your computer a design theme. In the baseball theme, for example, your computer beep is replaced with the crack of a bat, the flat cyan background changes to an aerial shot of a big league game, you see a different typeface and border, and incidental screen colors change to match the field.
- **Display:** Allows you to change a number of visual attributes of your PC (we cover the Display options in detail in the next section).
- **Fonts:** Shows you all the different typefaces that are currently available on your PC and allows you to add new ones at any time.
- **Mouse:** Allows you to adjust the speed of a double-click, the movement of the pointer, the button assignments (for you southpaws out there), and several other settings.
- **Sounds:** Allows you to change the sounds that you hear when you perform some action on your PC, such as the shutdown sound, the system beep, or the sound that accompanies an incoming e-mail.

Each of the Control Panel options is accessed by double-clicking the corresponding icon. The following section delves further into one of those options, namely, the Display option.

Changing the PC Display Options

To start changing the appearance of your screen, double-click the Display icon (it looks like a little monitor) in the Control Panel window. After you double-click, the Display Properties window appears, as shown in Figure 9-8.

TIP

You can also click the right mouse button and select Open to access Control Panel features.

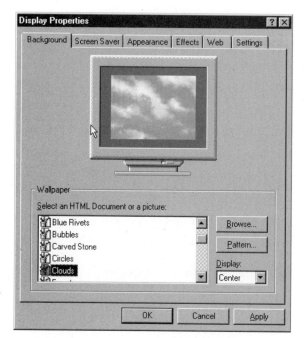

Figure 9-8
Your display can be changed via Control Panel. This is the Display window for Windows 98, which is slightly different for Windows 95

T*he background is an image that serves as the backdrop for your desktop.*

Each tab at the top, which look like tabs that you would find in a notebook, offers a different set of customizable options. Click each tab to see what it offers. For now, just change the background screen (under the Background tab). The background is an image that serves as the backdrop for your desktop. Each entry in the list represents a different background; use the scroll bar to see the entire list. When you click one of these, you can see a preview of what your new background will look like. Find one you like, click it with the mouse, click the OK button, and take a look at your desktop.

If the background you choose doesn't fill the entire preview screen, you can adjust it by selecting Tile or Stretch from the adjacent

Display field. Tile or Stretch "create a full background by plastering the smaller image, like a quilt, across your screen. You can experiment with both of these options and see what you like best.

Changing Your Screen Saver

Have you ever walked past an idle computer and seen a fascinating animation? That's a screen saver, a little program that becomes active when no one uses the PC for a specified period of time. Touch the mouse and the hypnotic graphic disappears. Screen savers were originally intended to extend the life of a monitor, but they really don't offer any utility anymore except for a fun visual effect for your inactive PC. You can also assign a password to your screen saver. If you wander from your machine and use the password option with your screen saver, you can help keep information on your computer private; when the screen saver goes on, you must enter your password to return to display what you were working on.

Your PC comes with a number of different screen savers, also available through the Display option of the Control Panel. Here's how to choose one and start it up:

1. Open the Control Panel window, and double-click the Display icon.

2. Click the Screen Saver tab. The Screen saver window appears.

3. Click the arrow to the right of the field labeled Screen Saver to see the screen savers that are available to you.

TIP

Don't set your screen
saver come on in too short
a time, or else
you will constantly be
interrupted as the screen
saver kicks in while
you're working.

4. Use the scroll bar to see all your options, and click the one you would like to try. A small preview of your selection appears on the little screen.

5. When should the screen saver come on? The Wait field enables you to set the length of time your PC must be inactive before the screen saver comes on.

Turning Off Your PC

Now that you've been through the basics, you can turn off your machine and take a well-deserved break. Here's what you do:

1. Click the Start button.

2. Click the Shut Down option at the bottom of the menu. The Shut Down Windows window appears. Select Shut Down The Computer? and click OK. The machine either turns itself off, or an on-screen message tells you that it is safe to turn off your machine.

You've passed the first hurdle of turning your machine on and becoming familiar with some of its features. Now you can move on to an introduction to software and see how to open a program, create a document in a word processing program, and find out other basic concepts that you need to know for working with the documents you create.

Chapter Ten

The Basics of File Management

Like many others, you have perhaps felt intimidated by the seeming complexity of a computer. Maybe you have been put off by the level of difficulty or the fear of doing something irrevocably wrong. But as powerful and grand as your PC may be, it pales in comparison to you. You are much more in charge of it than you may feel when you first approach it. Keep this in mind: your computer isn't the driving force here. Your computer isn't capable of creativity; it has no muse or inspiration.

Your PC can't independently write letters, manage your finances, or trace your genealogical roots. Whatever your misgivings, you are a vastly more complex being than your computer, and you have everything the computer doesn't have to allow you to reach your goals. You can simply reach some of them a lot faster using this machine that exists to make your life easier.

This chapter walks you through how to get real things accomplished with your computer. We cover how you can use software as a tool in everyday projects. In addition, we show you the importance of keeping all of your work organized and some good tricks to ensure that you stay organized. In the course of this chapter, you'll find out that, when you get the hang of it, using a computer is not so intimidating after all.

Understanding Software: The Tools of Your Trade

No matter what your interest or vocation, no matter what you want to achieve, the computer can help you better realize your goals. Used properly, your computer can simplify and accelerate many of the mundane and time-consuming tasks associated with your day-to-day responsibilities. The computer helps you accomplish your goals with the use of "software," which consists of a set of instructions that transforms your PC, chameleon like, into whatever tool you need. The software, however, can't do anything on its own; like a hammer or a saw, it requires someone with the skills and know-how—and the direction—to perform the task.

No matter what your interest or vocation, no matter what you want to achieve, the computer can help you better realize your goals.

The Right Tool for the Job

Software programs, referred to as "programs," "applications," or "apps" for short, are designed to help you with a particular task. Before performing your task or starting your project, you need to decide what program is best suited for the particular job. Software comes in a number of different categories. Here are some of the most popular ones:

- Word processing software used for writing
- Spreadsheets/personal finance software for taking care of bookkeeping, accounting, and financial chores
- Graphics software for all types of imaging, including drawing, animation, photo editing, and design

- Games software for, well, games!
- Shareware/freeware for the budget conscious—available in all categories
- Utilities for assistance in a variety of computing chores
- Internet software/browsers to allow easy access to and exploration of the Internet

After you decide what to use, based on what programs you have, what you need, and what you're willing to buy, you have to start the program.

Programs on Your PC

When you open the Start menu, the Programs option provides a list of all the programs that are currently available to you on your PC. Although your own list depends on what software you have purchased or what came with your PC, numerous fun, scaled-down programs come with every copy of Windows 95 and Windows 98. These programs let you experiment and get a good feel for what more advanced programs, such as Microsoft Works and Microsoft Word, can really do for you.

Opening a Program

When you want to use a program, you first must open it. Start by opening WordPad, a word processing program that comes with Windows 95 and Windows 98. To open WordPad, follow these steps:

1. Click the Start button to open the Start menu.
2. Move the mouse to the Programs option and, when the submenu appears, move the mouse up to the top entry, Accessories.

When you open the Start menu, the Programs option provides a list of all the programs that are currently available to you on your PC.

3. The Accessories option also has a submenu associated with it. When it appears, navigate to the last entry, WordPad, and click it. The WordPad program opens and you are now working with a word processor. Figure 10-1 shows the opening screen for WordPad.

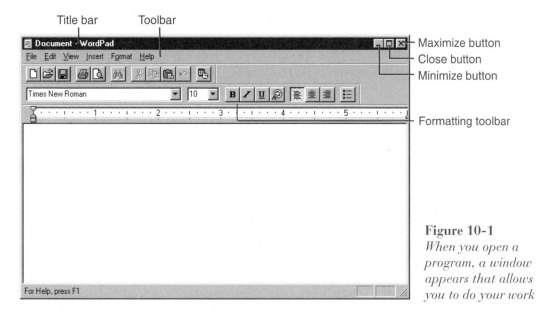

Figure 10-1
When you open a program, a window appears that allows you to do your work

The program window appears, showing the same elements as any other window. The title bar, for example, identifies this as a document in WordPad, and the menu bar appears right below the title bar.

We don't go into the details of word processing here; that comes in the next chapter. For now, we introduce the basics of opening a program, creating a document, saving, and exiting.

TIP

Make it easier on your eyes: maximize the program window by clicking the Maximize button in the upper right corner.

Creating a Document

You've found the Start button. You've clicked the name of a program and opened it. You're staring at a large, white space in the middle of the screen. What do you do now?

That white space is the "document window," which is where you type whatever you want. See the blinking vertical line at the top left corner of the document window? That blinking line, called a "cursor," marks the spot where the first character you type will appear. As you type, the cursor moves with your text. When you reach the end of the line where the margin is set, the cursor automatically jumps down to the next line. This feature is called "wrapping," and it serves the purpose of the Return key on a typewriter for moving down to the next line. With the wrapping feature, you can type as much as you want without having to worry about pressing a carriage return.

The "Enter" key that you see on your keyboard, where a typewriter's Return key is, functions differently on a computer. (Some keyboards label the Enter key as "Return.") Pressing Enter tells the word processing program that you want to begin a new paragraph.

The Enter key has another purpose as well, which is to execute a command. You'll find out more about commands in subsequent chapters. Also, when you move on to creating a document with Microsoft Word in the next chapter, you'll experience the magic of the spelling checker—a utility that finds your errors—and discover one of the best features of using a computer.

Pressing Enter tells the word processing program that you want to begin a new paragraph.

NOTE

Don't press Enter when the words you type reach the end of the screen.

Meanwhile, there it is: your first document. Whether you typed one letter or 10,000 words, you have a document. Now what?

With a typewriter, you can leave the paper on which you're typing right where it is, turn off the machine, and go do something else. When you return, the document you left in it will still be there (unless someone yanked it out). Unlike a piece of paper in a typewriter, however, your computer document does not yet truly exist. If you just close the word processing program and go away, you won't see that document when you return. To make a document "real," you must go through some simple—but critical—steps, discussed next.

Getting Help with a Program

If you find yourself frustrated and unable to do something in a program, check out your online Help options. Almost all programs offer some form of online Help, and the procedure for accessing it is the same, regardless of the program. To get help, click Help on the toolbar to open the Help menu, and then select Help Topics or some similarly named option in that menu, depending on the program.

Saving Your Work

Every program that allows you to create something also allows you to save what you have created. Fortunately, many programs are designed for you to follow the same procedure to save your work.

TIP

Dialog boxes give you the means to communicate to the computer program the task you want to perform.

Here's how you save a document in WordPad to make it be there when you come back:

1. Click File and then click the Save option. The Save As dialog box appears, as shown in Figure 10-2.

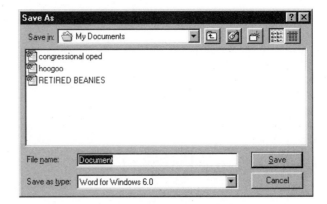

Figure 10-2
The Save As dialog box prompts you for a name and a place to save your work

2. Give your document a name.

3. Click the Save button.

That's all there is to it. Well, almost. Step 2 needs some elaboration. The next two sections give you more information on this simple but important step.

Naming Your Document

In WordPad, near the bottom of the Save As dialog box is a rectangular box with the words "File name" to its left. The box shows the text "document.doc" highlighted within it.

The name "document.doc" is the "default" name, or the name the program automatically assigns to your document. The three-letter extension identifies the type of program you're in; in this case, it's a word processing program that uses .doc. Every time you start

TIP

Highlighted text shows up on-screen in a different color. Text highlighted in a dialog box shows up with a different background color, such as dark blue.

a new document with a program, a default name will be assigned to your work. When you save your work, however, you are better off giving your document a name that's more meaningful to you.

Say, for example, that you write a letter to the editor of your local newspaper. You need to give the letter a name that indicates its contents to you and distinguishes it from any other letters or documents that you write. Including a date along with the name might be helpful, as in "Editor08-09-00.doc" for August 9, 2000. You can use whatever naming system is best for you. Bear in mind, however, that you can't use slashes in a file name. Slashes are reserved for another use that we don't need to go into yet.

Filing Your Document

Another aspect of naming your document to save it involves giving it a place to reside within your system. Just as the program assigns a default name, it also assigns a default location for a document unless you direct it to a different one. Similar to the way you file documents in folders in a filing cabinet, the program deposits your document into an electronic "folder." When you open the File menu and choose Save in WordPad, you can see icons that look like tiny file folders. Those folders constitute the heart of the organization system of your computer.

Notice the area next to the words "Save in" in this dialog box. In that area, called a "list box," you see an icon that looks like an open folder. That folder is the default location that WordPad assigns to your document. For now, just leave this location as it is. We cover how to change this location later in this chapter, in the section "Keeping Your File System Organized." Click the Save

NOTE

Don't use the slash character (/) in file names.

WARNING

If you don't give your document a meaningful name, you will never be able to find your work; all your documents will appear on your hard drive like so many canned goods without labels!

button with your mouse; your document, newly named, is now saved. The document's new name appears in the WordPad title bar.

At this point, you've already worked your way through the basic steps of opening a program, creating a document, naming it, and saving it. With luck, you're beginning to feel less intimidated and realize that you truly are the one in charge. With that in mind, you can go ahead and print your new document and then delve more deeply into the workings of your system.

Printing Your Work

If your printer is on, connected, and has paper in it, you might be ready to print. Here's what you do in WordPad:

1. Click File. The File menu opens.
2. Click Print. The Print dialog box opens.
3. Look in the rectangular box, or list box, that appears next to the word "Name." This list box shows you what printer your software program plans to send your document to. If your printer's software has been configured correctly on your system, its name appears in that list box.
4. Click OK. Your printer obediently churns out your document.

Opening Saved Documents

When you want to work on a previously saved document, click the File option and select Open from the File menu. The Open dialog box appears with a folder icon showing in the Look In list box. If that folder isn't the one containing the document you need, use your mouse to double-click one of the folders that appears in the set of folders below the Look in box, or possibly above the Look in box.

Exiting a Document and Program

When you complete your work, save it, and are ready to exit the software program, almost every program you use offers three ways to do so:

- Click the Close button in the upper right corner.
- Double-click the small icon in the left corner of the title bar.
- Click File and, in the File menu, select the Exit option.

If you exit without saving your work, a message appears on-screen asking whether you want to save your work. Click the Yes or No button. Or, if you change your mind and don't want to exit yet, click Cancel.

Backing Up Your Work

Your PC will save you hours of time on your various projects, but always keep in mind that accidents happen and work can be accidentally deleted or overwritten. Play it safe with your hard work by backing up your projects onto floppy disks or your Zip drive. Here's the easiest way to back up your work:

1. Return to the Desktop.
2. Double-click My Computer.
3. Move the My Computer window to the right side of the screen.
4. Open another window, and navigate to the files you want to back up.

TIP

Even if your project is not completed — and you don't anticipate finishing for days or weeks—be sure to back up your work in progress.

5. Click the files to highlight them, and drag them to the floppy disk icon or the Zip drive icon as they appear in the My Computer window. Don't be shy about backing up your work!

Using Other Types of Software Programs

Although many programs have similarities, the fundamental purpose of each program can be very different. To see an example of a different type of program, follow these steps to open Paint, a beginner's drawing program that comes free with Windows 95 and Windows 98:

1. Click the Start button to open the Start menu.

2. Move the mouse to the Programs option and, when the submenu appears, move the mouse up to the first entry, Accessories.

3. The Accessories option has its own submenu. When it appears, navigate to the Paint entry and click it. When the Paint program opens, the screen shown in Figure 10-3 appears.

With Paint, you can pick a color from the color palette at the bottom of the window. You also can choose a brush or tool from the Tool palette that appears on the left edge of the window. As you can see, the purpose of this program is obviously different from a word processing program. Despite this difference, the File menu still provides you with the same fundamental functions, including Open, Save, Print, and Exit.

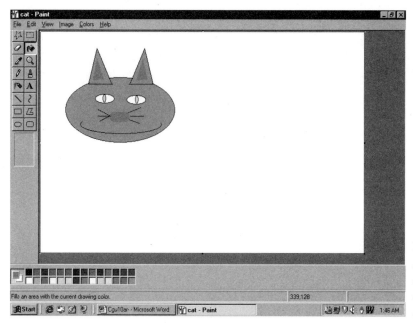

Figure 10-3
*Microsoft Windows comes
with a fun, beginner's
drawing program called
PC Paint.*

Sometimes a program doesn't seem to follow the rules exactly.
Many games, for example, have no File menu. But even without
the File menu, an Exit or Quit option typically appears in a menu.
To see an example of a typical game menu (and to take advantage
of an excuse to play), try opening Solitaire, one of the games that
ships with Windows 95 and Windows 98:

1. Click the Start button to open the Start menu.

2. Move the mouse to the Programs option. When the submenu appears, move the mouse to the top entry, Accessories.

3. The Accessories option has its own submenu. When it
   appears, navigate to the entry "Games" and await the appearance of yet another submenu. Drag the mouse to the Solitaire

option in this last menu and click it. Solitaire opens, as shown in Figure 10-4.

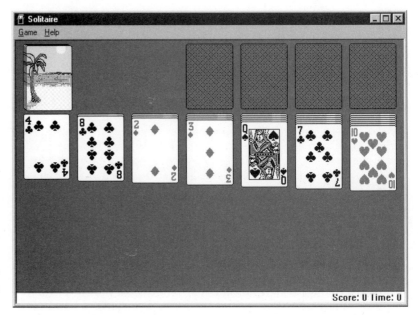

Figure 10-4
Games on your PC often have nonstandard menu options

Notice that the File menu is missing from the menu bar; in its place is a simple Game menu.

As you can see, the Game menu in Solitaire provides the means to start a new game or exit the game. The window in which the game appears also contains the same Minimize, Maximize, and Close options that you find with every other window.

Multitasking

Your Windows operating system is capable of running more than one program at a time. Called "multitasking," this feature means that you can, for example, open your word processor to write a letter, open your drawing program to create an accompanying sketch, and start a game of Solitaire to occupy you when you feel like taking a break from whatever else you're doing. You don't have to close one program to go into another. The easy way to manage all the various programs you have running is to use the taskbar.

Multitasking with the Taskbar

The taskbar consists of the row of buttons at the bottom of your screen. When you minimize an open program, document, or window, that element shrinks to become a button with an icon on the taskbar, awaiting your order to make it reappear on your screen.

To see what happens when you place an item on the taskbar, open the document you created in WordPad and follow these steps:

1. Click the Minimize button in the upper right corner of the window. It's the first one, going left to right, in that little row of buttons.

2. Look down at the taskbar to find the button that reads "Document – WordPad." Your document is still open; it just doesn't take up space on your screen.

3. Click the Document – WordPad button once. The WordPad window—with your document—is back.

As you can see, when you want to access the item or task that you minimized, you can click the corresponding button in the taskbar and bring the item back up instantly. You don't need to track it down on your computer and reopen it. The taskbar allows you to toggle among programs instantaneously.

Keeping Track of Open Windows

In addition to using the taskbar to keep more than one program running at a time, you can have many windows open on-screen simultaneously. But you can rid your screen of the clutter of too many windows by clicking the Minimize button on the windows that you don't need immediately. The windows fold up and appear as buttons in the taskbar. When you need one open, just click once on the corresponding button in the taskbar and the window reappears on your desktop.

Keeping Your File System Organized

You've heard the maxim that success is 1 percent inspiration and 99 percent perspiration. Success in using a computer, however, requires at least 50 percent organization.

Imagine if, in your day-to-day life, you just threw everything into a big container. Your clothes, gifts, family photos, undeveloped film, bank statements, bills—everything. Soon the container would overflow. Now imagine trying to find something when you needed it. Fortunately, no one operates like this, at least not without some major catastrophes! To organize, you filter, you sort, you discard, and you prioritize, based on a system that lets you find the things you need to find quickly.

You need to bring the same concept of organization to your computer. You will create many different kinds of documents on your computer and, without a means of organization, you'll have a difficult time finding your documents. Although your Windows operating system takes care of some of the organization without your help, it doesn't know the best place for the documents you

NOTE

Having too many tasks open on the taskbar simultaneously can slow down your computer. If it seems sluggish, close one or two programs or windows.

create. Only you know how best to organize your own space. Windows 95 and Windows 98 give you the means to build an organization; you just need to know how that works. This section shows you how.

Understanding Your Computer's Filing System

To start, take a look at how your PC is currently organized. To do so, go to the desktop and double-click the My Computer icon at the left side of your screen.

When you click this icon, the My Computer window appears, similar to that shown in Figure 10-5.

The icons we are interested in provide access to the floppy drive, your hard drive, the CD-ROM drive, and any other storage devices

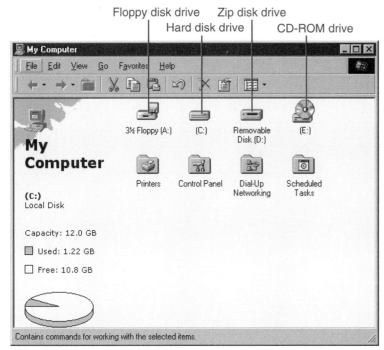

Figure 10-5
The My Computer window is your gateway to everything stored on your computer.

you might have, such as a Zip drive. To access information on any of these drives, you must double-click them. The drive labeled "C" is your hard drive. Double-click it, and you see a number of files and folders. Use the scroll bar or maximize the window if you need a better view.

TIP

You can also access an icon using the right mouse button to click it once (right-click); then select Open from the menu.

Excel

Mspaint

Winword

Identifying Programs

Besides naming your documents and creations, Windows 95 and Windows 98 help you keep organized by assigning different icons to different kinds of programs. For example, WordPad has its own icon; Microsoft Word has another; Paint has yet another.

When you see these icons, you know immediately what program was used to create them. You may not recognize some file icons on your PC, but that just means that you aren't yet familiar with the program that was used to create them.

Using Windows Explorer

Sometimes, all the icons can be difficult to read and to navigate. Windows 95 and Windows 98 provide several different ways for you to view what's on your hard drive, but probably the easiest is to use Windows Explorer.

To see your file system through Windows Explorer follow these steps:

1. Click the Start button. The Start menu appears.
2. Point your mouse to the Programs option. The Programs submenu appears.
3. Find Windows Explorer and click it.

TIP

With Windows Explorer, you can see where all the files on your computer are located.

Now you can see your entire organization of programs, folders, and subfolders in plain view. Click the scroll bar to navigate the system quickly.

Creating Folders

Previously in this chapter, we touched on saving your documents to "folders," the storage areas that function much like an electronic filing cabinet. Your computer already has some folders, but to truly organize your documents, you need to be able to create your own folders as well, giving them names that make sense to you.

To create a folder, follow these steps:

1. Click the Start button. The Start menu appears.

2. Move your mouse to Programs to make the Programs sub-menu appear.

3. Click Windows Explorer. The Exploring window opens, showing an alphabetical list of all the folders that exist on your hard drive.

4. Click the File menu in the Exploring window. The Windows Explorer File menu opens.

5. Move your mouse to the New option. A submenu appears with "Folder" at the top.

6. Click the Folder option. Look to the right side of the window. A folder icon with a highlighted box next to it showing "New Folder" appears at the bottom of the folder list.

7. Type a name for your new folder and press Enter.

TIP

Organize your computer files just as you organize a file cabinet—using folders.

TIP

To rename an existing folder, select it, choose Rename from the File menu, and then type the new name.

TIP

To rename a folder or file quickly, click the name once and press the F2 key.

N*aming a folder is as easy as creating it.*

Naming Folders

As with your document files, you want to give your new folders more specific names than just the generic "New Folder" moniker. Naming a folder is as easy as creating it. Move the mouse to your new folder (or the folder you want to rename), and click in the box where "New Folder" appears. The highlight (or colored background) vanishes. Now you can delete the text that is already there and type whatever you want to name the folder, such as "Letters" or "Taxes." You can make a folder name as specific as you want: "Letters to John"; "1999 Taxes." As time goes on and you become more comfortable with your computer, you can continue to adjust your folders' names and organization, naming and renaming as much as you need to.

Creating Folders Within Folders

With a regular filing cabinet filled with paper folders, trying to store folders inside other ones would be awkward and inefficient. Your computer's electronic filing cabinet, however, makes this kind of storage efficient and desirable.

A folder that you name "Taxes," for example, can contain numerous subfolders that further sort and organize your tax-related documents. You can have subfolders labeled "1997 Taxes," "1998 Taxes," and so on. Or you can deposit documents in Taxes subfolders labeled "Household Expenses," "Charities," "Home Maintenance," and so on. Your subfolders can in turn have their own subfolders, which can have *their* own subfolders . . . and if we go on like this, the description will make an easy process sound confusing!

To create a subfolder, simply go to Windows Explorer, as explained on page 124. Click a folder under which you want to create a subfolder. In the Exploring window, click the File menu and move the mouse to New to open its submenu. Click Folder and type a name in the folder's box that appears on the right side of the dialog box. Press Enter, and you have created a subfolder.

Moving Folders and Files

You can move files wherever you want within a window, between folders, from one window to another, or even from your hard drive to a floppy disk. To get files where you want them, click the file you want to move, and drag it to the desired location.

Finding Files

Keeping track of where you put all of your files, even if you're the most organized person in town, is a challenge. With files, like your car keys, you can expect to forget where you've stowed them from time to time. Fortunately for all of us, Windows 95 and Windows 98 have a built-in private detective that can help you find anything and everything—and in a lot less time than it takes to find your keys!

To find a file that you have misplaced on your PC, follow these steps:

1. Click the Start button. The Start menu appears.
2. Point the mouse to the Find option. The Find submenu appears.
3. Click Files or Folders. The Find: All Files dialog box appears.
4. Click in the Named text box, and type as much of the name as you can remember.

TIP

Always choose folder names that describe the folder contents.

NOTE

To "drag" something means that you click the item and continue pressing the mouse button while using the mouse to move the item to a new location. Release the mouse button when the item is in place.

TIP

Don't worry if you don't remember where you filed something. That's what Find is for.

5. The Look In list box shows the drive on which your file will be searched. If you want to search a drive other than your C hard drive, such as a floppy disk drive, click the down arrow next to this list box, and select the desired drive.

6. Click the Find Now button.

A window appears with a list of all the files that meet your search criteria.

When you type the file name in the Find: All Files text box, be sure to spell the file name correctly. If you misspell it, your search won't find the file or files you're looking for. If you can't remember the full name, you can just enter a fragment of the file name, and you'll find your file just as quickly. Be careful not to make the fragment too short, or you'll be awash in files that share part of the same name but aren't what you're really after.

Deleting Files and Folders

We know someone who has a good rule for keeping tidy: if he has an unread magazine in his house for more than three months, it goes into the circular file. You should tidy up your hard drive on a regular basis, and that should include throwing away, or deleting, unwanted or outdated files. Are you holding on to all three versions of that letter you sent to the phone company a few months ago? Time to do some housecleaning.

Two ways to rid your system of outdated files are as follows:

- Click the file or folder you want to delete, and press the Del (Delete) key in the lower right corner of your keyboard. When you do so, you are asked whether you really want the

TIP

When a file is located by Find, you don't have to hunt it down in the folder where it is buried. Instead, take the shortcut: double-click the file name when it appears in the list of found files.

TIP

To find a Word document that you think begins with the word "Report," for example, type Report*.doc in the Find dialog box.

NOTE

A file in the Recycle Bin isn't really deleted until you empty the Recycle Bin.

file to go into the "recycling bin" (even Windows is environ-mentally minded!).

- If you prefer, you can also drag the file or folder to the recycling bin located on your desktop. Either way, pruning and weeding your hard drive of unwanted files will make staying organized much easier.

As you become more versed on the ins and outs of your PC, it will, like a well-worn chair, mold to the contours of your personality. Everyone likes having things set up and organized a certain way, and the more you use the computer, the more you will be inclined to customize and personalize it. Eventually, you'll begin to feel at home with your computer.

WARNING

If you discover a file or document that is of mysterious origins, don't delete it. A number of files appear in various folders on your PC that are important to the operation of Microsoft Windows or other programs.

Chapter Eleven

The Golden Age for (Your) Writing

How many times have you heard that computers are making books go the way of silent movies?

Computers have not killed the written word. In fact, computing has done more to prove the importance of writing than any other modern technology. Writing is required to communicate on the World Wide Web, to compose e-mail to colleagues, friends, or relatives, to create polished and professional reports, and a whole lot more.

Writing is a critical skill, and more than likely it will be the mortar of your computing experience. In this chapter we survey a few of the tools available to help you with the writing process. When you finish this chapter, you'll have a good understanding of how to most effectively use these tools in all your writing projects.

Welcome to ~~Typing~~ Word Processing 101

A word processor is arguably the most important and the most popular application available today. With its impressive array of features, it is responsible for making its once-proud ancestor, the typewriter, obsolete.

In the early days of computing, people were burdened with word processors that were complicated, hard to use, and user-unfriendly. Those days are happily past. You'll find that you can produce very impressive-looking documents faster while spending less time on the drudgery of typing, correcting, and editing. And less drudgery means more time devoted to the creative process.

The Big Picture: What a Great Word Processor Offers

The best way to learn is to do, so it's time to get started. One of the most popular word processors is Microsoft Word, so we use that program for this chapter. Your computer may already have Microsoft Word on it, so check your Start menu to confirm this.

To open Microsoft Word, open the Start menu, point to the Programs option, and select Microsoft Word from the Programs menu. Word appears on your screen, as shown in Figure 11-1.

Word can do just about anything for you, but what makes it great is that its most important features—the ones you need and can really use—are always right at your fingertips.

Befriending the Toolbars

The two rows of buttons below the menu bar, as shown in Figure 11-2, are called "toolbars." The top toolbar is called the Standard toolbar; below that is the Formatting toolbar. The toolbars give you fast access to the most commonly used features in Word. Those same features are accessible from the menu bar, but the toolbars are a lot more convenient.

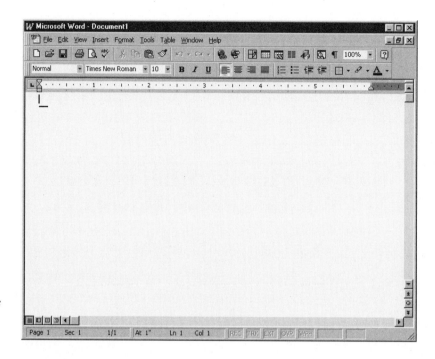

Figure 11-1
Microsoft Word fulfills the needs of the most demanding user

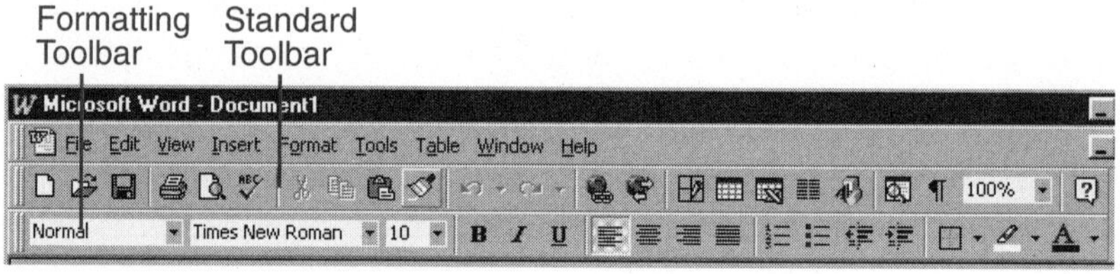

Figure 11-2
The toolbars give you fast access to whatever you need

TIP

Hold your mouse over a button if you don't know what it's for.

For a quick preview of the tools available on the toolbars, slowly move your mouse over the toolbar buttons, stopping briefly on each one. When you stop, the name of the button pops up in what is called a "ScreenTip." ScreenTips are helpful reminders even after you've grown more familiar with the program.

When you're ready, head into the next section to take the plunge into working with your first Microsoft Word document.

Creating a Document in Microsoft Word

Chapter 10 introduced you to some of the basic concepts of working with documents in WordPad. As promised, these same concepts apply to some other word processing programs, such as Microsoft Word.

In the Word document window, click the mouse and begin typing. Remember that, with the "wrapping" feature, you don't need to press the Enter key until you want to begin a new paragraph. Done? Now click File on the menu bar, and choose Save to save the document as *"your name* #1". Congratulations! You've created your first Word document.

The Basics of Editing: Cut, Copy, and Paste

Introductory Anthropology courses teach that the human opposable thumb and forefinger distinguished humankind from the apes. We could say that computers distinguished themselves from the typewriter when they allowed us to cut, copy, and paste. These are the simplest of features and, in many respects, some of the most powerful because Cut, Copy, and Paste allow you to reorganize and rearrange your document with the touch of a button. Here's how:

1. Click in the left margin of one of your lines of text. The highlight lets you know that that line of text has been selected.

2. Click Edit and select Copy from the Edit menu.

3. Click your mouse on the scroll bar to move to the end of your document, and then click the cursor in the document.

4. Click Edit and select Paste from the Edit menu.

TIP

See Chapter 10 for a review of creating, naming, and saving a document. The steps are the same in Microsoft Word as they are in WordPad.

You just copied the first line and pasted it to the end of your document.

The Copy and Paste features allow you to select any size portion of your text. You can copy a word or a whole page, or more. Cut and Paste works the same way, except that cutting completely removes the original piece of text from its starting location so that it appears only where you decide to reposition it in your document.

Formatting for Fun and Profit

Besides allowing you to edit your document on the fly, Microsoft Word also helps you transform your document visually so that you can better communicate your thoughts. As an example, Figure 11-3 provides a taste of what you can do just with options from the Formatting toolbar.

Figure 11-4 shows what's available to you on the Formatting toolbar.

Using the following tools provides some of the ways you can give your own document a custom makeover. Just select the text you want to format, and then choose one or more of the following:

- Bold
- Italic
- Underline
- Center
- Type Size
- Typeface (font)

Formatting really is fun. So many ways are available to change the appearance of a document. One very popular way is to change typefaces, commonly called "fonts." A font is the collection of

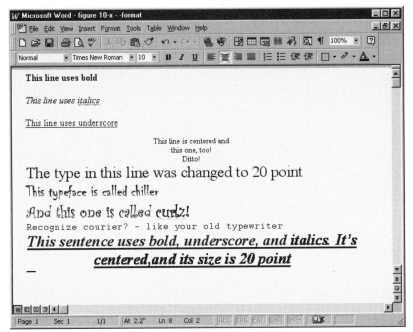

Figure 11-3
Word has a wide range of formatting options that help you make your document look as dashing as you want

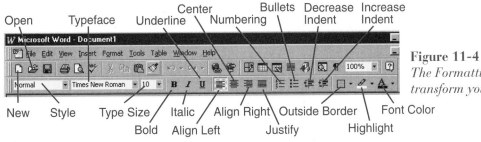

Figure 11-4
The Formatting toolbar lets you transform your documents effortlessly

letters, numbers, and other characters that have the same design and style. To get a sense of your options, just look at the list of fonts! But as you experiment, you'll make formatting choices that you don't like and that you'll want to take back. Have no fear; you're not stuck with anything. Getting rid of a format change requires, in many cases, the same procedure you used to apply it. For example, if you want to change bold text back to regular text, select the text and click the Bold button again. If you don't like a particular font, select the text and opt for a more appropriate typeface.

Drawing the Line: Starting a New Page

Remember how, with your old typewriter, you had to gauge the end of the page? Remember the kind of trouble it caused when you tried to squeeze in one more line? With Microsoft Word, you don't have to think about the end of the page. Word takes care of the number of lines that can fit—even when you mix up the type sizes on any given page—automatically. Word starts a new page when the current one is full and inserts a "page break" where the old one ends. You can identify an automatic page break by the thin, dotted line that appears across the document window (don't worry, it doesn't print).

You can start a new page before your current page is full. To do so, follow these steps:

1. Click Insert and click Break on the Insert menu.
2. Page Break is the default choice—it's already selected—so click OK. Word automatically begins a new, clean page for you, indicated by a darker line within your document and across the document screen.

Figure 11-5 shows both types of page breaks: the dotted one that Word places when you reach the bottom of your page, and the one you put in when you want to jump to a new page.

TIP

Would you like to change the length or width of a document's page size? From the File menu, select Page Setup.

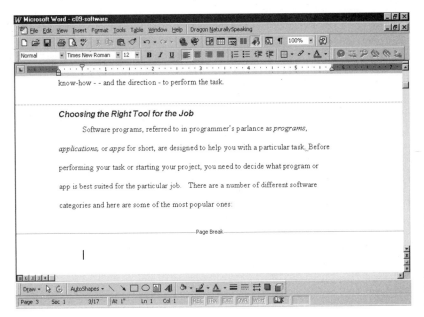

Figure 11-5
Word takes care of meticulously filling your pages but also allows you to decide how much should go on a page

Scrolling Through a Document

As your document grows in length, you'll need access to all pages even though your screen can display only a small part of the document at a time. The easiest way to move around in your document is with the scroll bars. To move up in your document, use the scroll bar to go up. To move down in your document, scroll down. If you don't remember how to scroll through the document, you can refresh your memory in Chapter 9.

Undoing Mistakes with Undo

If you make a simple error or a string of blunders, Word can help you out of the mess. Just follow these steps:

1. Click Edit.
2. Click the Undo Typing option on the Edit menu.
3. Repeat as necessary.

TIP

If you make a mistake, it's easy to undo it!

Watch your document as you perform the Undo command to make sure that you don't undo too much. If you goof and go back too many steps, you can remedy that error:

1. Click Edit.
2. Select the Redo option!

Katching Your Typos

If you use the Microsoft Word spelling checker, you're sure to become a big fan. As your constant companion (if you choose), the spelling checker gently points out when you make an error by underlining the word or words with a colored scribble. In fact, Word even has a marvelous grammar checker that points out issues with the mechanics of your writing—as you write!

To turn the spelling and grammar checkers on, follow these steps:

1. Click Tools and select Options (at the bottom). The Options dialog box appears.
2. Click the Spelling & Grammar tab, and the Spelling and Grammar options appear.
3. To activate the spelling checker, make sure the box next to "Hide spelling errors in this document" is not selected. If this box is selected, click the check box to remove it.
4. To activate the grammar checker, make sure the box next to "Hide grammatical errors in this document" is not selected. If it is selected, click the check box to remove it.

Now go back to your document and search for any misspellings by clicking Tools and then Spelling And Grammar on that menu. If

NOTE

Word can't help undo mistakes you may have made in your personal life. Many of the software products available out there are great, but they aren't that great!

WARNING

Microsoft Word's grammar and spelling checkers can't always catch usage errors when the words are spelled correctly, so be careful: "ewe and eye" has quite a different meaning than "you and I," but Word will accept both.

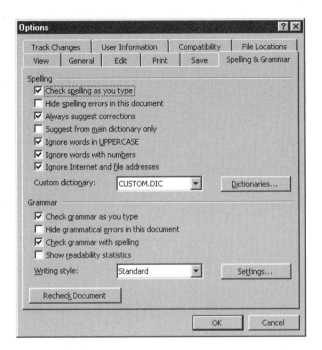

Word highlights a word, right-click that word and watch as a list of possible corrections pops up. Click the word you intended to use, and it instantly replaces the mistake.

Saving Before Your Retirement

Most computer users learn the hard way about saving work. Here's the lesson the easy way: *save your work frequently!* All you have to do is click File and click Save. An even quicker method is to click the Save button on the Standard toolbar. That's the whole enchilada (after you've named a document, of course).

Don't wait until you are done with your work. Save repeatedly as you work. If you have toiled away at your masterpiece, not saved your work, and something happens—you lose power or your

NOTE

A computer "crash" is the term used to describe when a program or disk drive unexpectedly fails to operate properly. Sometimes a crash requires that you restart your computer. Either way, a crash results in the loss of any unsaved work.

TIP

Microsoft Word does have an autosave feature. On the Help menu, select Contents And Index and look up "AutoSave" to see how this feature works.

TIP

Checking Print Preview can save time and wasted paper.

computer crashes—you will curse your infernal machine for losing your labor of love. But doing that won't bring back your work (and it's not your PC's fault). So, to say it yet again: save your work frequently during a session and, if your machine goes down for any reason, you won't have nearly as much to regret.

Printing: Enjoying a Sneak Preview

Printing in Word follows the same procedure as that in WordPad covered in Chapter 10: click File and select Print. Printing can, however, take some time, and because it also uses ink and paper — all valuable resources—previewing what your document looks like before you print it doesn't hurt. For a sneak peak, click File and select Print Preview. When you select Print Preview, your document appears on-screen, as shown in Figure 11-6.

If you want to go through a long document, use the scroll bar to see your other pages. To change how big or small the pages appear in the Preview window, click the (%) Zoom box on the Standard toolbar, and select an option from the drop-down list. The percentage you select here does not affect the size at which the document is printed.

You can't edit your document from this screen, but rather can only see a preview of how your printout will appear. To exit the Preview screen, click the Close button on the toolbar.

We've talked about some of the basic and powerful features of Word, and we've hardly scratched the surface. If you want to learn

TIP

Microsoft Word offers a very thorough online help feature (accessible via the Help menu) that can provide a wealth of information when questions arise.

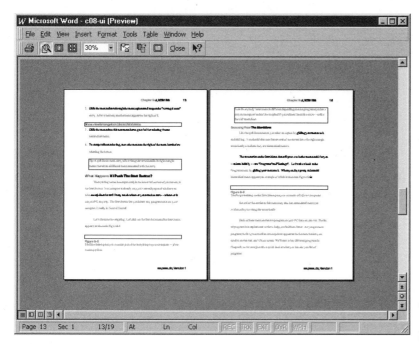

Figure 11-6
Print Preview lets you see how your pages will look before you print them.

a lot more about Word, you can and should experiment with it. If you are interested in more written information, you'll find many books that detail everything Word can do. When you find yourself searching or reaching for a feature that seems hard to grasp, you would do well to reach for a Microsoft Press book such as *Microsoft Word Step by Step, Running Microsoft Word*, or *Microsoft Word At a Glance*. For a list of books published by Microsoft Press about Word, see *http://mspress.microsoft.com/findabook* and select "Word" as the subject.

✒ Chapter Twelve ✒

Sprouting Wings:
Flying with the Global Community

The much-ballyhooed Internet. Is it all that it's cracked up to be? Fewer than 10 years ago, the Internet was almost exclusively the domain of scientists, engineers, government/military personnel, and students. Now it has transformed itself, the culture of computing, and the way the world communicates.

In a few short years, the Internet has proven to be a profound agent of change, both technological and social. The Internet is all that it's cracked up to be and more. It is astonishing.

In this chapter, we take the long view of the Internet: what it is, what you need to connect to it, what to guard against when you do go online, and how you can benefit from it. The Internet is as compelling as computing can be and this chapter will show you why.

What in the Heck Is the Internet, Anyway?

The U.S. Department of Defense laid the foundation for the Internet back in the 1960s but did not intend to create what the Internet has become. The Defense department wanted to connect its computers to a network that would enable its computers at remote locations to exchange information and resources. One critical requirement was that the network be impervious to catastrophic events—such as nuclear attacks. The way to satisfy that requirement was to decentralize the network so that if part of the system went down, communications could be rerouted and still reach their intended destinations along other lines.

The Department of Defense succeeded in meeting its requirement, and we see the result today: the Internet exists without a central hub or any sort of Master Computer. Over the years, the Internet began to grow with more and more people getting connected and no one setting artificial boundaries or rules to participate. It was only a matter of time before it exploded into the lives of nontechnical people everywhere, and the Internet has since become *the* new and largely unexpected channel for communication. Figures 12-1 and 12-2 show a couple of Web sites aimed at different segments of the population.

Underneath it all are countless computer networks interconnected by phone and transmission lines. The system is based on a "client/server" approach whereby servers are computers that hold information and are accessed by client computers looking to access that information. Your own PC is a "client." You can sign on to the Internet using a PC in Piscataway, New Jersey, for example, and are free to roam unfettered about the globe. Without so much as a toll call, you'll find yourself reading the Prague daily paper, getting marital advice from a mate down under, or chatting with someone from Kenya about your next safari adventure. You can even keep up with some of the FBI's most wanted (see Figure 12-3). And you don't even have to get out of your pajamas. The Internet is anything but a static phenomenon, and it is evolving at a break-

T he Internet is anything but a static phenomenon, and it is evolving at a break neck pace.

Figure 12-1
*The Internet has
something for kids...*

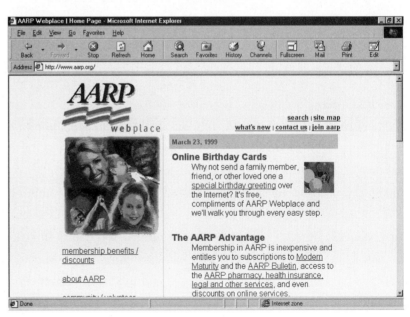

Figure 12-2
*...and grown-ups
alike!*

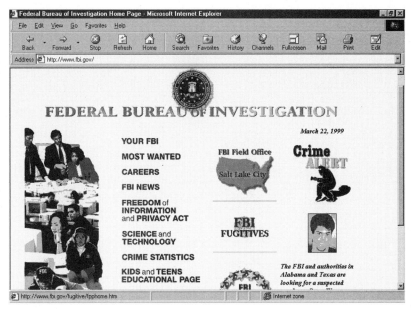

Figure 12-3
The Federal Bureau of Investigation uses the Web to publicize its most wanted

neck pace. Like a kaleidoscope, the Internet is different each time you look at it. It is as glorious as it is historic.

Why Some People Fear the Internet

The undeniable reality is that the Internet, like every other aspect of modern life, does have some negatives, including that of people who use the Internet to try to take advantage of others.

The other undeniable reality, though, is that the Internet is safer than real life.

When you go to the corner market, for example, you take the risk of meeting a grifter who wants to con you out of your life savings, or worse. Such risks don't mean that corner markets are a bad idea or that going outside and having social contact is a bad idea. It just means you must follow some basic rules and keep your eyes open. Can you have bad encounters with people on the Internet? Of course. Can you get addicted to the Internet? Perhaps, if you are predisposed to such excesses. Can you encounter pornography online? Yes, just as you can elsewhere. To live full lives, we have no choice but to accept the dangers of living and interacting in society, and so it goes with the Internet. The fears shouldn't act as excuses to remain disconnected; they should be the motivation to behave responsibly while connected.

The Internet is really about freedom. People can say what they want, and they can say it however they want, for the most part. People from all over the world participate on the Internet, representing countless lifestyles and belief systems. You can be sure that you will disagree with at least some of what's out there. You can also be sure that you will come to embrace many good people from around the world who show us all that different is sometimes bad, sometimes good, sometimes better, and sometimes it's just different.

People from all over the world participate on the Internet, representing countless lifestyles and belief systems.

Do You Meet the Internet Requirements?

The Internet is anything but an exclusive club. What is so confusing to so many people—and vexing to many oppressive governments—is that the requirements for getting online consist solely of a computer with a modem, a phone line, a little software, and an Internet connection (which we discuss in Chapter 13).

A dominant factor in these few requirements is speed. the process of sending and receiving information on the Internet is slower than it has to be if you have older equipment. If you're in the market for a new PC, try to get the fastest processor you can afford, at least 64 megabytes of RAM, and the fastest modem available. As of this writing, that's a V.90 56 Kbps modem (see Chapter 8 on buying a new computer). You can find some other modem options, such as cable modems, but these require special hookups and can prove to be difficult for a beginner.

What You Need When You Pack Your Software Bag

To go online, you need some software with your hardware. Here's a list of what to pack to prepare for your first online trip:

- Microsoft Windows 95 or Windows 98
- Microsoft Internet Explorer (available with Microsoft Office 2000 and easily accessible from Windows 98—see Chapter 14)
- Microsoft Outlook or Microsoft Outlook Express (see Chapter 13)
- Virus software (see next section)

Most new computers come with these programs already installed on them. Check your computer to confirm that you have them also. On the Windows taskbar, click Start and point to Programs. You'll see a full listing of all your installed software.

Your Computer Needs Its Shots

When you begin your Internet journeys, you'll quickly discover how much information and software are available and how freely it is passed around. The vast majority of Internet travelers have come to embrace this philosophy of sharing and generosity of spirit. Unfortunately, this generosity has not gone unnoticed by some less-than-stellar individuals. Some programmers see the free dissemination of information and software as an opportunity to

The vast majority of Internet travelers have come to embrace this philosophy of sharing and generosity of spirit.

cause mischief and even harm. They do this by creating computer viruses. A "virus" is a small hidden program that rides piggyback on another program or file that you download. When you open the program, you wake up the virus, and it installs itself on your computer without your knowledge.

Viruses can cause a number of problems, some relatively innocuous, others quite malicious. Viruses are not exactly rampant on the Internet; they aren't waiting to get you at every turn. They are, however, out there, and you might encounter one. To guard against this possibility, you need to install anti-virus software on your PC (it comes installed on many new PCs). The anti-virus software guards against the surreptitious activation of such a program, alerts you to the problem, and then "disinfects" your machine by eradicating the virus from it. If your computer didn't come with virus protection software installed, you can find popular programs—Norton Anti-Virus and McAfee Virus Scan are two examples—at just about any store that sells software.

Keep in mind that new computer viruses, like their biological counterparts, continue to appear. To counter these new strains, you can update a virus protection program by visiting the respective Web site, as shown in Figure 12-4.

Benefits of Going Online

The benefits of surfing the Internet are so wide-ranging and dependent on individual tastes that you have to try it on for size. One thing everyone on the Internet agrees about, though: the Internet has

TIP

Visit Microsoft on the World Wide Web (http://www.microsoft.com) to get more information about maintaining your computer and pick up some great tips on using Windows 98.

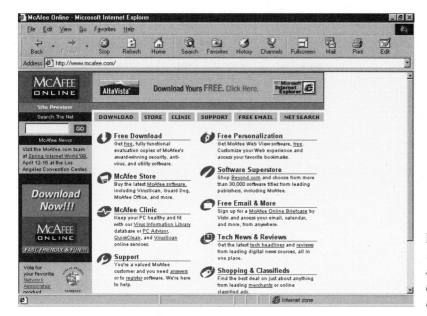

Figure 12-4
Virus protection software can be updated anytime on the Internet

ushered in a new age of global communication, discourse, and information access from which no one should be excluded. The only way to take advantage of it all is to get connected.

Chapter Thirteen

10,000,000 Tin Cans and a Lot of String: Getting Connected

Back in the 1800s, people were understandably taken by the wondrous technology of their day, the telephone. Imagine the excitement it generated when people realized that they could communicate with people over an incredible distance in an instant, without traveling any distance themselves. What nobody thinks about, though, are the kinds of hoops the earliest users had to jump through to get connected!

Sound familiar? For someone who's already wired to the Internet, getting connected is simple, but for a novice, the "Internet connection" can be as elusive as the Loch Ness monster. In this chapter, we show you how to evaluate which kind of Internet connection is best for you and how you can get it.

What Is an Internet Service Provider?

When you move into a house or apartment, you need phone service. You probably have a few phones that you brought with you from the old house, so you already have the hardware you need. You know what you have to do next: call the phone company. For a monthly service charge, it connects your phone to the giant global phone network that allows you to communicate with other people who also have phone service. Phone companies offer a list of additional services such as call waiting and caller ID, but without basic service, you can't use the phone at all.

The Internet works the same way. You already have the hardware you need: a computer, a modem, and the phone connection (via the phone company). Now you need to find an Internet service provider, or ISP. An ISP is a company that, in exchange for a monthly fee, connects you to the Internet through its computer system—just like the phone company.

How Much Internet Service Do You Need?

All sorts of dealers out there claim to get you on the Web cheaply, and some do so by offering service that is limited in some way. Don't start out by shortchanging yourself. Here's what you should get from your ISP:

- Basic dial-up access to the Internet (access to the Web)
- Toll-free access from your home (no toll call!)
- E-mail
- Usenet News (newsgroup access)
- Host services for your own Web page, should you decide to create one
- Technical support

NOTE

The Internet is free. Your monthly ISP service charge is not a fee for using the Internet; rather, it's a fee for facilitating your connection to it.

Big Name vs. Little Name: Choosing Your Team

Service providers fall into two distinct classes: the big name class and the little name class. Each class has advantages and disadvantages, and your decision should be based on your particular needs.

The Big Name Service Providers: Advantages

The big name providers are distinguished first by their size. Each boasts of having a million-plus national customer bases and offering numerous access numbers (phone numbers) around the country called "POPs," or points of presence. These features afford you three big advantages:

- With their millions of customers, the larger ISPs have a track record; they know what's required to deliver service.
- Because of the provider's large customer base, you should be able to find someone who uses its service and can offer an opinion about it.
- If you want to get your e-mail messages or go online when you travel, an ISP with many local access numbers around the country ensures that you can do that with just a local call.

Probably the most attractive feature about going with the big names is that they make it easy. The big names have software that walks you through the setup procedures and automatically configures your computer. Not surprisingly, Microsoft is one of the big names and offers Internet service via MSN (The Microsoft Network). It's as convenient as it gets: you sign up right from your desktop, and the

Probably the most attractive feature about going with the big names is that they make it easy.

software walks you through the entire sign-up procedure step-by-step. The introductory screen for MSN registration is shown in Figure 13-1.

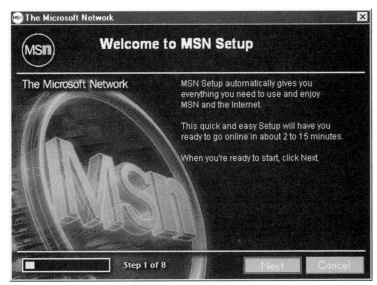

Figure 13-1
Need an Internet service provider? Microsoft can have you there in less than 15 minutes

The Big Name Service Providers: Disadvantages

We told you the advantages of big providers, but you also need to know the disadvantages. Here are the two biggest:

- Because the big names are so big, many people can be vying for a connection simultaneously. This glut of users can make connection difficult and service slower.

- Big names may have great online technical support, but when you have a problem or you can't get online, you're looking at long-distance phone charges and potentially long waits for help. Those instances should be infrequent, but sometimes you might want to hear a human voice when you need help, and that will cost some money.

- It may be a problem to get the exact e-mail address you want. If your name is Jack Someone, for example, and this is a popular name, you might have to settle for just *someone@microsoft.com* or even *jsomeon@microsoft.com*, which is not nearly as easy for your friends to remember.

The Little Name Service Providers: Advantages

Smaller, locally based service providers have advantages, too. Here are three:

- Smaller, local service providers don't have access numbers around the country, so if you travel, you have to place a long-distance call to get online.
- Sometimes, smaller is better. With a smaller service provider, you don't have to worry about millions of other users trying to get access simultaneously, although this can still be a problem if the provider is taking on more customers than it can support.
- You stand a better chance of getting the e-mail address you want because fewer people are vying for names.

Little Name Service Providers: Disadvantages

That old adage that "less is more" is not always true; going with the little names has some disadvantages as well:

- Smaller, local service providers don't have access numbers around the country, so if you travel, you have to place a long-distance call to get online.

Smaller, locally based service providers have advantages, too.

- Local service providers are subject to local problems. If a power failure or other unforeseen occurrence knocks out their system, for example, you're stuck without service until they get their power back.

How to Locate a Service Provider

The easiest way to find a service provider is to check with connected friends or relatives about what service they use; talking to people about their own experiences often proves invaluable. You should also ask them for the names of other service providers they are familiar with. The Yellow Pages of the phone book can be a good source to find out what's locally available to you. If you can, get on the Web with someone you know and ask that person to help you do some online research to locate online guides and directories of local and national service providers. Some Web sites even rate the different providers.

The easiest way to find a service provider is to check with connected friends or relatives about what service they use

Evaluate Potential Service Providers

One of the best ways to evaluate a service provider is, as we mentioned, to talk to people who use its service. For local service providers, you should get online with a friend if you can and check the ISP's Web sites. Review its corporate client list, and see what caliber of corporate client it attracts. If its site is a mess and it doesn't have corporate clients, you probably want to look elsewhere. If you are looking at a smaller service provider, be sure to call and talk to someone there about the provider's services and what it offers, making sure that includes everything on the list that started this chapter.

WARNING

Some service providers offer 1–800 access numbers, but these may not be toll free! These lines can be quite expensive, so check with the service provider to find out about the toll rates, if any, on such numbers.

NOTE

If you have voicemail service, incoming calls will automatically be picked up by your voicemail.

Determine the Costs

You can expect to pay $20 to $25 a month for Internet service that includes everything we have mentioned (Web access, e-mail, newsgroups, and so on). Can local service be a bit cheaper? Sometimes, but make sure you know exactly what services you'll be getting. Beware of services that claim to give you the company store.

Do not accept a service plan that offers you an hourly rate ("30 free hours per month! — $5 each additional hour!"). You will spend more time online than you anticipated, and those charges will pile up faster than you ever dreamed.

Be aware that these companies don't send you bills in the mail; your monthly charges are automatically billed to the credit card you designate, so don't be surprised if you're asked for your credit card number. (With some providers, you can have your charges added to your phone bill.) Also, some ISPs offer substantial discounts for prepayment, so you might find that worth inquiring about.

Consider an Extra Phone Line

In light of all that time you might be spending online, you should consider getting an additional phone line for your Internet adventures. Here's why: if you use the only phone line in your home for your Internet session, people can't reach you by phone when you're online. You can't receive incoming phone calls. You can't hear call waiting when you're online, and the call waiting signal actually disrupts your Internet session. (You can disable call waiting for just the duration of your Internet session, however.) So, if you are concerned about hampering people's ability to reach you by phone and would like to keep your phone line open, add a cheap, no-frills (no call waiting!) line for your by-modem travels.

You can disable call waiting by accessing the Dialing Properties dialog box. Follow these steps:

1. Double-click My Computer on the Desktop. My Computer opens.

2. Double-click Dial-up Networking. The Dial-Up Networking folder opens.

3. Double-click the icon for the dial-up connection you would like to modify. The Connect To dialog box opens.

4. Click the Dial Properties button. The Dialing Properties dialog box opens.

5. Click to place a check mark in the To Disable Call Waiting, Dial: check box.

6. Select *70 in the drop-down list.

NOTE

Dialing *70 does not always disable call waiting. Check with your telephone service provider if it doesn't work.

A Little Advice

This whole Internet business can be a little tough, so make it easy on yourself. Don't choose a provider just because the name is familiar, and don't choose the first one you find in the phone book. Weigh all the factors—convenience, ease of use, costs—and go with a provider with a proven track record of reliable service. After you have a little experience, you might find that you want to do some more shopping around. You *can* switch to another service later.

Chapter Fourteen

Your E-Ticket to Ride: The Browser

Information comes in many forms on the Internet. To travel the Internet
and read, view, or listen to the sites and sounds, you need a program called
a "browser." In this chapter, you'll learn what Web pages (HTML files) are,
how to use Microsoft's browser, Internet Explorer, and how to "surf" the
Internet by following links between Web pages.

What Is a Browser?

A browser is a program that displays files that are in the HTML file
format (in contrast to .doc files or .txt files that you view in your
word processing program). The files may be located on the World
Wide Web or on your own computer. Files in HTML format are
often called "Web pages" because they are the "pages" you view as
you move about the Internet. The browser also opens the next page
you've selected when you click a hyperlink. A Web site is simply a
collection of related Web pages.

It is easy to create a Web page today because many programs,
including Microsoft Word, allow you to type information as you
would for a letter or document, add pictures or sounds, and then
save the file in the HTML file format. The HTML (Hypertext
Markup Language) file contains special codes that tell the browser
how to display the words or images you have added to the page.

You can create HTML files on your computer, but no one else can see them unless you put the Web page on a "server." A server is any computer that has been set up so that others can access the information stored on it with their computers. Your ISP (Internet service provider) maintains servers so that there is a place where you can store Web pages you want others to see.

What, and Where, Exactly, Are We Browsing?

When you connect to the Internet and open your browser, the browser window opens a Web page. Literally millions of Web pages are available on the World Wide Web. The content and nature of these pages range from kindergarten class joke pages to highly charged political commentary. Anyone can produce a Web page, and the diversity of the existing pages is testament to that. You can, too, if you're game. See Chapter 33 to learn how to create your own Web page.

The "World" in World Wide Web

The World Wide Web is actually a collection or web of pages linked together around the globe to form a worldwide information web. The Web is truly global; when you start exploring, you may find yourself hopping between Web sites that are actually on servers located on several different continents. Your journey can take you around the world—not in 80 days, but in 80 *seconds*.

Isn't Global Travel Expensive?

Global travel is expensive, if you have to pay for airfare. But travel on the Web is not at all expensive. For many of us, this is difficult to grasp: how can I live in the U.S. and visit a Web site in France or Japan or Australia, without being charged long-distance fees? The easiest answer: That's how the Internet works! Accept it graciously and know that the only time you'll be charged for a long-distance call is if you dial a long-distance access number for your service provider. Some Web sites, although not many, do charge an access fee. The actual location of the Web site you visit has no effect on your monthly fee for your service provider, however.

Taking a Magic Browser Ride

How a browser works "behind the scenes" is really secondary to traveling on the Web. The most important aspect of your browser is knowing how to use it. That said, try using it!

A Look at Internet Explorer

The two most popular browsers currently available are Microsoft Internet Explorer and Netscape Navigator. Most computers allow you to connect easily using either browser, but we use Internet Explorer for our discussion here.

There are two easy ways to open Internet Explorer:

- Double-click the Internet Explorer icon on your desktop.
- Alternatively, open the Start menu and select Internet Explorer from your list of programs.

If you aren't connected to the Internet when you open Internet Explorer, it will automatically dial up and connect you. When the dial-up/connecting process finishes, Internet Explorer appears, displaying your "home page," which is your Internet home base.

TIP

If you haven't established an Internet account with an ISP (see previous chapter), you won't be able to use a browser in any meaningful way. Be sure to get yourself connected before continuing with this chapter.

You can change your home page as you please (we show you how later in this chapter). Figure 14-1 shows our home page.

Menu Bar   Address Bar

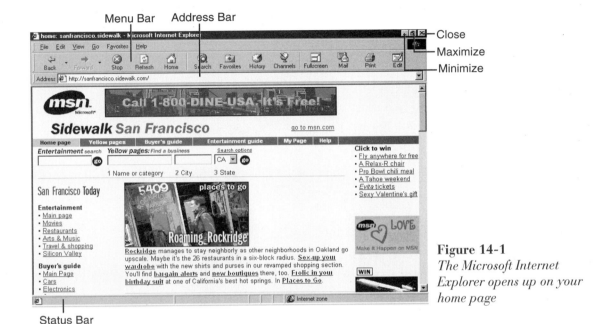

Close
Maximize
Minimize

Status Bar

Figure 14-1
The Microsoft Internet Explorer opens up on your home page

Browser Window Anatomy

The browser window, like other windows, has a title bar, a menu bar, and a toolbar. The title bar includes Minimize, Maximize, and Close buttons. The toolbar looks different than that of, say, Microsoft Word because these two programs serve very different purposes. Like the Word toolbar, however, the Internet Explorer Standard toolbar gives you access to the most commonly used options in the program. The menu bar includes options unique to the functions of a browser. We describe the Standard toolbar a little later in this chapter.

The browser window includes an Address Bar on which you can see the address of your current location. A Web address is commonly referred to as a URL (which we pronounce as "U-R-L" but you may also hear pronounced as "earl.") URL is short for Uniform Resource Locator. Every Web page has a unique address, so you can always find a favorite page and return to it easily at a later date. You can always type a new address into the Address field to check out a different Web site. We come back to addresses a little later in this chapter.

Finally, the bottom of the window sports a status bar. When you go to a Web page or Web site, Internet Explorer may take a little time to access the page and display it for you. The status bar shows you where you are in the process.

Some of the sites are like buried gems: you have to dig a little to find them.

Exploring the Labyrinth

The Web can be dizzying. It's teeming with great sites and discoveries waiting to be made. Some of the sites are like buried gems: you have to dig a little to find them. We want you to be as impressed with the Web as we are, and as a way of helping you learn about your browser, we visit a few of the not-so-buried gems with you.

First Stop: The Library of Congress When it comes to an information resource, you don't find any better than the Library of Congress. Here's how to go to it:

1. Move your mouse up into the Address field of the Address Bar, and click once to highlight the current address.

2. Type the address for the site you are headed for; in this case, type *http://www.loc.gov*. (Actually, most browsers no longer

require you to type the "http://" part of the address, so try entering an address without it first. If you don't locate the site, enter it again with the "http" part.)

3. Press the Enter key, and soon the Library of Congress's Web site home page begins to appear on your screen, as shown in Figure 14-2.

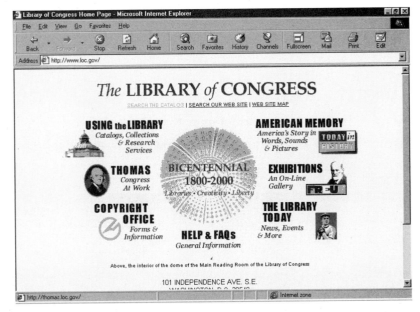

Figure 14-2
Welcome to the Library of Congress site

As the Web page loads, watch your status bar to see a gas gauge that shows the progress of the Web page transfer.

A Web Page: What's Hot and What's Not   When you visit a Web site, the site's home page may be just the tip of the iceberg, so be sure to check out what hyperlinks are available to you. A "hyperlink" is an area or spot on a Web page that, when clicked, takes you to another Web page or a different section of the current

Web page, as designated by the link. To find the hyperlinks on a Web page, move your mouse across the screen. When the cursor changes to a pointing hand, you have reached a link. Links can be found in text (typically colored), in pictures, even in empty screen space, so a little detective work usually pays off.

To go a little deeper into the maze, click the Web site map link, right below the banner, as shown in Figure 14-3.

Figure 14-3
The Library of Congress site map link is just below the home page masthead

> ## The LIBRARY of CONGRESS
> SEARCH THE CATALOG | SEARCH OUR WEB SITE | WEB SITE MAP

This is an impressive Web site! The Library's site map, as shown in Figure 14-4, provides a list of more than 200 links (you can tell they are hyperlinks because of the colored text) to different areas of the Library's site.

TIP

When you visit a new page, make sure to get the whole story. If a scroll bar appears on the right side, it means that the page is longer than your screen can display. Scroll down to see what else the page provides.

Figure 14-4
The Library of Congress offers a Web site map on its home page

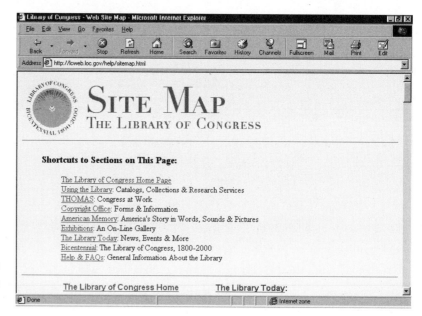

164

Marking the Trail

With a few hyperlink clicks of your mouse, you manage to wind quite a distance into the World Wide Web. Traveling to destinations near and far is undeniably part of the fun of the Web, but it would become frustrating fast if the browser didn't provide good navigation tools.

The Standard Toolbar for Internet Explorer Enter the Standard toolbar. Internet Explorer provides you with the tools you need to effectively explore the Web without becoming hopelessly lost. The toolbar is shown in Figure 14-5.

Figure 14-5
The Standard toolbar makes navigation easy

Following are brief descriptions of the buttons as they appear from left to right:

1. **Back:** The Back button returns you to the previous page. You can click the Back button repeatedly to backtrack to a page you visited previously. The Back button goes back only to sites that you visited during your current session.

2. **Forward:** The Forward button reverses the action of the Back button. If you went back too many pages, the Forward button enables you to move up to where you were. The Forward button goes forward only to sites that you visited during your current session.

3. **Stop:** The Stop button stops a newly selected page from loading. When a page is taking a long time to load, or you see that it is not a page you want, clicking Stop will save you the time it would take to finish loading.

4. **Refresh:** The Refresh button retrieves the page again and reloads it. If you are interested in pages that include information that is constantly being updated—real-time stock quotes, for example—the refresh button updates the screen with the most current information available.

5. **Home:** The Home button removes you from the maelstrom. No matter where you find yourself, the Home button brings you back to your home page, that is, the page Internet Explorer first opens to.

6. **Search:** The Search button helps you find subject matter when you don't know where to look (see Chapter 17).

7. **Favorites:** The Favorites button displays a list of Web sites to which you can go without typing the URL (see the following section).

8. **History:** The History button shows you all the sites you have visited, listed by date. If you click one of the entries, you jump right to that site.

9. **Channels:** The Channels button offers a diverse selection of Web sites, categorized by topic.

10. **Full Screen:** The Full Screen button allows you to view a maximized Web page without the menu showing.

11. **Mail:** The Mail button helps you manage your e-mail.

12. **Print:** The Print button allows you to print the current Web page.

13. **Edit:** The Edit button allows you to edit the currently displayed in Notepad.

TIP

Later versions of Internet Explorer may have buttons and features added or modified, so don't panic if you don't find something we describe on your toolbar. Internet Explorer 5.0, for example, doesn't have a Channels button.

Returning to Favorite Sites When you find a Web site that you know you want to return to easily, you don't need to follow a Web trail to find it again, and you don't have to memorize or write down that unbelievably convoluted URL that fills the Address field.

Instead, take advantage of the Favorites menu. When you find yourself at a site that you want to revisit or explore at a later date, follow these steps:

1. Open the Favorites menu.
2. Select Add To Favorites.
3. Click OK in the Add Favorite box.

When you select Add To Favorites, the Add Favorite box appears, as shown in Figure 14-6.

NOTE

The Favorites menu conveniently lists your chosen Web sites with names that are easy to read and understand, rather than with hieroglyphic URLs.

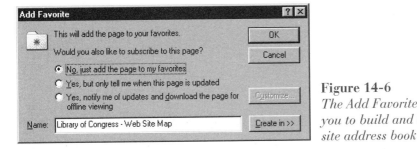

Figure 14-6
The Add Favorite dialog box allows you to build and keep a favorite Web site address book

Now your favorite Web site will be listed in alphabetical order with any other favorite site addresses that you place in the list. When you want to return to a site on the list, open the Favorites menu and select the site from there.

There's No Place Like Home: Changing Your Home Page

TIP

Try ThirdAge.com as a home page to take advantage of the site's rich set of features for older adults.

Each time you open Internet Explorer, you open on your home page. But where do you feel most at home? If you'd like to change your home page, you can do it easily. Open the View menu and select Internet Options. The View menu appears, as shown in Figure 14-7 (If you are using Internet Explorer 5.0, open the Tools menu and select Internet Options from there.)

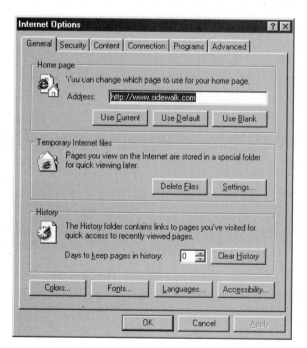

Figure 14-7
You can change your home page from the Internet Options dialog box

Put your preferred home page address in the Home Page Address field and click OK. That's it. The next time you click the Home button or open Internet Explorer, your new home page will appear.

Web Addresses: Knowing What Side of the Tracks a Site Is On

As peculiar as some URLs may appear, there are some standards built into them that can give you some sense of what you'll encounter at the address. For example, Web site addresses that end with one of the following higher-level domain names (a "domain" is roughly the equivalent of a category). You are likely to encounter addresses with the domain names that appear in the following table.

Higher-Level Domain Names

Domain Name	What It Signifies
.com	A commercial address
.gov	The federal government
.int	International
.mil	Military
.net	A network provider
.org	Some type of organization

There are also domain names that indicate the country of origin (*www.culture.fr*). Here's a partial list.

Country Domain Names

Domain Name	Country of Origin
.au	Australia
.ca	Canada
.fr	France
.cn	China
.il	Israel
.it	Italy
.jp	Japan
.uk	United Kingdom

Sorry, Wrong URL

Most people want their Web site URL to communicate the site's purpose to Internet travelers. Do people ever try to mislead you with an address? Let's just say that some folks have found a way to exploit honest mistakes. Here's one mistake that's quite common. You type in the URL to visit the White House Web site, except that, rather than type *http://www.whitehouse.gov*, you type *http://www.whitehouse.org*. Guess what? Somebody selling pornography on the Web was waiting for you to make that mistake. As another example of winding up in the wrong place, remember that the URL for the Library of Congress is *http://www.loc.gov*? If you enter *http://www.loc.org* instead, you may find yourself on a fishing expedition: this URL is for the Lake Ontario Sportfishing Promotion Council site!

NOTE

Pick the most interesting site, and it appears in the right portion of the window. If you like it and you want to close the Channel Guide, click the Channel button (in the toolbar) again.

Using Channels to Find Great Sites

Internet Explorer offers a rich selection of preselected destinations that you can reach with the click of the Channels button on the Standard toolbar. Click Channels and the Channel Listing appears on the left side of your Explorer 4.0 window, as shown in Figure 14-8. (There is no channel bar in Internet Explorer 5.0.)

When the Channel Guide appears, click the topic or area of interest that you want to pursue. When you do, a list of opportunities awaits, as shown in Figure 14-9.

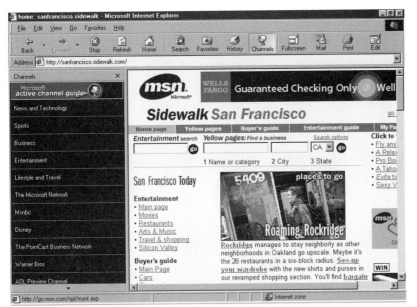

Figure 14-8
Channel surfing on the Web

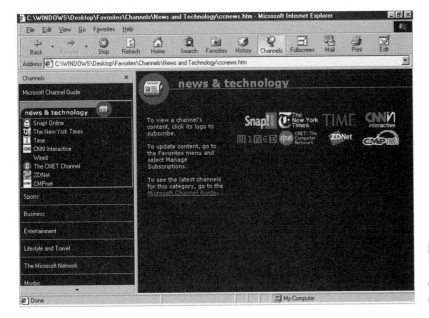

Figure 14-9
The Channel Guide gives you a great selection of Web sites you can go to without knowing any URLs

Great Sites for Grown-Ups

In addition to the Thirdage.com site, there are many other Web sites with a wealth of information for older adults. Sites you may want to explore include the following:

- *http://www.aarp.or,* an information-rich site sponsored by the American Association for Retired People
- *http://www.seniorsite.com,* a site with information on and links to many topics of interest for seniors
- *http://www.seniorlaw.com,* access to information about elder law, Medicare, Medicaid, estate planning, trusts, and more
- *http://www.50plus.org,* a site dedicated to physical fitness for older adults
- *http://www.seniornet.org,* a nonprofit organization dedicated to providing access to computer technology to older adults

Also check the Resource Links on Microsoft's site for seniors: *http:www.microsoft.com/seniors/olinks.asp* and *http:www. micro soft.com/seniors/organizations.asp*

When you finish here, we'll meet you in the next chapter. Happy exploring!

Chapter Fifteen

Rediscovering the Joys of Correspondence—With E-Mail

There was a time when letter writing was an art form. Correspondence by post gave you the opportunity to distill your thoughts and feelings and, after crafting your message, share your sentiments with others. It involved a wonderful chemistry between two people.

The span of time between a literary call and response used to add a grand anticipation to the equation. With the emergence of e-mail as a medium of communication, the equation has changed somewhat, but the art form is back, and with it are the feelings correspondence can evoke.

This chapter shows you what e-mail is all about. You'll see what it is, how it works, and how you can get the most out of it. We also show you how to guard against people who use e-mail for the wrong reasons.

Understanding E-Mail

E-mail, which is short for "electronic mail," is a special computer messaging system that lets you communicate with people all over the world via the Internet. Everyone with an Internet account has an e-mail address to which you may send messages. Some folks have more than one e-mail address. As with the mail that the regular postal service delivers to your home, you send and receive e-mail based on a person's address. Although a person can have multiple addresses, no two addresses can be identical; something must appear in the address to distinguish it.

In addition to a message you can send to someone, e-mail allows you to include "attachments," documents or files that you can share with another person electronically. If you have grandkids scattered around the country, for example, e-mail attachments offer the perfect way to receive a steady stream of pictures.

Unlike mail sent through the U.S. postal service, e-mail doesn't cost anything. In fact, you can send the same message to numerous people simultaneously, at no cost other than the service fee you pay for your Internet connection.

What You Need to Send E-Mail

If you don't yet have an Internet account, you need one before you can send any messages. Your e-mail messages can't go anywhere until you have an account and an address. To send e-mail, you need the same things you need in order to get online, plus a good e-mail program. You'll use your own address for the exercises in this chapter.

An e-mail program is sometimes called a "mail client." Microsoft Outlook and Microsoft Outlook Express are both excellent choices for an e-mail program. If you recently purchased your PC, one or both programs may have come preinstalled. Check

NOTE

Your e-mail address is assigned to you, not to your home or a specific computer, so your address doesn't have to change if you travel around the country.

M*icrosoft Outlook and Microsoft Outlook Express are both excellent choices for an e-mail program.*

your Programs list (from the Start menu) to see whether you do indeed already have one of these programs. If you don't have them, you can purchase them at your local computer store. We use Microsoft Outlook throughout this chapter.

Starting Out with Microsoft Outlook

Microsoft Outlook

To open Microsoft Outlook, double-click its icon (or that for Outlook Express) on your desktop, or open it from the Programs list on the Start menu. (You can also right-click the icon and select Open.)

Microsoft Outlook appears, as shown in Figure 15-1. As with all windows, Outlook has a title bar, a menu bar, and a toolbar.

Figure 15-1
Microsoft Outlook—welcome to the world of e-mail!

Figure 15-1 shows the different areas of the screen and what they have to offer. The screen shows a good deal of text, but navigating through the program is easy after you learn a few of the basics. Here we focus on the parts that you need in the beginning, namely the Information Viewer, the Preview pane, and the Folder list.

You can consider this Outlook window as your own personal mailroom. You'll see separate boxes (folders) for incoming mail, outgoing mail, and deleted messages (a trash bin). The Inbox holds the messages that you receive. The Outbox holds e-mail messages that you have written but have not yet sent, and the deleted items are e-mail messages that you have discarded. Unlike a regular mailroom, Outlook also has a Sent Items box that automatically stores a copy of everything you send. To see the contents of a folder, click its name in the Folder list, and a complete listing of the associated e-mails appears in the Information window. The Preview window gives you a sneak peak at any listed e-mail messages when you click the e-mail item (in the Information window). When you first open this screen, the Preview window shows you a preview of the first message in the Information list.

Filling In the Address Fields

You can now create your first e-mail message! For starters, click the New Mail Message button at the left end of the Outlook toolbar. Figure 15-2 shows the e-mail form that appears on-screen.

The e-mail form contains four separate address-related fields that you can fill in. You can move between the different fields of your message by using the mouse or the TAB key.

NOTE

If all the mail in your Inbox has disappeared, make sure that you have the Inbox folder selected from your Folder list. If you have a different folder selected, you'll see only the e-mails in that folder.

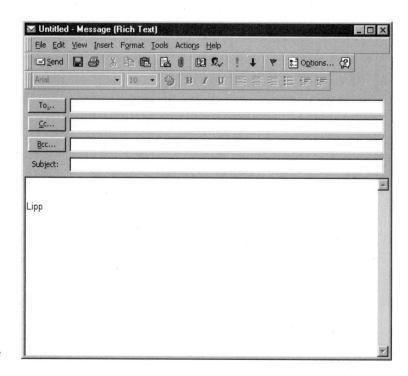

Figure 15-2
Outlook's e-mail message form; just fill in the blanks

- **To:** The To: field requires the e-mail address(es) for the person or persons to whom you are sending your message. You can include more than one e-mail address here, separating each address with a semicolon (or a comma, depending on your mail program; some accept both). You must provide at least one address.

- **Cc:** The Cc: field is optional and is used the same way as the To: field. Cc stands for "carbon copy," from the old days. You can also put multiple addresses in the Cc: field. When a person receives your e-mail, he or she sees the list of recipients, including everyone on the Cc list.

- **Bcc:** The Bcc: field, short for "blind carbon copy," is for additional recipients whom *you* want to remain anonymous. When people on the To list and the Cc list receive this e-mail, they are left unaware of who has received a Bcc. (If you are using Outlook 2000, the Bcc: field is not shown by default. To display the Bcc:, select Bcc field from the View menu of the message window.)

- **Subject:** The Subject field is used to describe the message's subject matter. It should be a few words or a short phrase. You don't *have to* provide a subject, but it's bad manners—against the rules of netiquette, as some users would say—to dispense with it; people appreciate getting some sense of what the message is about before opening it. You'll probably feel the same way when you begin receiving e-mail messages.

Composing Your First E-Mail Message

To practice sending e-mail, send yourself a message. Here's what to do:

1. Click the To: field, and enter your own e-mail address.

2. Click the Subject field, and enter "My first e-mail message" or whatever you want.

3. Click in the message field, and type a couple of sentences to yourself. Figure 15-3 shows our message.

To send an e-mail message, just click the Send button. When you do, Outlook whisks your message to its destination; in this case, your own mailbox.

NOTE

The message form has no From field because Outlook and other e-mail programs automatically tell the recipient whom the e-mail is from. Outlook uses the e-mail address you specified when setting up your Outlook Options. The form also has no date field because the date is automatically inserted, based on the time you send your message.

Figure 15-3
*To learn about e-mail,
you can send some messages
to yourself*

Reading Your Mail

Typically, a message to you *from* you will arrive almost instantaneously. In fact, most messages will arrive in a short time, regardless of where they are from geographically.

When you receive an e-mail message, it appears in the Information Viewer. When the message appears in the Viewer in bold, it indicates that you haven't looked at it yet. Figure 15-4 shows a number of e-mail messages in the Information Viewer. The top three messages have not been viewed yet.

To see a preview, which displays the first few lines of a message in the Preview pane (if it's open), click the message you want as it

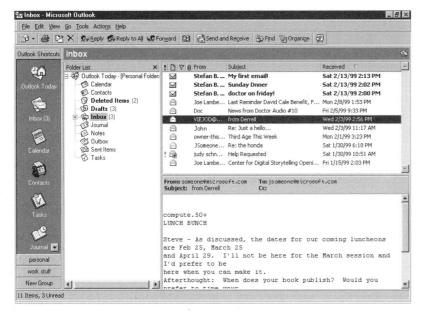

Figure 15-4
You can access any of your e-mail messages in Table View

appears in the Information Viewer. To open a particular message in its own window, double-click the message in Table View. Figure 15-5 shows your e-mail message in full bloom, after you double-click it.

Responding to E-Mail

Now that you have your message open, you have the option of responding to it. When you open an e-mail message, you see a slightly different toolbar with four important buttons:

- **Reply:** Sends your reply only to the person who sent you the message. The message is marked in the Subject field with the prefix "RE:".

Figure 15-5
*Reading your mail
the luxurious way*

- **Reply to All:** Sends your reply to everyone who received the message, including those on the Cc list. When the list of recipients is long, this is an enormous time-saver.
- **Forward:** Sends an e-mail message you received and sends it, in its entirety, to whomever you specify. The message is marked "Forward."
- **Delete:** Designated in the toolbar as an "X," this command takes the open message and puts it in the trash.

There is one very important option that is not on the toolbar: making no response or a delayed response.

The message may not require a response, and, if it does, you may want to spend some time thinking about and composing it. Waiting awhile before responding is okay, and Outlook lets you reply when you want.

Another great advantage of e-mail is that, when you do reply, your reply appears at the top of the page, and the original e-mail message appears at the bottom of the message. If your reply is met with a reply, you wind up with a two-person journal in which the dialog box is captured.

When the Mail Doesn't Go Through

Sometimes your mail may not get delivered. Here are the three most common reasons:

- The address is not a real address. Your e-mail message can't be delivered because nobody has the address you specified. You receive a reply that says your message was undeliverable.

- You send e-mail to the wrong address. Perhaps you send an e-mail message to your friend, at what you think is his address: *someonej@microsoft.com*. Your friend's address, though, is *someone@microsoft.com* . Another person has the e-mail address to which you just sent your note, so it did get delivered, but your friend will never respond; he never received your message.

- Your message never gets sent. You may get disconnected unknowingly as you write your message. When you click Send, the message goes into your Outbox folder instead of being delivered. Check your Outbox on occasion to confirm that all your e-mail messages have really been sent.

TIP

The response to an e-mail may be no response. You don't have to respond to an e-mail when you read it; you can put it away until you're prepared to reply.

Subject:	Returned mail: User unknown
Date:	4/29/99
From:	Mail Delivery Subsystem
To:	someonej@microsoft.com

NOTE

If you send an e-mail to a number of people and you receive an "undeliverable" message, be sure to check which e-mail address didn't work. You don't have to re-send the message to everyone; Outlook still sends the mail along to all the other people on your mailing list.

The Advantage of Instantaneous Delivery

The advantage of instantaneous e-mail delivery is that it goes to its destination immediately. You can communicate all sorts of information to as many people as you want, and they all get it—*fast*.

The Disadvantage of Instantaneous Delivery

The disadvantage of instantaneous e-mail delivery is the same as the advantage. When you are angry or upset and your emotions are doing the driving, a hastily sent e-mail can be regrettable.

Good Etiquette in Correspondence

E-mail manners are really in the realm of *netiquette*, the code of Internet civility. We cover netiquette in greater detail in the next chapter ("A Block Party with 30,000,000 of Your Closest Friends"). Almost everyone who corresponds via e-mail, however, encounters the issue of a delinquent e-pen pal.

Awaiting a Response

If you've sent e-mail to someone and haven't received a response as quickly as you expected, don't assume that your correspondent is ignoring you. Give your recipient the benefit of the doubt, and check whether your message ever arrived. A follow-up message is easy and innocuous: "I didn't get a reply, and I was worried that you didn't receive my last e-mail." It works pretty well. If your e-mail message or the other person's e-mail message was, in fact, lost, you've done your correspondent and yourself a favor. And if it wasn't, you'll alert that person to the fact that you're waiting for a reply.

Reading Other People's Mail

Having good manners on the Internet is important; respecting other people's privacy is fundamental. Reading other people's e-mail without their consent is no different than reading their regular mail without their consent.

There's not much you can do when you get an e-mail that is addressed to you but is clearly intended for someone else (see "When the Mail Doesn't Go Through," earlier in this chapter). The only way to know it's not for you is to read it! Good form in such a case is to send a simple reply to the sender: "Sorry, I received your message in error. You sent your message to my e-mail address, but I am not the person you meant to send it to."

In the event that you share an e-mail account with someone, try to find a way to have separate accounts. Many service providers offer added e-mail addresses at no extra charge, others for a nominal, additional monthly fee, and it works out better for all parties. You don't get upset because someone is reading your mail, and other people don't get upset if they misunderstand something they have read in your private e-mail.

Junk E-Mail and Some E-Mail Scams

Every night at dinner, the telemarketers start to call trying to get you to refinance your house or install a new roof. Each day's post brings offers and contests and solicitations promising big money and a rosy future.

You should not be surprised that junk mail has invaded the Internet ecosystem as well. In the e-mail domain, you deal with

Having good manners on the Internet is important.

TIP

*The best way to respond
to junk mail is to just
delete it. Replying
confirms for the sender
that your e-mail address
is accurate and active.*

junk mail the same way you deal with it every day: ignore and discard it.

Scam artists will try to lure you with promises of big money, easy money, and free gifts. In case you are tempted, here's a list of the top e-mail scams as compiled and published by the Federal Trade Commission:

1. Phony business opportunities that entice you with promises of fast and big money.

2. Bulk e-mailing lists that offer mailing lists for potential customers (this violates most service provider agreements and you'll get ejected from the game if you try doing this yourself).

3. Chain letters that promise wealth or success.

4. Work-at-home schemes that require some charge up front and result in no work for you.

5. Health and diet come-ons that promise you can lose weight with a pill or an herb.

6. Get-rich-quick schemes that claim you can make buckets of money without working hard.

7. Investment opportunities that are really Ponzi schemes set up to rob people of their savings.

8. The promise of free stuff if you pay an initiation fee. Later, you're told that you have to enlist others to get anything.

9. Cable (signal) descrambler systems so that you don't have to pay for cable subscription rates. When the descrambler

doesn't work, you can't complain about buying something that you use for illegal purposes!

10. Credit and loan scams that profess to get your good credit back or offer low-interest loans. They can't and they don't.

11. Grand Prize pronouncements that are aimed at getting you to respond so that they can lure you into a "better" deal—at a price.

E-mail is one of the highlights of being online, and having a strong working knowledge of your e-mail program will make your e-mail experience all the more enjoyable and rewarding. If you want to learn some of the nifty tricks you can do with Microsoft Outlook, take a look at Chapter 18 in Part III.

TIP

The Federal Trade Commission has free publications about recognizing fraudulent unsolicited commercial e-mail and other Internet-related subjects. Contact the FTC at 202–FTC–HELP (382–4357), or write: Consumer Response Center, Federal Trade Commission, Washington, D.C. 20580.
***The URL:** http://www.ftc.gov/bcp/conline/pubs/alerts/doznalrt.htm*

Chapter Sixteen

A Block Party with 30,000,000 of Your Closest Friends

The Internet has turned the world of telecommunications on its ear. Now people from all walks of life and from every corner of the earth can meet on the Internet to exchange ideas, beliefs, and opinions, and to help others.

The Internet is a big place and, like a bustling metropolis, you need to know how and where to meet people. In this chapter, we explore how to find people and how to communicate with them. We discuss how communities are formed on the Internet and how you can become involved (see also "The Art of Living on the Edge," Chapter 3). Finally, we discuss Internet discussions and Internet chat, two of the most popular Internet offerings, and how you can use these two features to have some fun and meet new people.

Connecting with Your Kind of People

Millions of people may be online, but are they the kind of people you want to be involved with? No one has the time to start sorting through the millions of online subscribers to find a few people with whom you *might* potentially have something in common. Fortunately, you don't need to do that—we show you some easy ways to hook up with the kind of people you *are* interested in meeting.

Defining Community on the Internet

The *American Heritage Dictionary*, third edition, defines community as

1. A group of people living in the same locality and under the same government

2. A group of people having common interests: *the scientific community; the international business community*

3. A group of people sharing similarity or identity: a. *community of interests.* b. *sharing, participation, and fellowship*

In your Internet travels, you will inevitably come upon the word "community" to describe a group of people who interact in some way on the World Wide Web. "Community" is a term we all know and use, but the connotation for online travelers is most accurately described by the third part of the preceding definition: "sharing, participation, and fellowship."

A community on the Internet does not need to be bound together by locality or municipality, but it can and does sometimes happen that two members live near each other. No rules exist concerning how many communities you can belong to on the Internet. In your day-to-day life, you may be active in several communities: as a professional, you may be involved in a community of your peers; as a swimmer, you may feel a part of a community of weekday swimmers at the local pool. If you are active in a church, mosque, or synagogue, you may be involved in activities to help strengthen

TIP

You can connect with other older adults online at ThirdAge.com, the Web community about mid-life transitions and lifestyle; it's located at http://www.thirdage.com. *Just type its Web site address, or URL, into the Address field at the top of your screen, to arrive at the ThirdAge home page.*

the community in which you live. The same multicommunity rule applies on the Internet.

Finding Folks with Common Interests

Thousands of communities continue to sprout up on the Web. Microsoft is host to an ever-growing list of communities that are built around a broad range of interests. When you click the Web Communities option at MSN (*http://www.msn.com*), you open MSN's Web Communities home page. From the Communities home page, select List Communities in the left margin to see what's available. Figure 16-1 shows a portion of that scrollable list.

Unlike with some regular (offline) communities, the Internet community does not require dues or fees for you to take part. In fact, most online communities will welcome you with open arms;

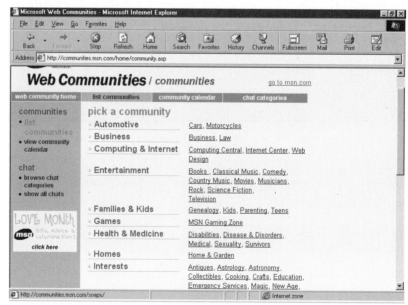

Figure 16-1
All sorts of communities are available to join at MSN

Web communities and the people who sponsor them are eager to see their communities grow, and your participation contributes to that growth.

You can also access the MSN Seniors Community site from the Microsoft Seniors & Technology page *(http://www.microsoft.com/ seniors)*. Click MSN Seniors Community on the lower left to see a page similar to the one shown in Figure 16-2.

The Internet is host to as many diverse communities as there are users. From pet lovers to stock market wizards, you can find a group where you'll fit in and find friends. For instance, Thirdage.com is a community site, focusing specifically on the issues and needs of active adults 45 and up. The site includes comprehensive and easy-to-follow tutorials on computing and on the Internet. The

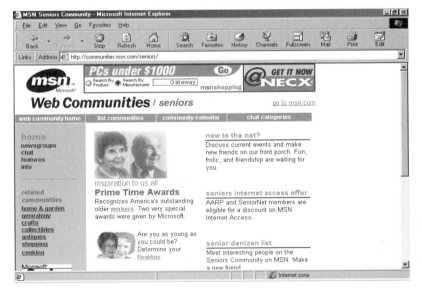

Figure 16-2
The MSN Seniors Community site has links to many interesting related communities

easy-to-use features, which include Chat, Discussions, Free Home Pages, and more, are designed with the novice user in mind. ThirdAge uses simple tools and compelling content to create an electronic community among older active adults.

Jumping into the Discussion

A community isn't a community if you can't share, contribute, or interact in some way. An important vehicle for community interaction is a discussion. A discussion on the Internet (called a "newsgroup" on the MSN site) is an area to which individuals come to:

- Express ideas
- Learn
- Pursue a hobby
- Voice opinions
- Offer support
- Help others
- Debate issues
- Have fun
- Find romance
- Find/offer solace
- Meet people

You can choose any topic or avenue for discussion based on your interests. MSN allows you to jump into a discussion at any time by selecting the Newsgroup option from a Web Communities home page. When you click Newsgroups, a scrollable page of available discussions appears, as shown in Figure 16-3.

On the MSN site, each newsgroup includes one or more hosts. A "host" acts as moderator, ombudsman, and ambassador. If you have a problem concerning a particular newsgroup, you should share your concern via e-mail with the newsgroup's host.

Your $0.02: It Adds Up!

Start by exploring a newsgroup devoted to making friends with Australians. Clicking this newsgroup brings up an expansive list of

Figure 16-3
Discussions—also called newsgroups—are open to you at any time of the day or night

messages in a window that looks a lot like Microsoft Outlook. Clicking one of the messages displays the contents in the Preview pane, as shown in Figure 16-4.

The program you use to read newsgroups looks a lot like Outlook because it is a lot like Outlook. This is the cousin to Microsoft Outlook, Outlook Express. Express is also your discussion reader.

When you read a message, or "posting," you can send a reply directly to the author of the message, or you can post it to the newsgroup. These two options are represented by two different buttons in the Express toolbar. If you click the Reply To Group button, your reply will appear as a message to the newsgroup for everyone to read. You can identify messages that have replies by the plus (+) sign that appears in the left margin of the Information list. Click the + to see a list of all the replies. If you click the Reply

When you read a message, or "posting," you can send a reply directly to the author of the message or you can post it to the newsgroup

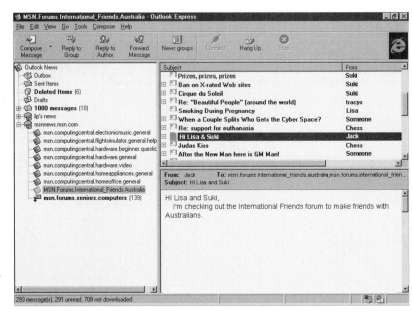

Figure 16-4
When you read these messages, you can respond to them at any time

TIP

When you enter a discussion or a newsgroup, you are under no obligation to participate. If you can shed some light on the subject at hand, however, your participation and contribution are greatly appreciated by others.

To Author button, you send a (private) e-mail to the author of the original message.

Many people visit discussions just to read the posts. The vast majority of readers don't ever post, instead relying on a few active participants to do the talking. If you frequent one discussion group, you will learn the personalities of the participants and eventually become comfortable enough to post yourself, if you want.

Finding Topics of Interest

When you don't find exactly what you are looking for in a particular discussion, you should bring it up! Let's say your son and his family are moving to Sydney, Australia, from Ft. Worth, Texas. You comb the Australia friends discussion, but there is nothing about relocating in Sydney from the States. That doesn't mean the discussion participants don't know anything about this; it just means that no one has discussed the subject—yet. To help yourself and others, you can post a new message in the Australian Friends discussion with the hope of obtaining some very specific information to help the kids (and you!) make the transition.

To post a new message, click the New Post button in the toolbar, and compose your message as you would an e-mail message. When you are ready, click the Send button to deliver your message to the newsgroup.

Waiting for a Reply

If you are hoping for replies to your message, be patient. You never know when someone will respond to your post. It could come in an hour; it could also come in a couple of weeks. The person who may be the most helpful to you may not sign on for a while—for whatever reason—so again, you need to be patient.

Getting Back Home

After you become comfortable with one discussion, you almost certainly will want to check out a few more. Discussion hopping is popular. So, where did the browser go? Outlook Express appears automatically when you enter a newsgroup, so don't be surprised when you lose sight of Internet Explorer and the community page you were on previously; just minimize or close the Outlook Express window (or just click the Internet Explorer icon on the taskbar), and you'll find your Internet Explorer window open and waiting for you.

Talking over the Fence: Chat

Besides offering discussions and newsgroups, Internet communities also allow you to communicate with members of an Internet

NOTE

In order to chat, you need an additional program that lets you chat (don't worry, it won't cost you anything extra!). When you move into MSN's chat area, you are prompted to download the software. The download is fast and the program installs automatically. After it's installed, you are able to chat away!

TIP

Intelligent talk is the hallmark of conversation in the ThirdAge community—with chat rooms offering topics on everything from rekindling romance in midlife to igniting your stock portfolio. Go first to: http://www.thirdage.com/join and fill out the brief form to join.

community *live*. Unlike newsgroup discussions that can meander and last for months, a *chat* is dynamic and immediate. Chat is the Internet's equivalent to CB radio or the old phone company party lines. With an Internet chat, however, you can be chatting with people from all over the world. Chat's informal nature has made it one of the most popular features of the Internet.

To get your feet wet, follow these steps for easy chatting:

1. Go to MSN's community home page.
2. Click the Chat Categories button, below the masthead.
3. When the Chat home page appears, click the last entry, Show All.

Finding a Chat That's Right For You

Each community page has numerous scheduled chats associated with it. To participate in a scheduled chat, go to it at the scheduled time and place. Scheduled chats can have special guests and include question-and-answer sessions, so you should keep your eyes peeled for the ones that are of particular interest to you. If you enter one of these areas off schedule, however, you'll probably be the only one in the room.

By going into the Show All area, you can find all the chats that are currently in session. To get into a chat, you choose a nickname that will identify you to other chatters. When you enter a chat, it might strike you as stream-of-consciousness melées, because that's how many of them are. Figure 16-5 shows the Seniors Chat, which offers you some fun and the chance to meet and get to know a number of regulars.

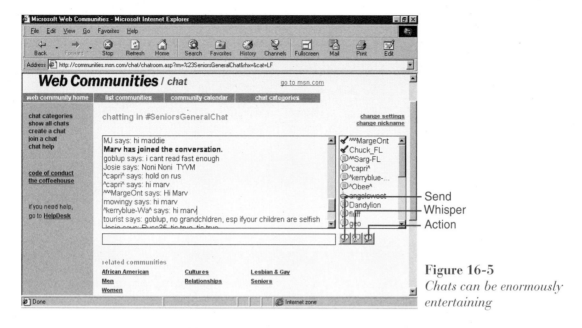

Figure 16-5
Chats can be enormously entertaining

Pushing All the Right (Chat) Buttons

Jumping into the chat fray is easy as long as you know what buttons to push and what windows to watch. Here's a brief guide.

- The window on the left side is the Chat window, where you can watch the banter as it flows.

- The Guest window, to the right, lists all the chatters in attendance.

- When you enter the chat, your arrival is announced in the Chat window.

- When you exit a chat, your departure is announced in the Chat window.

- The small text field at the bottom of the screen is where you enter your message.

- To post your message for all to see, just press the Enter key, or click the left talking balloon.
- To "whisper" a message, that is, to send a message that only one person or a select few people can see, you enter the message, select the recipients, and click the Whisper button—the middle talking balloon.
- To indicate an action, enter it and click the Action button, the right talking balloon. Your action statement appears in the chat window in italics. For example, if your name is Pat and you enter "wonders what this button does," clicking the action button posts "Pat wonders what this button does."

TIP

Your name automatically appears before your post. You don't need to enter your name with each line that you contribute.

Netiquette: Your Guide to Good Manners

Your Internet community experience will be a positive one if you remember that good manners and consideration of others applies as much to your online interactions as they do offline. Following are some of the more important rules to follow.

Communicate Clearly Communicating with people in discussions and newsgroups can be liberating because no one knows what you look like. Your appearance—the color of your skin, your race, your physical attributes—is not a part of the social equation, and others are left to judge you by what you say and how you say it. In discussions, saying what you mean as clearly as you can is of paramount importance. Above all, be sure that you are accurate in what you are stating; don't trumpet rumors or hearsay as fact. As you judge others on the Internet, so they judge you. By presenting yourself in the best possible light, you make yourself a shining example to others, and you will, in turn, be respected by those you meet online.

Don't make up stuff about a subject. If you're in a debate and you start to fabricate because you believe your side is the right side, you take the chance that a real smart chatter will check in, read your posts, and take you to task. You'll receive an upbraiding that can make you uncomfortable, you won't advance your argument, you won't look smarter, but you will sully your reputation. Stick to the facts.

Be Tolerant Golden rules apply everywhere on the Internet, especially when interacting with others. Keep in mind that people you meet on the Internet come from different backgrounds, have varying levels of education and experiences, and have as many different opinions on a given subject as you can imagine. Try giving people the benefit of the doubt in discussions, or at least point out sensitive issues privately and quietly—via e-mail.

Don't SHOUT! When you see a post in all capitals, that's shouting. Shouting is rude and unnecessary—and we apologize for shouting this heading at you! Try to steer clear of shouters. Maybe you inadvertently hit the Caps Lock key on your keyboard, or you just like the way all capitals look. Unfortunately, it comes across as yelling. Multiple exclamation points have the same effect. If you're saying, "CONGRATULATIONS!!!," or expressing a similar sentiment, however, it's okay.

Respect the Rules To ensure a hospitable and inviting community, Web sites have rules and regulations. Every site alerts you to its usage contract, the code of behavior and conduct to which

TIP
Edit your work before posting, and be sure to check your spelling.

S*tick to the facts.*

W*hen you enter a site, as when you enter a restaurant or any business establishment, you must follow the rules as defined by the establishment.*

you must conform in order to enter the site. When you enter a site, as when you enter a restaurant or any business establishment, you must follow the rules as defined by the establishment. Figure 16-6 shows the beginning of the MSN code of conduct posted in the Chat area.

People do have the right to express their opinions on the Internet, but not when their posts violate the rules and regulations of the site.

Look Before You Leap Unless you want to be the Web's Daniel and throw yourself to the digital lions, consider what neighborhood you are in before jumping into a battle. Two important rules to remember if you visit a discussion in which you clearly hold the minority point of view: don't be thin-skinned, and don't be surprised if people gang up on you.

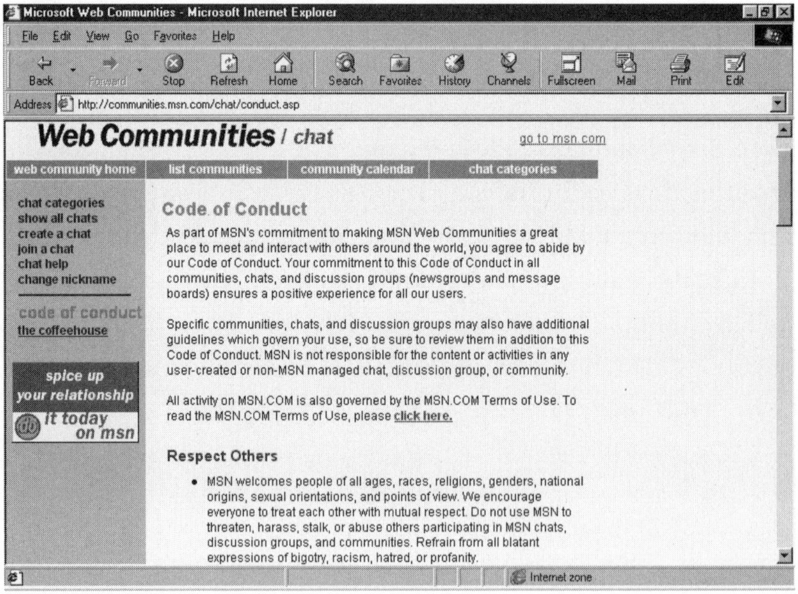

WARNING

Some sites, including MSN, include designated discussions that are unmoderated. Translation? No holds barred. If you don't have the constitution for verbal slugfests, steer clear.

Figure 16-6
Everybody can benefit in the MSN community area, as long as they play by the rules

Avoid Flaming "Flaming" is the act of sending someone an insulting reply to a post or statement made on the Web. You'll often see a discussion derail if a flame war gets going. It's dispiriting to all participants to lose a discussion to a war of insults and personal slanders. The best idea is to avoid flaming and ignore people who engage in it.

Respect Different Opinions The range of opinions voiced in Internet communities is as vast and diverse as the people who hold them. You may find that some viewpoints defy any sort of logic, others may seem particularly candid and heartfelt, and others smack of adolescent naivete. Whatever the opinion, remember that people have feelings, and being overly harsh when responding to them will earn you a bad reputation. You'll find millions of people on the Web who agree with you. You'll find millions who don't. If you don't like the opposition's point of view, look for discussions that are peopled with participants who have the same stripes as you.

Help Others Help Themselves The great thing about participating in online discussions is that you can learn an enormous amount from people who are willing to share their expertise. To help continue the spirit, help others when you know the answer to their question.

Use Common Sense Like rules at the swimming pool, community rules and netiquette are very much common sense rules. You'll always find people who are emminently sensible on the Web, as well as people who make you wonder how they have managed to survive this long in our often unforgiving world.

To help continue the spirit, help others when you know the answer to their question

Along with the posted rules of your community's discussion area, you should bring a few rules of your own to the party.

1. Just because someone addresses or baits you personally doesn't mean you have to respond. Some people, for whatever reason or psychological hang-up, get pleasure in goat herding; they try to get your goat and everybody else's! Ignore them.

2. If you see something getting out of hand—and it can—drop a line to the host, manager, or "sysop," the person who is supposed to be monitoring these conversations. Going toe-to-toe with aggressive types can quickly spiral out of control, and you can find others complaining about your behavior as well. To contact a sysop or discussion host on the MSN site, click Info on the front page of the community in question, select Meet The Staff, and send e-mail to the appropriate contact.

3. Never assume too much about a person with whom you are communicating. Remember, some people take advantage of their anonymity and are not always truthful about their identities. You can't be sure, for example, that newcomers Suzanne or Debbie in the Romance Chat room are *women* any more than you can guarantee that Gustav or Frank are men. It's a fact of life on the Internet: some people like to play weird games.

Privacy: Are Your Secrets Safe?

Privacy on the Internet is an issue of epic proportions. The global dissemination of information is welcome in many ways, but not

TIP

If you feel like sending a heated reply, type it into a Word document fiist instead of your e-mail program. You might feel differently later and then you don't have to send it.

when it comes to violating your right to privacy; most of us don't want our credit histories or our personal lives posted for all the world to see. The issues regarding privacy and freedom of speech are passionately argued and confronted all over the Web. Every good community site recognizes the importance of this issue and has a privacy policy posted. MSN's detailed privacy policy, the beginning of which is shown in Figure 16-7, can be found at *http://home.microsoft.com/privacy.htm*.

You can better familiarize yourself and learn a lot about this topic by visiting the Electronic Frontier Foundation (*http://www.eff.org*). It's an important topic that affects us all. As it is our civic duty to stay informed about current events, it is the cyber-duty of every netizen to stay informed of these issues as they apply to the Internet.

WARNING

Protect your privacy! Don't reveal information of a personal nature—such as Social Security or credit card numbers—in a chat or discussion.

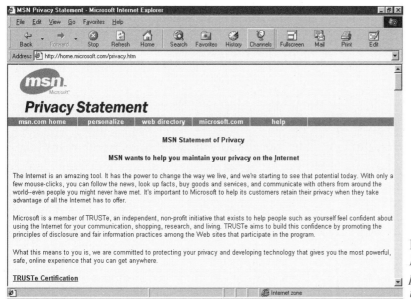

Figure 16-7
Know your community's privacy policy by reading it online

Chapter Seventeen

Search: Finding What You Need on the Internet

The Internet truly is the biggest information haystack of all time, and it grows larger every hour of the day. As the haystack gets larger, finding needles buried in it can pose a real challenge to someone searching through it, especially when everyone is looking for something different.

A portal site typically offers the full set of Internet features, all available from one starting point.

This chapter shows you how you can find what you're looking for and how to use the Internet tools to help you succeed in your search. You'll see how to take advantage of a "portal" site, which is a one-stop Web site to cover your basic needs, and how to search the Web for more information, right from the portal.

Start with a Portal

Comparing shopping in a large, busy city's downtown area to a shopping mall is like comparing the Internet to a portal. A shopping mall can offer more convenience, less confusion in finding your way around, and a more focused set of shopping choices. This is similar to what a portal can do for you. A portal site typically offers the full set of Internet features, all available from one starting point. Features include Web search capabilities (a search engine, detailed in this chapter), a community area, perhaps free e-mail, some editorial content, perhaps an area to park your own Web page, and a variety of shopping options. More and more portals are springing up, but the one we explore here is Microsoft's Sidewalk (*http://www.sidewalk.com*), shown in Figure 17-1.

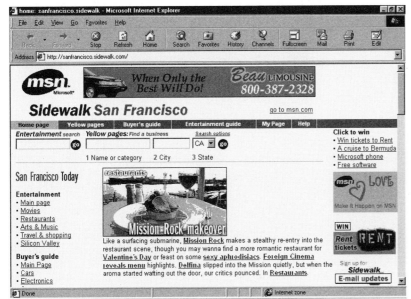

Figure 17-1
Sidewalk.com—Microsoft's well-rounded portal you can set up for your own city

When you enter sidewalk.com, you can personalize it by entering your postal code. After you personalize sidewalk.com, it will always provide news and information that is local for *you*. Portal sites are popular home pages because they offer so much flexibility and maneuverability when you connect. If you need to search or to shop for something, the tools are right there. If you want to share your opinions or hear someone else's beef, community options are also right there for you.

Figure 17-2 shows the lower portion of the sidewalk.com site. Everything is just a click away from this portal, including an entertainment guide, a search option, yellow pages, free e-mail, and a buyer's guide.

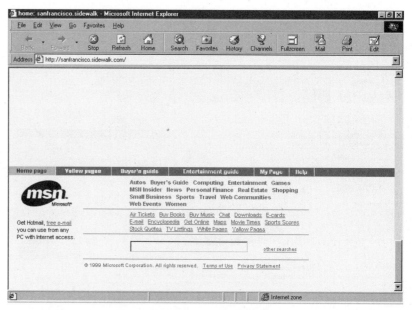

Figure 17-2
Sidewalk.com provides access to many of the goods and services associated with a portal site

It's Out There Somewhere

You may want to make a portal site such as sidewalk.com your home page because it provides a good subset of all the important categories of information, is well organized, and is easy to access. When you need more information on a topic or subject, however, you'll want to explore outside the range of the portal. At that point, a search engine is the tool you need.

Using a Search Engine

A search engine acts as your own personal detective agency. You tell it what you are looking for, and it goes out on the Web, scours millions of pages in search of the word or words you asked it to find, and returns with its results in breathtakingly fast time. How a search engine does what it does is not important here; knowing what a search engine can do for you and how best to use one is.

Beginning the Search If you've never accessed a search engine, follow these steps:

1. Go to the Microsoft Sidewalk site at *http://www.sidewalk. com/*.

2. Scroll to the end of the home page to where you see "Search the Web."

3. Enter a subject you want to research. For an example, type *jazz*.

4. Click the Go button.

The search engine finds an avalanche of pages listed that somehow reference jazz on their site. Figure 17-3 shows what the search engine returned for us.

The search engine provides details of what it finds. In our example, it located 374,725 pages that could be relevant to this search! It displays a list with a brief summary of what the site offers, with 20 of the located sites on the page. You can move to the next set of 20 by clicking the Next button, and return to a set you already viewed by clicking the Previous button.

To see more of the search results on the screen at one time (see Figure 17-4), clear the Show Results Summaries check box and increase the

TIP

Search is a good way to find other sites and resources developed specifically for seniors.

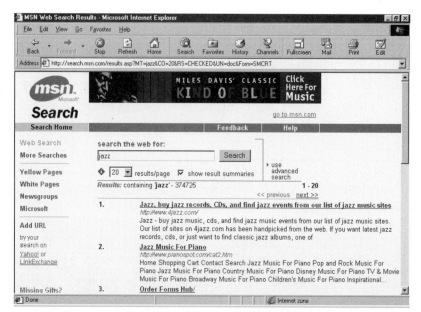

Figure 17-3
The MSN search engine is fast, but you need to keep your searches narrowly defined, or else you'll be buried in page links

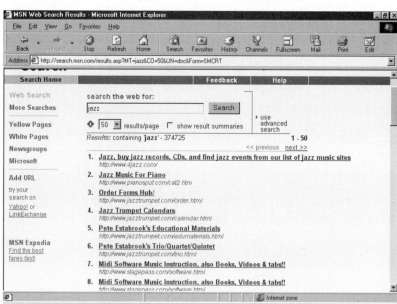

Figure 17-4
You can change how you view your search results

number of results per page. Figure 17-4 shows the jazz search without a summary and with 50 results to the page (many do not show on-screen).

Narrowing Your View The big problem with this broad topic search is that it returns an overwhelming number of avenues to pursue. If you are interested in a particular aspect of jazz or a particular performer, try entering the aspect or the performer's name. Figure 17-5 shows the results of a search on Count Basie that brought the total down to 4,582 possible site references.

Translating the Hieroglyphics of Your Search The search engine's field of vision doesn't stop at the horizon. The first entry that you see in Figure 17-5 is unreadable because it is a Taiwanese

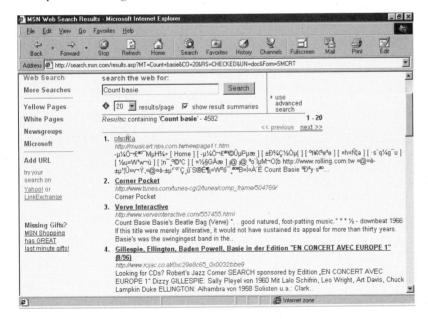

Figure 17-5
Basie's band was big, but our search on him came up bigger: nearly 5,000 results!

Web site that is not in English. Depending on your search, you might run into international entries that use a foreign alphabet, so don't be taken aback by them.

Refining Your Search . . . Again A list of more than 4,000 results is still too large to manage, so try narrowing the search again. If you want, you can search by adding more (relevant) words to the search, along with using one or two of these tricks:

- Search on additional words: *jazz + swing*
- Indicate words that should not be included: *jazz – bebop*
- Include quotation marks to indicate a phrase and not a collection of words: *"Count Basie Orchestra"*

The plus sign (+) tells the search engine to find pages containing the topics of both jazz and swing. This search rules out some pages that may not cover the topic of swing. Using the minus sign (-) tells the search engine to leave out pages that discuss bebop under the general category of jazz. To ask the search engine to find a certain phrase, use quotation marks to surround the phrase you want to locate. These options can be found on the Use Advanced Search option after your search engine produces a page of search results to view.

Filtering Your Search Results When you've refined your search and you're still coming up with a galaxy of matches, you need to decide what sites to investigate. Performing this search with the Show Result Summaries check box selected will help immensely because the brief description of the content often reveals whether the site is of value to you without your having to visit it. You may find that your search has correctly captured a completely

TIP

Use "+," "–," and quotation marks ("") to narrow your search options.

unrelated set of sites that also match your criteria! For example, a search on jazz is especially large because it also picks up references to the Utah Jazz, the basketball team in the NBA. As you view the list, the result summaries help you choose to ignore sites that appear completely unrelated to what you're looking for and instead investigate those that look most interesting.

The result summaries help you choose to ignore sites that appear completely unrelated to what you're looking for

Trying a Local Search Sometimes your search may come up with a site that sounds promising but, when you visit it, the treasure's not there. When you want to find information or a term on a particular Web page, try this approach: do a local search! Here's how:

1. Go to the page you want to search.
2. Click Edit on the Internet Explorer toolbar.
3. Click the Find (on this page) option. The Find dialog box opens.

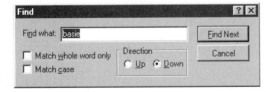

4. Enter a word to search, and click the Find Next button. If you want your search to match the case you provided, select the appropriate check boxes.

5. The search is nearly instantaneous. Internet Explorer finds the word and highlights it. If you can't see it, drag the Find box to the side.

6. To find additional occurrences of the word on the page, click the Find Next button.

With a little practice and some ingenuity, you'll find ways to obtain results even if your first attempts don't work.

TIP

As you become comfortable with various search engines, take advantage of the Help option that accompanies them. The Help screens include excellent pointers on how best to use the search engine in question.

Coming Up Empty-Handed: Don't Quit Yet!

The Count Basie search was easy and bountiful. But sometimes a search will wind up with no results. That doesn't necessarily mean nothing on the search topic is out there; it just means that you should alter your search words. With a little practice and some ingenuity, you'll find ways to obtain results even if your first attempts don't work.

One strategy when you come up empty-handed is to try another search engine. Numerous engines are available, and they all perform searches at least slightly differently. One search engine can often turn up different results from another, so you might want to perform your search with a few different ones to find what you're looking for and to find which search engine works best for you.

To access a different search engine, return to your portal home page, in our case, sidewalk.com. On the sidewalk.com site, just to the right of the Search the web search field is the Other Searches button. Click it and you see the MSN Search home page, and then click More Searches link (see Figure 17-6).

The World's Biggest Phone Book

The phone companies now charge a small fortune for information, but the Internet offers an inexpensive alternative. You can use a special search engine designed specifically for phone and address information to obtain telephone numbers for individuals, organizations, and businesses.

Searching the White Pages

1. To locate someone in the white pages, you don't even need to know what area code the person you want to contact lives in.

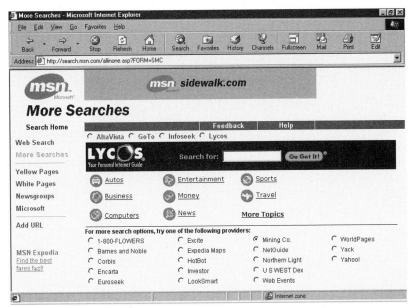

Figure 17-6
Even when your search proves fruitless, try another search engine to see what might be out there

Here's what to do: Click the White Pages link at the bottom of sidewalk.com, located to the right of Quick Links. The White Pages search window appears, as shown in Figure 17-7.

2. Enter as much information about the person as possible, and click Find People.

3. The search returns with a list of people who fit your search information.

The Yellow Pages

If you are tracking down a place of business, portals such as sidewalk.com offer a yellow pages directory option alongside the white pages. These online yellow pages, however, are super-charged.

TIP

If you're curious about someone you knew, such as a high school friend, try entering his or her name. The white pages can do an outstanding job of helping you locate him or her.

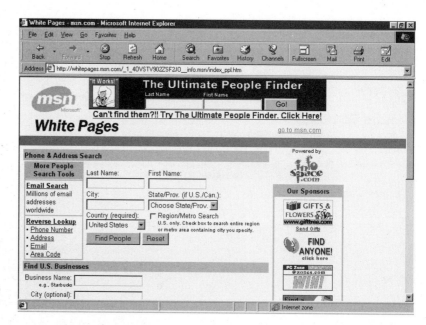

Figure 17-7
*Search the
white pages to
locate somone*

Here's how to use them:

1. Click the Yellow Pages link at the bottom of the sidewalk.com
    page, listed next to Quick Picks. The Yellow Pages search
    screen appears, as shown in Figure 17-8.

2. Fill in the business you are interested in locating, or select a
    category from the left margin (this example shows
    "Community" for Berkeley, California). Figure 17-9 shows
    the associated subcategories that appear for "Community."

We picked Senior services from this menu and received a rich
listing of local resources, some of which are shown in Figure 17-10.

3. And now, the coup de grace: When your list of businesses
    appears, click the button that appears to the left of the entry
    you are interested in. A detailed map appears, as shown in
    Figure 17-11.

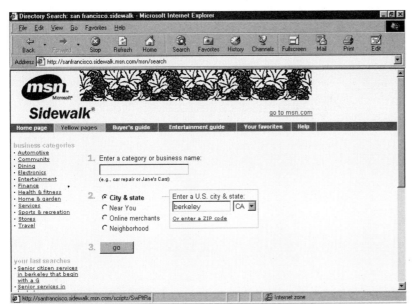

TIP

Print the directions that the sidewalk.com yellow pages provide before setting out for your destination—and take them with you!

Figure 17-8
The sidewalk.com yellow pages

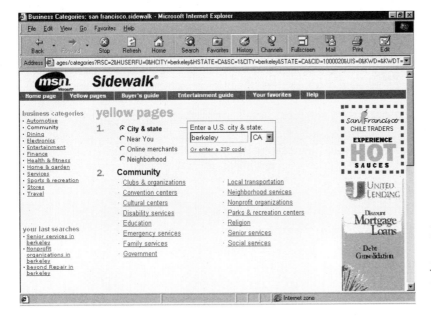

Figure 17-9
The sidewalk.com yellow pages are updated constantly, as are its categories

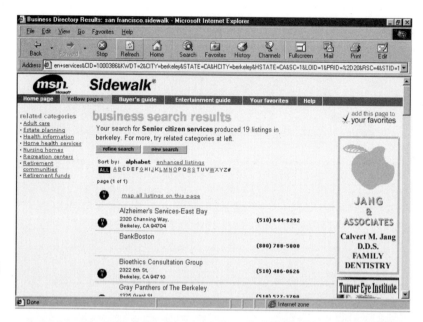

Figure 17-10
The yellow pages don't divide government listings, so you'll find all the resources you're seeking in one search

Figure 17-11
These yellow pages give you a lot more than directory assistance—at no extra cost

Tell me what you eat and I will tell you who you are.
—Jean Anthelme Brillat-Savarin

Part Three

Ten-Minute Recipes for Successful Computing

Chapter Eighteen

Keeping in Touch with Friends and Loved Ones

If the chore of addressing envelopes, getting stamps, and taking a letter to the post office keeps you from writing letters often, you will love e-mail. Oh, you still have to write the letter because your computer can't read your mind—yet! But the process is fun and fast if you follow this recipe.

This recipe shows you how to take advantage of e-mail, including how to address e-mail messages with just the click of a mouse, and you can even send your message to lots of folks at one time. When the recipe is complete, expect to receive many responses. Read, enjoy, repeat!

What You'll Need

- A modem
- Microsoft Outlook (or comparable e-mail program)
- E-mail addresses for a few friends and relatives
- A desire to receive lots of letters from friends and relatives

Simple Recipe for Becoming a Conscientious Letter Writer

1. Open Microsoft Outlook.
2. Begin a new e-mail message.
3. Fill in your friends' e-mail addresses.
4. Create a mailing list in your address book.
5. Write your message.
6. Send the e-mail message to your gang—with an attachment!

Filling in Your Little Black E-Mail Address Book

E-mail addresses might look strange and be hard to type, let alone remember, but the good news is that you need to type one only once. The way to avoid retyping e-mail addresses is to build an address book. After an address is entered in your personal address book, you can just select the address each time you need to address your e-mail message.

Follow these steps to add an e-mail address to your personal address book:

1. Open Microsoft Outlook, and click Tools in the menu bar.

2. Click the Address Book option, and the Address Book window appears.

Show Names
drop-down list

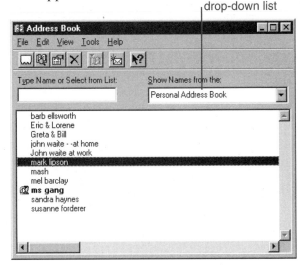

3. The Show Names drop-down list should show "Personal Address Book." If not, click the down arrow and select "Personal Address Book" from the list.

NOTE

Microsoft Outlook is used for these examples, so if you're using another e-mail program, the procedures will vary.

4. Click File in the Address Book window and click New Entry. The New Entry opens.

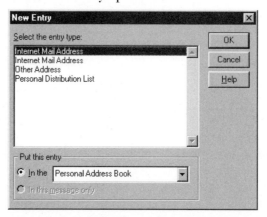

5. Select Internet Mail Address by double-clicking it. The New Internet Mail Address Properties window opens.

NOTE

When you enter a Display Name, choose a name that tells you whose e-mail address you're entering.

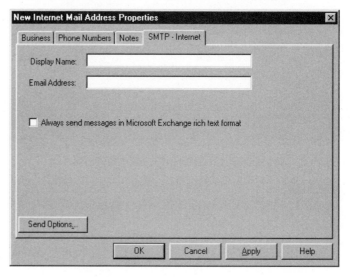

6. Enter your recipient's regular name (or nickname) in the display field and his or her actual e-mail address in the e-mail address field.

7. Click OK. The name and address are added to the list.

8. Repeat this process to add all the e-mail addresses you want to have in your address book. Don't forget to include your own address here (just in case you want to send something to yourself, too).

Congratulations! You've started your address book. When you have more addresses to add, repeat the first part of this recipe to include the new names in your address book. Once you add an address, you'll never have to enter it again!

Writing One Letter—Sending Many Letters

You may regularly write letters that you want to send to many friends or to all your kids located around the country. Do you make several copies and send each of them a copy? Do you address it to all of them? No, you make a distribution list by following these steps:

1. In Outlook, click Tools on the main menu, and select the Address Book option. (Or click the address book icon on the tool bar.)

2. Click File on the menu bar of the Address Book window, and select New Entry.

3. Double-click the Personal Distribution List option, and the New Personal Distribution List window opens. (See Figure 18-1.)

4. Enter a name for the group of people you plan to send to. For example, you might call a distribution list that includes your four children "Our Kids."

5. Click the Add/Remove Members button, and the Edit Members window appears. (See Figure 18-2.)

6. Double-click each name you want added to the list, and the names move over to the Members list.

NOTE

After you've entered an e-mail address in the Address Book, you can use it by clicking it when you're addressing e-mail.

TIP

Distribution lists make it easy to send e-mail to a group of people.

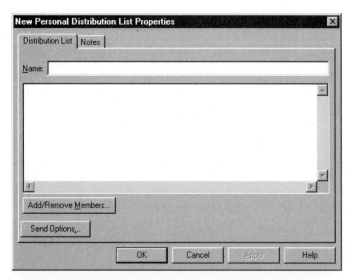

Figure 18-1
Here's what you'll see when you start a distribution list

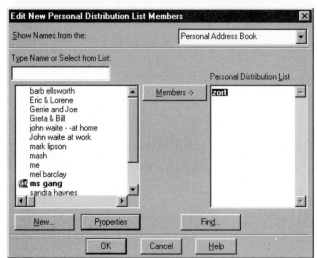

Figure 18-2
Adding and removing members is as easy as clicking a button

7. When you have completed the list, click OK and then click OK again. The group "Our Kids" now appears in the mailing list with a symbol indicating that it is a distribution list.

Mailing It to the Gang

Now that you have a personal distribution list, follow these steps to use it to make sending e-mail even more efficient:

1. Return to the main Outlook window by clicking OK in the windows.

2. Create a new message by clicking the New Message button at the left end of the toolbar. The New Message window opens.

3. Click the To button that appears below the Send button. When you do, your address book appears.

4. Double-click "Our Kids" to send the e-mail to everyone on that distribution list. If you want, you can click additional names, and the e-mail will be delivered to them as well.

5. Definitely double-click your own name (you did put it in your address book, right?), and send it to yourself.

6. When you're done, click OK and your message is addressed.

TIP

Remember that you added names and groups in your Personal Address Book. If the window opens and says "Contacts" or "Outlook Address Book," you need to change to the Personal Address Book.

TIP

You can fill in the Cc: and Bcc: fields by clicking the buttons right below the To button. (The Bcc: field sends a copy of the message hiding the recipient's name. The Cc: field sends a copy, and all names are displayed.)

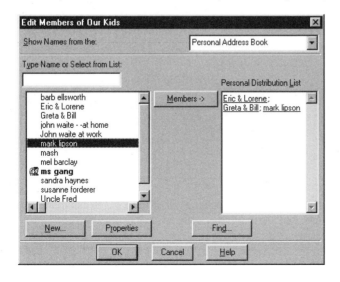

An "attachment" is any type of file accompanying an e-mail message.

Sending More Than One Message in the Bottle

In the past, many e-mail programs allowed only text messages to be sent. Today, most e-mail programs such as Microsoft Outlook allow you to add wonderful embellishments, including drawings or pictures. Sometimes these can be copied directly into an e-mail message. To try including a graphic, you can use Microsoft's Paint program to create a picture. (If you haven't used Paint before, you'll find it easy to use.) Select part of your drawing, and copy and paste it into an e-mail message. If your letter recipients use an e-mail program that has the same features as yours, they will receive your drawing or photo right in the e-mail message.

Another way to send photos, documents, drawings, or even sound or video files is with attachments. An "attachment" is any type of file accompanying an e-mail message. If the recipients of your e-mail message have an e-mail program that can process attachments, they will be able to view the file you send. To learn how to attach a file to your e-mail message, follow these steps:

1. Create a new e-mail message and address it to yourself.
2. Click the icon that indicates you have an attachment (in Outlook, the icon is a paper clip) in the toolbar, and the Insert File window appears.
3. Select a file from the directory, and double-click it. Your e-mail message now includes an attachment.
4. Click the Send button, and the document will soon arrive in your Inbox (depending on your server). When your message does arrive, it appears with a small icon in the left margin indicating that it has an attachment.

5. Double-click the e-mail message in the Inbox, and it opens.

6. To open the attachment, double-click the icon as it appears in your e-mail message, and presto! The item appears in the program in which it was created.

Sharing Your New Knowledge

After you have an address book, some distribution lists, and a grasp of how attachments work, you'll no doubt find that sending e-mail messages is truly an effortless way to stay in touch with people. Enjoy! Your friends—and everyone else—will be impressed with your new mastery of e-mail.

TIP

Your e-mail program may use another indicator for attachments—see the online Help system in the program.

Chapter Nineteen

Desktop Publishing

Publishing has always required an enormous amount of effort and expertise. It involves editors, typesetters, graphic designers, experts in page layout, and printers, to name a few. Publishing professionals use very expensive, very complicated software programs for desktop publishing, or DTP, that allow them to control every single detail in the design and production process. Fortunately, you can get great results with Microsoft Publisher, a desktop publishing program that is easy to learn and also a lot of fun to use.

What You'll Need

- A copy of Microsoft Publisher or similar program
- A printer, preferably a color one
- The desire to create a variety of artistic, entertaining, or professional documents

A Simple Recipe for "Do It Yourself" Publishing

1. Open Microsoft Publisher.
2. Use a Publishing Wizard to design greeting cards.
3. Impress your friends and family with your original greeting cards.
4. Apply your creativity in the publishing world beyond greeting Cards.

Donning Your Publisher's Cap

This recipe helps you to enter the world of publishing through Microsoft Publisher, Microsoft's DTP program for home users. You can create custom greeting cards and an award certificate with Microsoft Publisher and learn the ropes of publishing. By recipe's end, you'll know enough about Publisher to create a slew of different publications such as brochures, newsletters, or advertisements as you provide the creative ideas and experiment on your own.

Creating Your Own Personal Greeting Card Line

With greeting cards becoming more expensive these days, you can save a bundle by designing and printing your own.

Open Microsoft Publisher (if you haven't purchased it, check your Start menu; it may have been included on your computer). The opening screen appears, as shown in Figure 19-1 on the following page.

This is the Microsoft Publisher Catalog window. The Wizard window on the left lists the different types of documents that Microsoft Publisher can help you design. The Template window on the right shows all the "boilerplates," or starting designs, that are available to you in that particular category. Use the scroll bar to see the full range of available templates.

For this project, click the Greeting cards option in the Wizards column, and a list of card types appears in the Wizard window. You can scroll through the available greeting cards in the preview window. You'll find more than 80 cards here from which to choose, and you can customize them all.

*W*ith greeting cards becoming more expensive these days, you can save a bundle by designing and printing your own.

*Y*ou can scroll through the available greeting cards in the preview window.

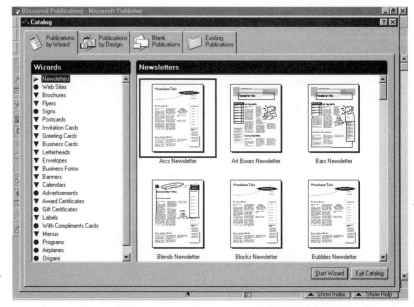

Figure 19-1
Microsoft Publisher opens with quite an offering: 28 newsletter styles from which to choose

TIP

Some cards are hard to see in the current view. To enlarge the on-screen image, click the plus (+) sign at the bottom of the Template window. Click the minus (-) sign to make it smaller.

Click the Birthday Card option in the Wizard window. When the birthday cards appear, double-click the Fireworks And Star Birthday Card option. The card fills the Template window, as shown in Figure 19-2.

When the greeting card appears, your wizard also appears on the left side of the screen to help guide you through the card-making process. Click the wizard's Next button to read your next instruction.

Designing: The Way of the Wizards

Wizards walk you step-by-step through all the stages of creating and personalizing a card. Here are the steps this wizard follows:

1. The wizard first asks you to choose a layout for your card. Click each button to see how each layout varies. We stick with Picture Squares in this chapter. Click the Next button.

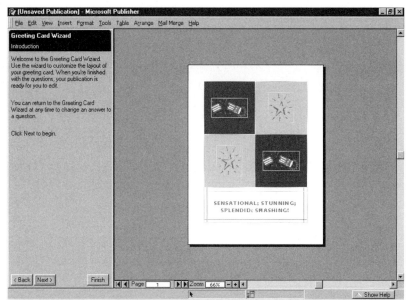

Figure 19-2
You can select any item from the catalog window and customize it as you want

2. The Size and Fold options describe how you will fold the page to form the card. The Quarter page side fold is perfect. Click the Next button again.

3. Choose a color scheme for your card. They all look good, but you should choose the scheme that you like best! Click Next again.

4. The verse window appears. Click the Browse button, and a list of verses appears, as shown in Figure 19-3. Click any one line to read the full verse. If you want to write your own, choose any one of these, and rewrite it if you wish. Click Next again.

5. In this wizard step, specify home/family for the personal information to be used on your card. This is the publisher's

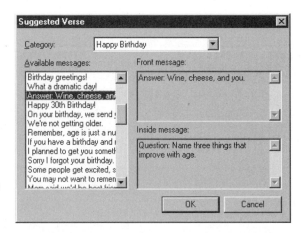

Figure 19-3
You can choose one of the many verses provided or write your own

information that appears on the back of the card (that's you). Click Finish.

6. The next screen, shown in Figure 19-4, is a summary of your card and the design elements you selected.

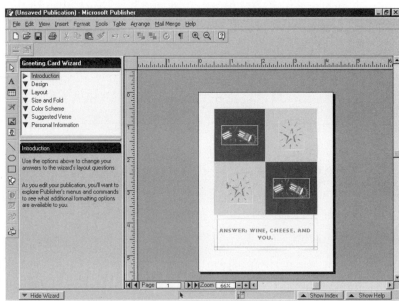

Figure 19-4
The last wizard screen is a summary of all of your design decisions

Revising Your Work

- You can change any of the design elements by clicking the item that you want to revisit and changing the associated setting. If you want to write your own text for the card, click the text as it appears *on the card* in the Editing window, and type a new message.

- To examine all the pages of the card, click the right- and left-pointing page arrows in the bottom left corner of the Editing window. If you want to really be creative, you can even incorporate your own graphics and photos into the card. To do so, double-click the picture you want to replace (in the Editing window), and the Microsoft Clip Gallery opens. The Clip Gallery is a selection of images that you are free to use in your publishing projects. Select the graphic you want to use by double-clicking it.

- When you are done, save your work, print the card, and fold it as intended. Three cheers! Your publishing house has created its first greeting card.

You Deserve an Award

In honor of your extraordinary work in the field of publishing, you deserve an award. As an independent publisher, though, you need to make it yourself!

To create your award certificate, follow these steps:

1. Open the Microsoft Publisher File menu, select New, and the Catalog window opens.

2. Select the Award Certificates Wizard. The award templates appear in the Template window.

TIP

Clip art is defined as small computer drawings and images used to enhance a document. Clip art can be found all over the World Wide Web. Some sets are free or very cheap. A collection of clip art images comes with Microsoft Publisher.

3. Scroll down and double-click the Great Idea certificate to select it. The award certificate appears, as shown in Figure 19-5.

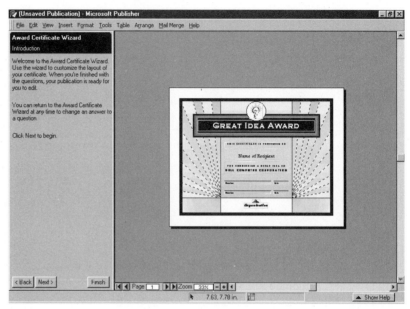

Figure 19-5
Microsoft Publisher enables you to produce anything and everything—newsletters to greeting cards to certificates

TIP

Click the different options that appear in the Wizards column to see some of the other types of publications Microsoft Publisher can help you create. Each document type in the Wizards column will display an array of design variations from which to choose.

Let the wizard guide you through the design steps. When the wizard summary screen appears, click the text fields you want to replace, and enter your own accolades. When finished, print the award and show your friends the kind of quality work you produce.

Don't be surprised if your friends start asking you to produce signs, cards, flyers, and newsletters for them!

Chapter Twenty

Bon Voyage! Planning Your Next Trip

Wherever you're headed, whether it's just a weekend trip to the country, an out-of-state sojourn, or an international adventure with intrigue around every bend, you can take advantage of what the World Wide Web has to help you plan and enjoy your trip.

What You'll Need

- A modem
- Microsoft Internet Explorer
- Microsoft Expedia (accessed online)
- The desire to save money on your next excursion

Recipe for the Perfect Getaway

1. Get online.
2. Go to *http://www.expedia.com*.
3. Plan the perfect getaway.
4. Comparison shop for airline tickets.
5. Change the message on your answering machine to: "On vacation. Call back later!"

Using the Internet to Plan a Trip

The travel industry has discovered the Internet in a big way. For years, ticket purchases were controlled by the airlines and by travel agents. Now, thanks to the Internet, you can find cheap flights and book them yourself! You can also learn about great cruises, reserve rental cars, make hotel reservations, and even find the coziest bed-and-breakfasts you could ever dream of, all from your PC.

The easiest way to start is to go to Microsoft's travel services Web site, expedia.com (*http://www.expedia.com*). Expedia.com's home page appears, as shown in Figure 20-1.

T*hanks to the Internet, you can find cheap flights and book them yourself!*

Registration button

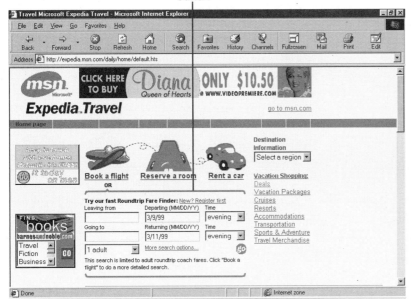

Figure 20-1
Microsoft's expedia.com Web site gives you access to travel-related information

To take advantage of what expedia.com has to offer, you need to register for the site, which takes only a minute to do. Under New Visitors, click Register With Expedia, follow the directions on the page to select your preferences, and click the Continue button. When you reach the Member Information page, shown in Figure 20-2, fill in the requested information to register.

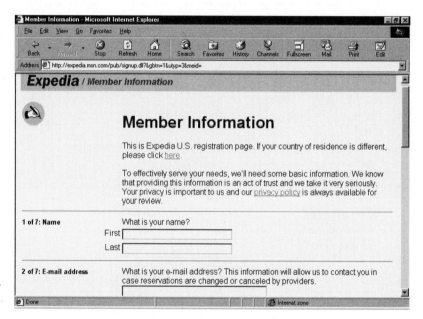

Figure 20-2
Registering with expedia.com offers you many benefits

After you have completed your registration, you should print the final page and keep it on file for your records.

On the Road Again

To familiarize you with the offerings on expedia.com, we take you on a quick tour.

If you're looking for the perfect vacation, *and* you don't want to pay a small fortune, click Vacation packages link, shown in Figure 20-3, for an easy, one-stop, hassle-free deal.

Figure 20-3
Don't worry about the big stuff; just enjoy yourself with a vacation package

Chatting with Others About Your Travel Plans If you aren't sure where or how you want to travel, you might want to chat with other older adults about their travel adventures. To meet with this circle of fellow travelers, go to *http://expedia.msn.com/forums/senior*. Here we take a peek at the "Loving Retirement" page, as shown in Figure 20-4 on the following page.

In the Seniors' Forum, you can join a travel chat and learn about some of the more adventuresome trips that some older adults

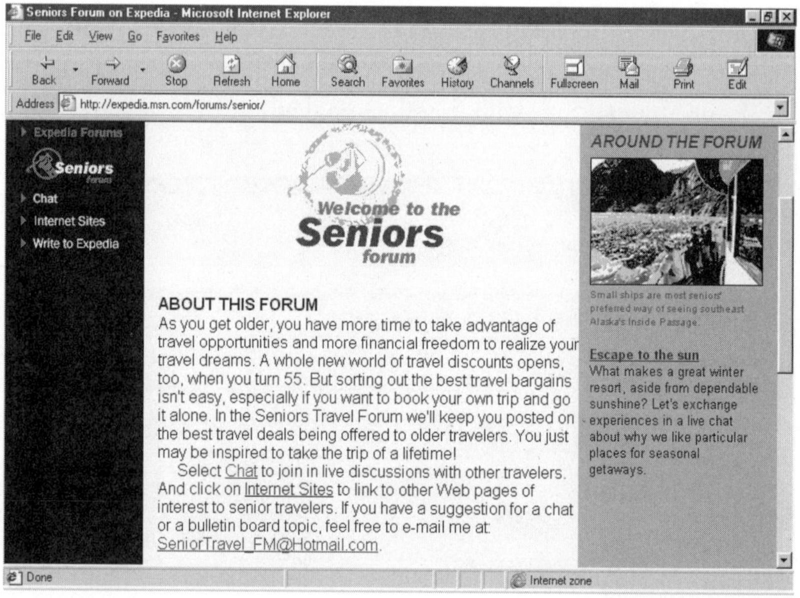

Figure 20-4
The best source of information on that trip you're planning? A peer who has already taken the trip! The senior travel forums are just what you need

I*f you know where you're headed, Expedia can help you get a good deal on airfares.*

are raving about: freighter travel, houseboating, African safaris, and even trekking in Nepal! If you don't like the idea of bungee jumping off Mt. Rushmore or kayaking over Niagara Falls, don't worry; you'll find plenty of folks to chat with here who prefer quiet, relaxing vacation alternatives as well.

Taking in More Sites—Before You Travel Expedia.com also offers you a good index of other travel sites that are intended specifically for the more mature Lewis & Clarks out there. The Forum's Internet sites link offers a list of such sites. Figure 20-5 shows a few of them.

Locating the Cheapest Airfares

If you know where you're headed, Expedia can help you get a good deal on airfares. From the Expedia Home page, try the Round trip

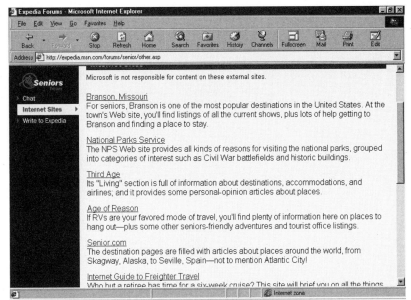

Figure 20-5
Expedia.com gives you an index of other Web sites to help you better research your travel plans

Fare Finder: plug in your arrival and departure dates as well as your arrival and departure locations. When you click Go, the Flight Wizard appears to gather more detailed information from you. Don't forget to indicate "seniors" to take advantage of significantly lower rates. Figure 20-6 shows the ticket prices available to us if we wanted to escape the tail end of Chicago's winter for the heat of San Diego.

The Elderhostel Adventure

If you want an adventure, and you'd like to take it with people with whom you share some common interests, then Elderhostel is another *great* find. Elderhostel, a nonprofit organization, has been running educational vacations since it was founded in 1975. We've heard only raves about its trips, its organization, and the people who participate. Figure 20-7 on the following page gives you a snapshot of its Web site *(http://www.elderhostel.org)*.

NOTE

It's certainly not in its literature, and we're not guaranteeing anything, but we know of some romances that got started on Elderhostel trips.

Elderhostel's mission statement identifies its members as those who "believe that learning is a lifelong process.

Chapter Twenty Bon Voyage! Planning Your Next Trip

239

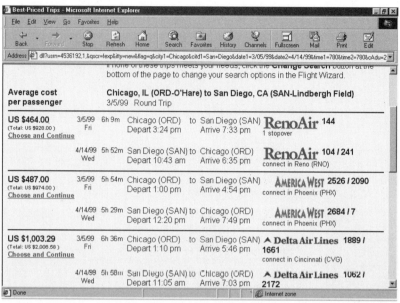

Figure 20-6
Expedia helps you choose the least expensive flight right from your PC

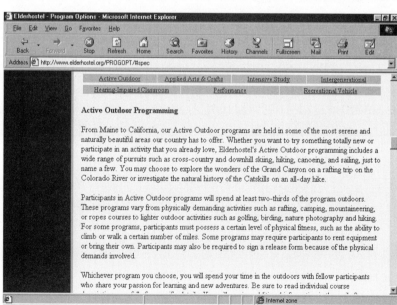

Figure 20-7
Elderhostel has regularly scheduled trips for older adults to all reaches of the globe

Elderhostel's mission statement identifies its members as those who "believe that learning is a lifelong process." Its trips are always educational, whether the focus is natural history, Shakespeare, or architecture. If that sounds interesting to you, visit its site and learn more about what Elderhostel has to offer.

NOTE

Try SeniorSearch (http://www.seniorsearch.com) and the AARP site (http://www.aarp.org) for access to travel information.

Chapter Twenty-One

Shopping on the Internet

Ah, the mail order revolution. You've surely seen the results of it: the mail carrier sagging under the weight of all those catalogs, the bulging recycling bins, and so on.

Now you can skip the paper catalogs and shop online instead. But if you haven't yet experienced shopping on the World Wide Web, you might not completely trust it. It's new and there are many unknowns. What if someone steals your credit card number? What happens if you don't get your merchandise? What if the order is incomplete? This recipe will put you at ease about using the Web to shop, and you'll learn how to be a savvy online shopper.

What You'll Need

- A modem
- Internet Explorer
- A valid credit card
- A friend or a relative who deserves something nice

  or

- An excuse to buy something for yourself
- Some self control!

Recipe for the Ultimate Shopping Trip

1. Connect to the Internet.
2. Visit online malls and window shop.
3. Learn the rules for safe shopping on the World Wide Web.

Shopping at the Biggest Mall This Side of Alpha Centauri

You don't typically need to think about how you shop. You've known how to do this since your first solo trip to the penny candy store. But you do have a system for shopping: you know where to go for what; you know who has the best sales and best prices, and you know who has the quality stuff and whose merchandise is a couple of floors south of the bargain basement.

The Web may seem at first like a completely different environment; the amenities are different and the concept of "service" seems different. So the idea here is to allay your fears, help you get comfortable with the basics of Web shopping, and show you how to make purchases via the Web.

Window Shopping

One of the great things about the Web is the ability to just window-shop. It's as though you were able to transport yourself across town to whatever store you think of, in the wink of an eye. Besides being fun, Web window shopping is a superlative way of gathering consumer information. All the car companies, for example, have Web sites, and you can do all your research about a potential purchase online, without a salesman pressuring you one way or another. When you have narrowed your choices down, you can *then* go into a showroom and wheel and deal.

Introducing the DTM: The Desktop Mall

The Web is a great source for all sorts of information, but how do you find Web sites that sell products? Portal sites include areas that

TIP

The Internet can help you if you want to purchase products from local merchants, too. You can use the online yellow pages, which can be accessed from any portal site to make searching for what you want or need quick and easy.

TIP

Check out the shopping available from the thirdage.com site.

are the equivalent of virtual malls where merchants of all sorts hawk their wares. If a site has something to sell, it typically contains a link on its home page that says "shop" or "buy" or "company store."

On portal sites such as the Microsoft sidewalk.com, access to its desktop malls featuring hundreds of "stores" is just a mouse click away. To see your store choices, go to *http://www.sanfrancisco.sidewalk.com*, as shown in Figure 21-1.

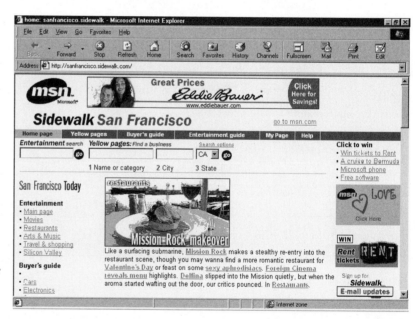

Figure 21-1
Sidewalk.com is the door to a mall with hundreds of stores

From sidewalk.com, click Buyer's Guide, just below the masthead, and the "mall directory" appears. Figure 21-2 shows a portion of the scrollable directory. New offerings appear on a regular basis, so be sure to check back regularly to see what's new.

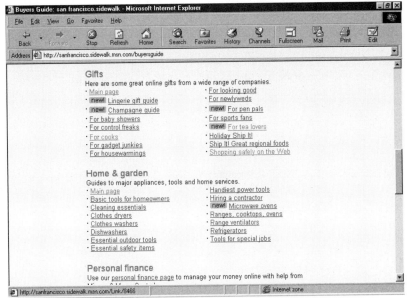

Figure 21-2
The mall directory. Every store is just a click away; no more running to the other end of the mall or across town

Shopping Outside the Mall If you want to leave the sidewalk.com mall, you can use the search engine to find other places to go. Finding stores outside the mall is a little more complicated because a search on "computers for sale," for example, will bring you a listing of about a trillion vendors selling everything and anything related to computers. Be sure to refine your search so that you don't have to wade through search results that aren't what you are looking for. (For information on how to refine your search choices, see Chapter 17 in this book.) One approach is to stick with merchants with whom you do business in person. If you search on specific merchant names, you should meet with success.

Classified Ads You'll find classified ads all over the Web. If you have a local paper with classifieds, *and* the paper is on the Web, you can bet that the classifieds are on it, too.

WARNING

First impressions are important, and not all sites are created equal. If finding your way around on a site is difficult, find another site that's easier to navigate.

The advantages to reading the classifieds online are phenomenal. First, you can read the ads without struggling to read the small newspaper print. Even more important, you can sort and filter on specific details of what you are looking for. For example, on the *San Francisco Examiner/Chronicle* site (*http://www.sfgate.com*), you can search the automotive ads based on make, model, year, and price. You can see part of the sorting tool in Figure 21-3.

T*he advantages to reading the classifieds online are phenomenal.*

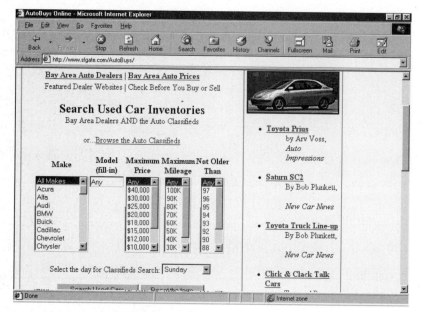

Figure 21-3
Search your classifieds for some good bargains

Seeing How the Other .001% Lives So who really shops on the Web? Apparently everybody! If you've just won the state lottery, you might want to trade in some of your winnings and your '92 Buick for a Ferrari. Get the Ferrari information you need at its Web site (*http://ferrari.com*). Figure 21-4 shows a little beauty in the Web showroom that will probably claim most of your lottery winnings!

S*o who really shops on the Web?*

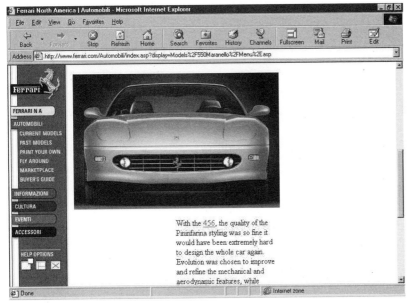

With the 456, the quality of the Pininfarina styling was so fine it would have been extremely hard to design the whole car again. Evolution was chosen to improve and refine the mechanical and aerodynamic features, while

Figure 21-4
Ferrari's 456M GT with a top speed of 186 miles per hour. Not very practical, but it will make you the envy of every teenager in town!

If you buy that Ferrari, you'll probably need a castle to go with it. If you use a search engine and search on "castle for sale," you'll be amazed at the number of choices. Castles are available in Italy, France, Scotland, and, well, California.

Is It Safe to Buy on the Web?

You probably have some reservations about giving your credit card number to a person or company via your computer. That's understandable. There are issues and guidelines to follow when making a Web purchase, and they are posted as part of the Microsoft

Buyer's Guide (Which you can find at sidewalk.com). To find them, click the Buyer's Guide, scroll down to the Gifts listings, and click, "Shopping Safely on the Web." This entry provides an excellent guide to becoming a smart Web shopper (see Figure 21-5).

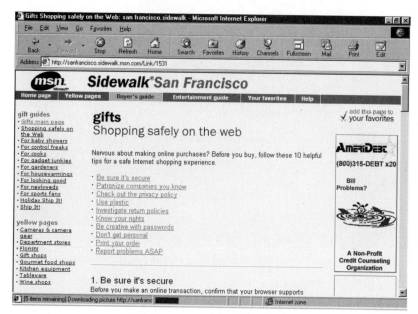

Figure 21-5
Be Web savvy—read Microsoft's guide to safe shopping

Ringing Up Your Purchase

In this section, we walk you through the steps required to purchase something via the Web (without actually purchasing anything). We start with the Gift section of the Buyer's Guide. The entries may be different when you read this, but any selection will work similarly. Here are the basic steps:

1. Click the item you are interested in (see Figure 21-6). We chose "For Tea Lovers" (see Figure 21-7).

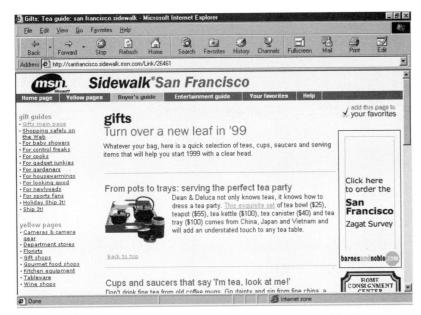

Figure 21-6
You can find almost any gift you can imagine

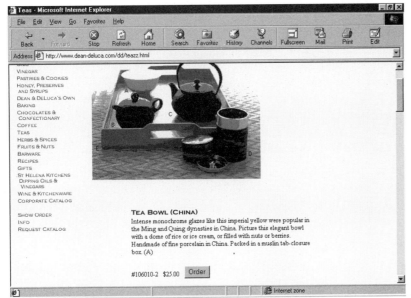

Figure 21-7
Here's a great tea bowl that took only a short while to find

2. To purchase the tea bowl, click the link. The merchant's 1–800 number is provided in case you prefer to order by phone. To order online, click the Order button as shown.

3. A security alert appears. Click OK.

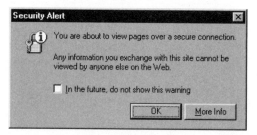

NOTE

The security alert is there to remind you that information you are sending or reading will be sent over a secure connection. Other Internet users cannot access it.

4. Your shopping basket appears. Specify the quantity you want, and click Update Cart for an accurate subtotal.

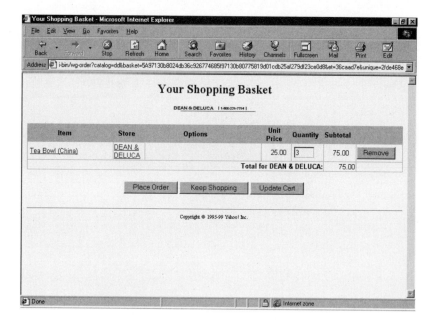

5. You may continue to shop or choose to check out and place your order.

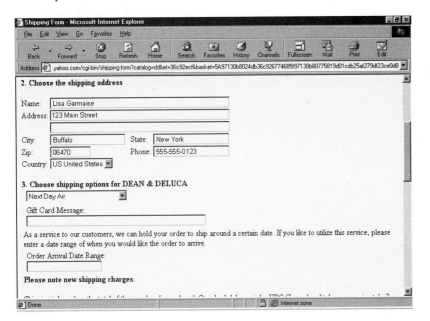

NOTE

When you click the Submit or Order Now button, your order will be sent to the online store. Don't do so now unless you really want to order items you've selected.

Do You Have to Buy Everything in Your Online Shopping Cart? You can add a million things to your shopping cart as you shop at a site. You can then either empty everything out of your cart, or remove selected items as you choose. Every item has a Remove button next to it; one click and the item is gone.

The total cost of your order is calculated based on whatever items remain in your cart. You enter all the address and billing information and your credit card number, and the site provides a confirmation number. If you fail to provide any required information (such as your state or your postal code), you will be prompted to correct the oversight. After you have corrected the

TIP

If you're having a problem getting merchandise out of your basket, or you don't want to make any purchases, click your Home button and exit the site.

WARNING

If you do put things in your online shopping cart, provide a credit card number, and submit the order, that means you are buying those products. Never provide a credit card number unless you are prepared to purchase the selected products.

information and received your confirmation number, you should print your order as a receipt. Merchants will typically send you an e-mail confirmation of your order as well, which also acts as a receipt.

When Will Your Merchandise Arrive? Many Web merchants offer you a variety of delivery plans, so you should have a sense of when your order will arrive based on what you were or weren't willing to pay for shipping. Whichever option you choose, however, your confirmation number often acts as a tracking number. When you enter the tracking number at the site, you will receive all the vital statistics on the status of your delivery. Ironically, you will often have a better sense of when a package ordered on the Web will arrive from across the country than you will from the furniture store around the block!

Complaints, Anyone?

Okay, no store would be complete without a complaint desk. All the sites you will visit via MSN and sidewalk.com are eager for feedback from customers, and they want to make sure that your experience with them was positive. So if you have a problem, don't be shy: let them know!

Here's a site you should visit immediately and bookmark: Consumer World (*http//www.consumerworld.org*), which is shown in Figure 21-8.

The Consumer World site is an incredible site with links to federal, state, and international consumer protection agencies that you didn't even know existed, as well as links to the complaint desks of an ever-growing list of companies. Even if you don't want to

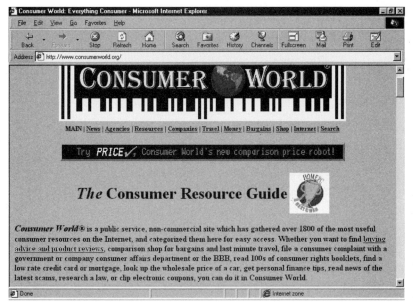

Figure 21-8
Consumer World is the spot for sharp consumers—and merchants

shop on the Web, this is a great site for every consumer, *and* it's entertaining!

Why Some Companies Don't Sell on the Web

Thousands of businesses are leaping at the chance to sell on the Web, but not all merchants are so inclined. In fact, some companies, for reasons of market strategy or maintaining good relations with their sales force, will not allow their products to be sold over the Web. You can use their Web sites only to get product information and to locate a retail outlet. Other companies are just a little slower, so if you look for a company that doesn't have a Web presence yet, let the company know that you were surprised at its absence.

TIP

When searching for a product or service on the Web, be sure to use more than one search engine if you have any problems finding what you're looking for. The results of multiples searches can be dramatically different.

Chapter Twenty-Two

Turning Your PC into a Home Stereo and Tape Recorder

You may be wondering why your computer came with stereo speakers, a sound card, and a microphone. These audio components enable you to listen to the audio segments of CD-ROMs and provide an air of realism when you play certain video games. But your computer can also be used as an audio CD player *and* as a tape recorder. This recipe shows you how.

What You'll Need

- Speakers connected to your PC
- A sound card
- A microphone (comes with most new PCs)
- An audio CD of a recording artist you enjoy
- A love of music and sound

Listening to Music and Recording Sound

1. Open the CD-ROM drive.
2. Load your music CD.
3. Enjoy your favorite melodies as you work.
4. Record sample messages with the microphone.
5. Play back and experiment with your tape-recorded message.
6. Save your recorded file.
7. Share your recordings with others.

Music to Your Ears

Much of the music that we enjoyed in earlier days is now available on CD, and it's not much different from using an LP on a phonograph. Here's what to do:

1. Open the CD-ROM drive by pushing the Eject button on it.
2. Make sure that your PC speakers are turned on.
3. Load an audio CD in the CD-ROM drive, shiny side down, and close the drive.
4. Go to your Windows desktop, and double-click My Computer. The CD drive indicates that a music CD is loaded.
5. Double-click the Audio CD icon. The first selection on the CD begins to play.

Deciphering Your New Stereo Components

When you clicked the audio CD icon, the music started, and a picture of the CD player appeared on-screen, something like that shown in Figure 22-1.

The CD Player has the following options:

*   **Transport controls:** Includes the functions for Stop, Play, Pause, Skip Backwards, Skip Forwards, Rewind Next Track, and Previous Track
*   **Eject:** Stops the music and ejects the CD

NOTE

The CD may begin to play without your having to click a audio CD icon if your computer has its "AutoRun" option enabled.

NOTE

Your stereo may look a little different from the one shown here, depending on which version of Microsoft Windows you have.

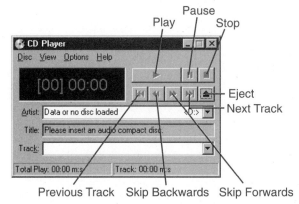

Figure 22-1
Use your PC as a stereo

Turning Your PC into a Tape Recorder

We keep describing your PC as a tape recorder, but that's not really very accurate: it has no tape!

Your voice can be recorded, but the sound is "digitized," or turned into binary information, that can be stored on your hard drive or floppy disk in much the same way as a word processing file. Most professional recording studios now have embraced this form of digital technology, forgoing the world of tape altogether.

Here's how you can record your voice:

1. Open your Windows Start menu, and select the Programs option.

2. Navigate up the Program List to Accessories, and open Entertainment.

3. Open the Sound Recorder option. The sound recorder appears on-screen.

4. Hold the microphone several inches from your mouth.

5. Click the Record button (the red circle), and speak or sing clearly. When you are finished, click the Stop button (next to the Record button).

6. Play your recording back by clicking Play, the right-pointing triangle.

7. Add special effects: open the Effects menu and select Add Echo. Click the Play button. Go back to the Effects menu, and select Add Echo again to increase the effect.

8. To save the file, open the File menu and select Save. Name the file to reflect what you have recorded. The file name should have a ".wav" extension.

How Audiophiles Can Play Audio Files

The tape-recorded file that you just created is now sitting in the "My Documents" folder, just screaming (silently) to be heard. If you want to play it, just double-click the file.

Your voice can be recorded, but the sound is "digitized," or turned into binary information.

TIP

To share your recordings with loved ones, send your file to family members (as an e-mail attachment) so that they can hear you and you can show off your new computer skills! In terms of byte size, sound files—even brief recordings—become extremely large, however, and take awhile to transmit online.

Chapter Twenty-Three

This Just In—Keeping Abreast of the News

Okay, we confess, we're news junkies. And if you're even half as addicted as we are, you'll wish you had gone online a lot sooner. As a news source, the Web is nonpareil. We show you why it's great and what you can do to keep your edge in any current events debate.

What You'll Need

- A modem
- Microsoft Internet Explorer 4.0 or higher
- A nose for news

No-Frills Recipe for Gathering News

1. Connect to the Internet.
2. Locate one or more of the following sites and bookmark them:
   - MSNBC
   - A set of national newspapers
   - A wire service
   - An international newspaper
   - Today's Papers from *Slate*
3. Visit your bookmarked sites once daily to stay current with the news.

Read All About It

In Frank Capra's movie classic *Mr. Smith Goes to Washington*, reporters swarm out of the Senate chambers, frantically attempting to get to pay phones to report on the idealistic Senator Smith's tumultuous experience. In today's world, reporters use modems, laptops, and the Internet rather than pay phones—and they are better served to do so. Unless some late-breaking news is so important that the major television networks interrupt a broadcast, it's available via the Internet first.

Why the Web Is So Good for News

Television, print journalism, and radio have logistical issues that prevent instantaneous release of information: newspapers and magazines must be printed and distributed, and radio and television shows must be scheduled. In addition, so much news is available that it must be filtered and prioritized before being made available so that the readers, listeners, or viewers aren't inured to the sheer volume. Finally, breaking into regularly scheduled broadcasts frequently would infuriate an uninterested public and would in turn wreak havoc on the economics that define broadcasting.

The Web is an unbelievably powerful medium because it is unfettered by many of the limitations associated with these other media. The advantages, such as its immediacy, that the Web offers have not been lost on journalists and publishers, so not only do most major publications and broadcasters offer Web sites, but a slew of new information sources has cropped up as well. Also remarkable is that, with few exceptions, these sources of information come at no extra cost beyond your Internet service fee.

Unless some late-breaking news is so important that the major television networks interrupt a broadcast, it's available via the Internet first.

For those of us who love news, the Web's free delivery means access to multiple sources and innumerable points of view, access to news at any time, and the opportunity to read as much on a subject as desired. You don't have to stop reading at the end of a story; you can continue to read about particular subjects as they are reported elsewhere.

Why Some Critics Say the Web Is Not Really Good For News Some Web critics predict the Web is too inconvenient to succeed. Critics note that you can't read the news on the Web while riding on the train, subway, or taxi as you can a newspaper. On top of that, you can't read it in bed without bringing your computer in, and that could be a problem.

The critics are right about portability, but nobody's saying that newspapers don't have a place; they do. Despite the Web's few shortcomings, getting your news online can be a joy; you can get up anytime in the night and read the morning paper on-screen *before* it's delivered to your home.

Getting the News You Want The biggest dilemma with getting news on the Web is deciding what news you are most interested in getting—including the slant. Every newspaper and every news-oriented Web site has some bias. Whatever your interest or bias, you can find the news you want from whatever source you want *and* find the columnists, political and otherwise, that suit your tastes and beliefs.

W*hatever your interest or bias, you can find the news you want from whatever source you want and find the columnists, political and otherwise, that suit your tastes and beliefs.*

A Fast Start

To get started, tune in to the MSNBC site (a joint venture between Microsoft and NBC News) at *http://www.msnbc.com*. When you go to MSNBC and you download the News menu. The home page appears, as shown in Figure 23-1. If it's a busy news day and lots of folks are trying to get the news, loading the table of contents as it appears on the left side of the page may take a moment. When the page appears, add it to your list of favorites by opening the Favorites menu and selecting Add To Favorites. (For information about how to add Favorites, see Chapter 14; for information about how to manage Favorites, see Chapter 24.)

Figure 23-1
MSNBC gives you a timely and complete view of the news: international, national, and local. Just click the section you want to read, and you're on your way

Combining Microsoft's online expertise and NBC's news-gathering expertise has resulted in an excellent Web site with a good blend of national, international, business, living, travel, and technology news. The site also offers some easy customization features. For example, if you enter your postal code, MSNBC provides you with impressive local news and information.

Another excellent site to add to your list of favorites is *The New York Times* (*http://www.nytimes.com*), whose home page is shown in Figure 23-2.

Figure 23-2
The New York Times, that bastion of journalistic integrity, is free online

The New York Times has succeeded in transferring its Pulitzer-prize-winning reportage and newspaper publishing acumen to the Web. If you are one of those out-of-New York-state people who has *The New York Times* delivered, you can see tomorrow's headlines on the Web before your paper is delivered in the morning.

Still hungry for news? Good! Although MSNBC and *The New York Times* could each be considered a main course, much more is on the menu. After you finish those in the morning, you can move on to other news sources that suit you.

The Local News Many of us feel that local news is every bit as important as national and international news. With MSNBC, you receive excellent local coverage along with national and international news. But what if you want news that's local to someplace else? Sure, you've been living where you are for ages, and you want to stay connected with your current local scene, but it would be great to get the local news from your old neighborhood.

Not a problem. The Web gives you local news from any region, including Web sites for local TV stations, radio stations, magazines, and local papers. To find your local news sources, follow these steps:

1. Go to *http://www.yahoo.com*. The Yahoo site appears, as shown in Figure 23-3.

2. Find the heading "News & Media." Click right below it on "Newspapers," and the Media page appears.

3. Click News & Media: Newspapers By Region, and the Region List appears.

4. Click U.S. States and the States Listing appears.

5. Click the state of your choice. Here, we click North Carolina.

6. When your state page appears, click "Complete Listing."

The number of local papers listed will astound you. Figure 23-4 shows part of a scrolling list of what's available for North Carolina.

Take your pick, and when you select one you like, be sure to open the Favorites menu and add it to your list of favorites.

NOTE

You can also find local news by clicking Local News on the MSNBC start page (http://www.msnbc.news).

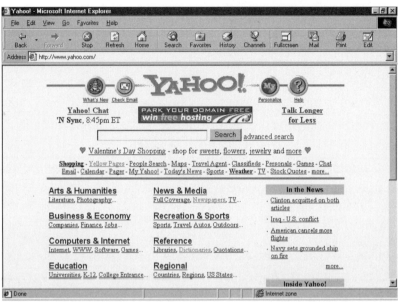

Figure 23-3
Yahoo! gives fast access to a variety of media

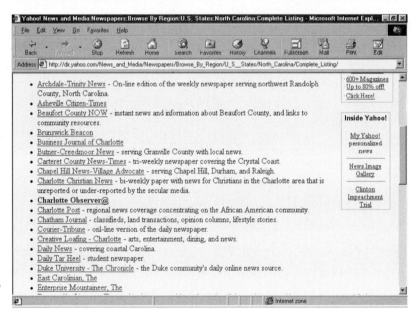

Figure 23-4
The local paper can't be delivered as fast as the Web; this listing offers 50 different papers local to North Carolina alone

More Papers Delivered If you want to load up with great papers printed all around the country, visit the Global Newsstand (*http://www.mcs.net/~rchojnac/www/tgn.html*). We know: it's a terrible URL for a Web site, but go to the site, and you can get a hundred different major U.S. papers with the click of your mouse. Figure 23-5 shows a portion of what's offered.

The Web gives you access to all the major wire services including AP, UPI, and Reuters.

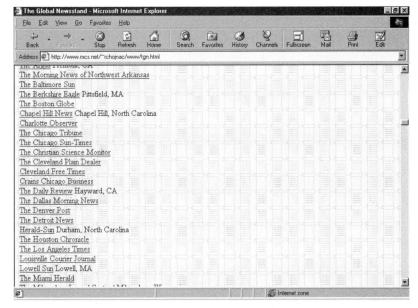

Figure 23-5
Your out-of-state papers always arrive on time on the Web

Click the papers of your choice. Be sure to mark these as Favorites when you find some you like.

Choosing a Wire Service Now you can get your news fresh off the wire at home. The Web gives you access to all the major wire services including AP, UPI, and Reuters. Figure 23-6 shows the AP

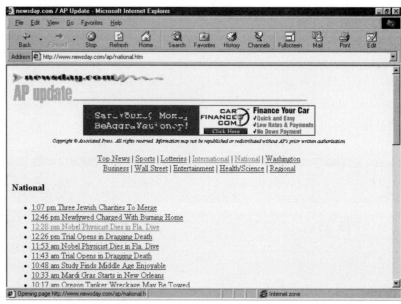

Figure 23-6
The AP National newswire provides up-to-the-minute news 24 hours a day

TIP

Add good sites to your Favorites menu as soon as you spot them. The URL for the Global Newsstand is so long and complicated that you don't want to have to enter it manually more than once!

National Wire (via New York's Newsday site: *http://www.newsday. com/ap/national.htm*). You can also access the Associated Press Web site directly at *http://www.ap.org*. The wire service news isn't always monumental, but that's the nature of the service; you get the news as soon as it happens.

Global News: International and Foreign Language Papers The Web has two outstanding sites where you can find international and foreign language papers, and you've already been to both! Return to the Yahoo Web site, again click the Newspapers link under News And Media, but select Countries rather than U.S. States. A list of countries appears, as shown in Figure 23-7.

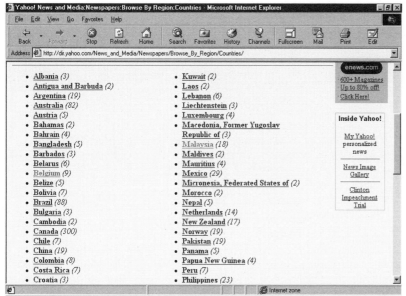

Figure 23-7
*You can reach thousands of
international papers on the
Web right from Yahoo!*

You can get another very generous list of foreign language
papers as well as foreign papers in English—or in any of five
languages—at the Global Newsstand (see the URL on page 265).

The Seasoning: Choosing Your Favorite Columnists

Besides the latest news, you probably would like a good ladle of
editorial flavoring. Many newspapers provide their columnists'
current columns as well as an archive of their previous work. *The
New York Times*, for example, provides a list of each columnist's
work over the last several weeks. If you have a favorite columnist,
find his or her newspaper home base, visit the newspaper, navigate
to that writer's columns, and be sure to bookmark them.

*If you have a favorite
columnist, find his or
her newspaper home
base, visit the
newspaper, navigate
to that writer's
columns, and be sure
to bookmark them.*

Today's Papers: Who Put *That* on the Front Page? One link that you absolutely have to bookmark or add to your list of favorites is "Today's Papers" from the online magazine *Slate* (*http://www.slate.com*). Click this and Scott Shuger's column appears, as shown in Figure 23-8.

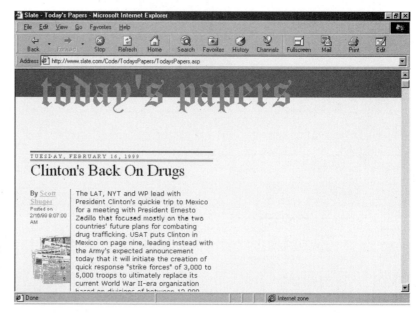

Figure 23-8
Scott Shuger's "Today's Papers" column gives you the low-down on how the nation's biggest papers present the news

Shuger's column is as refreshing as it is unique. Rather than report the news of the day, he compares *how* the major news agencies carry the news of the day; what stories get front-page play; what the major papers see as the core issues of any story; and more. It's an eye-opener. Printed daily, it is definitely a Web highlight and a must for any newshound.

Keeping Journalistic Standards High—Assorted Sites

Aside from all the mind-boggling choices you have in collecting news, several sites are ones you should visit because they consistently deliver news on all topics, and they do it with aplomb and unique styles:

- National Public Radio (*http://www.npr.org*)
- British Broadcasting Corporation (*http://www.bbc.co.uk/*)
- Christian Science Monitor (*http://www.csmonitor.com/*)
- CNN (*http://www.cnn.com/*)
- International Herald Tribune (*http://www.iht.com/*)
- PBS—Public Broadcasting Service (*http://www.pbs.org/*)
- Slate (*http://www.slate.com*)
- Weekly World News (*http://wwnonline.com*)—[we couldn't resist!]

News on the Internet: Probably Habit Forming

The Internet is a great source for news addicts, but be forewarned: if you relish reading your morning paper or you savor the nightly news, then when you've finished this recipe, you'll be hooked on the Web.

TIP

Add these news sites to your list of Favorites so they are easy to access.

Chapter Twenty-Four

Organizing Your Favorite Things

You'll do yourself a big service by keeping your Favorites menu well organized. This recipe walks you through the basics of how to do that. In the end, you'll be able to find everything in your Favorites menu quickly so that you can spend more time enjoying the sites.

What You'll Need

- A modem
- A browser, preferably Microsoft Internet Explorer 4.0 or higher
- A list of Web site favorites you have already added to your Favorites menu
- The ability to categorize

Quick Recipe for Keeping Track of Your Favorite Sites

1. Open your browser.
2. Open the Favorites menu.
3. Categorize your favorites.

Finding Your Favorites

As you become comfortable using the Web, and as you find more and more worthwhile Web sites, you'll find yourself adding more and more items to your list of favorites. The Favorites menu is an important place because it saves you so much time in getting to where you want to go, *and* because it is a very personal place; it is a map of your interests, your passions, and your pursuits.

Tending Your Favorites Garden

To get started, open the Favorites menu. Figure 24-1 shows a Favorites menu that is in dire need of a good weeding.

To help restore some order, click the Organize Favorites option, and the Organize Favorites window opens, as shown in Figure 24-2. If you are unable to see all your favorites, resize the window to make it larger.

NOTE

See Chapter 14 to see how to add a site to your list of Favorites.

T*he Favorites menu is a map of your interests, your passions, and your pursuits.*

Figure 24-1
With a Favorites menu like this, you'll never find that site you liked so much

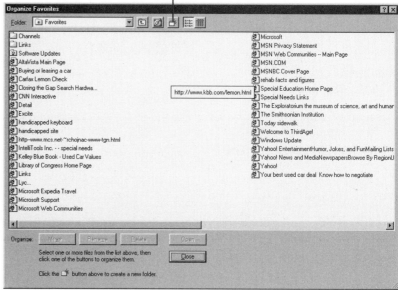

Create New Folder button

Figure 24-2
Your list of favorites can probably be classified into a few different categories

TIP

The Favorites menu provides an understandable name or description for the URL rather than the address of the Web site. Sometimes, however, the description is more complicated than the URL. If the description is still confusing and you're unsure of what site it represents, point the mouse to it and wait for a moment. A URL window then appears, displaying the associated URL. You can also change the description when you create a new favorite.

The easiest way to organize is to classify your favorites. Look at your existing list and see what categories seem most natural to you. In this chapter, we create six categories:

- Microsoft sites
- Special needs
- Culture
- News
- Search engines
- Auto info

After you have figured out what categories are most appropriate for you, click the Create New Folder button, and create a new folder for each category. Name each folder so that it reflects each category.

Sort your favorites into the appropriate folders either by dragging and dropping them into the appropriate folders or by highlighting them and clicking the Move button. Figure 24-3 shows the Microsoft Favorites before being moved.

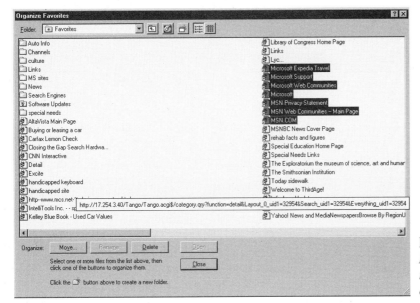

Figure 24-3
Favorites can be relocated in folders for easier access

Plowing Under Last Season's Crop

When you finish putting your favorites in their respective folders, there will still be some favorites that don't fit into any category. Go through these assorted favorites, and delete outdated or invalid entries.

To be especially organized, you can create another folder called "Miscellaneous" and move the remaining favorites to it. When you have finished all your rearranging, click the Close button.

When you are ready, open the Favorites menu again. With your Favorites menu still open, navigate to one of your new folders, and the newly ordered group of favorites appears, as shown in Figure 24-4.

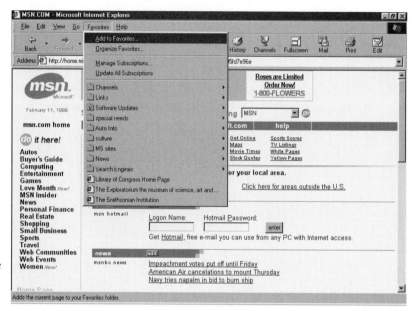

Figure 24-4
Finding your favorites is easy when your menu is well organized

Chapter Twenty-Five

Discovering References for Writers

The writing process is a difficult one to describe; like any creative act, it entails many approaches and no single "right way." People write about different things for different reasons, requiring innumerable formats, contexts, forms, and styles. One way to improve your writing is to make use of the many sources of information that are available to writers.

NOTE

Microsoft Bookshelf and Microsoft Encarta are available on the Microsoft Office CD-ROM.

What You'll Need

- Word processing software, preferably Microsoft Word 97 or Word 2000
- Microsoft Bookshelf
- Microsoft Encarta
- A writer's muse

Quick Recipe for Better Writing

1. Open Microsoft Word 97 or Word 2000.
2. Open Microsoft Bookshelf.
3. Begin your story.
4. Use the Reference works to fortify your words and enhance your writing.

So You Want to Be a Writer . . .

Regardless of the approach you take to writing or the style in which you write, you'll always need a good set of reference books on hand. This recipe introduces some excellent resources for your computer and shows you how to use them while you are writing.

To get started, open a story, essay, or letter you have been working on. If you don't already have a document going, open Microsoft Word so that you'll have a sense of how you can use Word in concert with Microsoft Bookshelf. Figure 25-1 shows a story in progress.

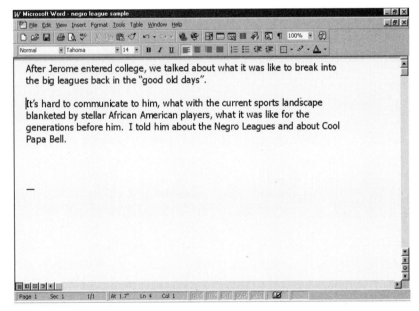

Figure 25-1
Microsoft Word accommodates whatever writing project you wish to undertake

Finding Just the Right Words

Often when you write, you need to grab the dictionary or thesaurus off the shelf. Now there's an easy-to-use alternative: load the

Microsoft Bookshelf CD-ROM into your CD-ROM drive. If it doesn't appear on-screen in a few moments, you can open Bookshelf from the Start menu by selecting Microsoft Reference from the Program list and then choosing Microsoft Bookshelf.

When you open Bookshelf, a screen similar to Figure 25-2 appears.

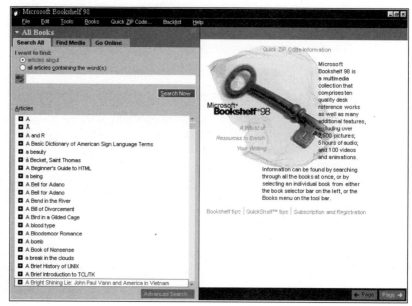

Figure 25-2
These books would take up a lot of space on an actual bookshelf

Here's the list of the reference books that are a part of Microsoft Bookshelf 98:

- *The American Heritage Dictionary of the English Language*
- *The Original Roget's Thesaurus of English Words and Phrases*
- *The Columbia Dictionary of Quotations*
- *The Encarta Desk Encyclopedia*
- *The Encarta 98 World Desk Atlas*

- *The People's Chronology*
- *The World Almanac and Book of Facts*
- *The Microsoft Bookshelf Internet Directory*
- *The Microsoft Bookshelf Computer* and *Internet Dictionary*

To use the thesaurus, open the Books menu and select Thesaurus. *Roget's Thesaurus* opens, as shown in Figure 25-3.

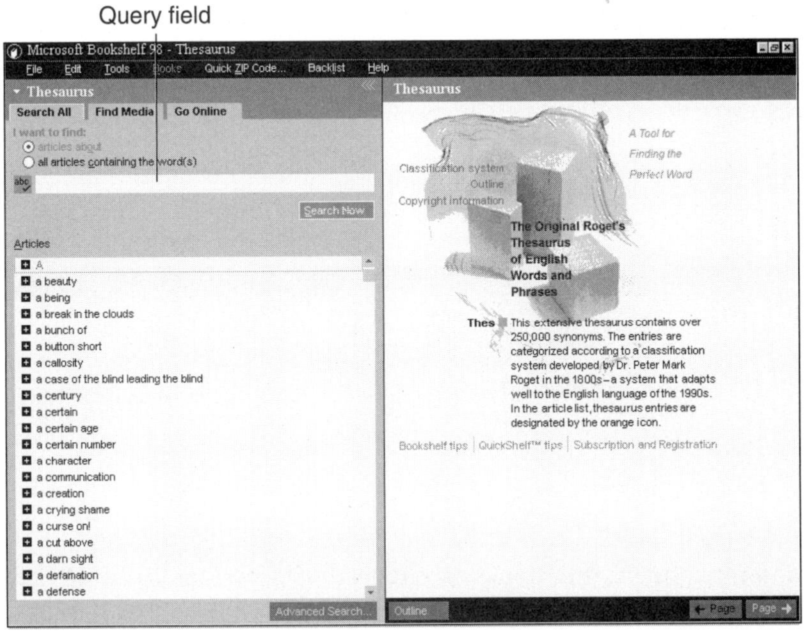

Query field

Figure 25-3
Roget's Thesaurus: *for use when you need a better word than the one you have*

Type the word you want to replace in the query field (we entered "conceal"), press Enter, and all the synonyms and related terms appear, as shown in Figure 25-4.

To use the word you have found, follow these steps:

1. Highlight the word.

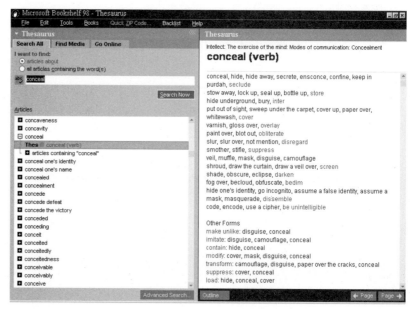

Figure 25-4
No more cross-reference problems when you use the electronic version of Roget's Thesaurus.

2. Open the Edit menu, and select the Copy option.

3. Go to your Word document, and use the Edit menu in Word to paste the word into your story.

When you want to strengthen your own words with a memorable quote, use *The Columbia Dictionary of Quotations*. To find a quote, open the Books menu and select Quotations. The Quotations window opens, as shown in Figure 25-5.

Enter a keyword or subject you want the quote to address, or enter the name of a person whose quotes you'd like to peruse. As an example, enter Marx (for Groucho, not Karl). When Groucho's name appears, click the plus sign next to it, and a list of all the quotes attributed to him appears, as shown in Figure 25-6. Click one of the quotes, and it appears in the Quote window.

TIP

If you don't see the perfect word on your first attempt, click one of the blue words in the Thesaurus window to view a list of synonyms and matching words for that term.

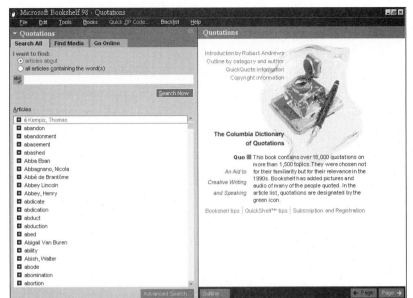

Figure 25-5
When you can't find the words, use someone else's!

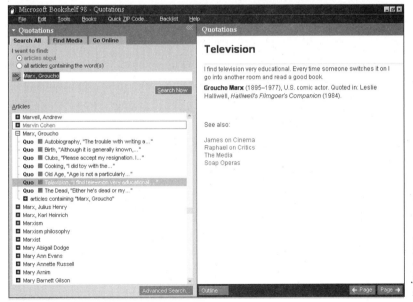

Figure 25-6
You can find quotes from everybody from Plato to Groucho

When you find the quote you like, you can highlight it in the Quote window and copy it into your Word document.

When You Need the Web as a Reference

Bookshelf is a fabulous compendium, but even Microsoft recognizes that you will want and need to do research on the Web. To help make your Web research easier and more productive, Bookshelf includes the Internet Directory, an alphabetic guide to quality Web sites addressing virtually every topic you can think of. To see just how thorough the Directory is, click Books to open the Books menu, select Internet Directory 98, and click a few entries. Clicking the URL automatically connects you if you aren't online, and then takes you to the associated Internet site.

Taking Advantage of Encyclopedic Knowledge

Although Microsoft Bookshelf offers the Encarta Desk Encyclopedia, it can't compare to the full CD-ROM of Microsoft Encarta 1999, a referential masterpiece. Reminiscent of the way that Americans used to purchase at least one year of the *Encyclopedia Britannica*, Encarta stands as a singular research achievement that *everybody* can benefit from owning.

For research, you'll find extraordinary depth to support and enhance your own writing. To see one facet of Microsoft Encarta, load the CD-ROM and, when Microsoft Encarta appears, enter a subject of interest in the Find field in the upper-left corner. As part of the story we opened in Microsoft Word, Encarta provided the X-Giants, the Philadelphia-based baseball team in the Negro League, as shown in Figure 25-7.

Bookshelf includes the Internet Directory, an alphabetic guide to quality Web sites.

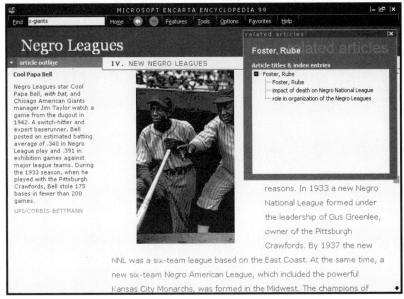

Figure 25-7
Encarta is an extraordinary reference for any writer —or family

When an image appears in Encarta that you want to use in your Word story, follow these steps:

1. Click the right mouse button on the image.

2. Select the Copy option.

3. Move to your Word document, and open the Edit menu.

4. Select Paste. The image appears as part of your word document, as shown in Figure 25-8.

TIP

Be sure to explore other options on the CD-ROM, such as the Atlas, Almanac, or People's Chronology. Don't be surprised if the hours pass quickly. Just consider it as research for your next writing project!

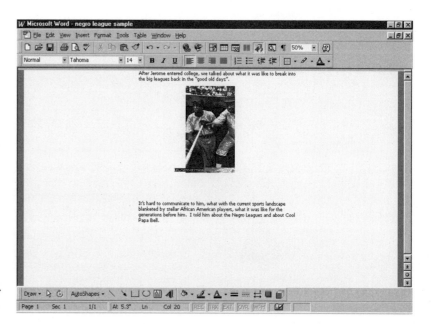

Figure 25-8
Encarta has thousands of pictures that you can copy into your Word documents

Chapter Twenty-Six

Researching Your Genealogy

Genealogy is the study or investigation of family trees. Its importance usually doesn't strike us until we're old enough to understand the significance of our own heritage. Genealogy helps us see from whence we came, and it gives our children and our children's children a map of their ancestry.

What You'll Need

- A modem
- A browser, preferably Microsoft Internet Explorer 4.0 or higher
- Microsoft Word or Microsoft Works
- Relatives whom you can interview
- Patience to perform thorough and detailed searches for relatives and family history
- A scanner (not required, but helpful)

Recipe for Tracing Your Family Tree

1. Sketch a basic family tree using the knowledge you already have of your lineage.
2. Interview at least one relative about your family tree. Take copious notes.
3. Confirm the information with other relatives.
4. Get online and check out genealogy sites.
5. Track your history.
6. Use your scanner to incorporate photos and other historical documents.

Using Your PC in Genealogical Research

The initial steps to begin the process will take more than 10 minutes, but your PC can make you far more efficient and your genealogical research more rewarding.

Outlining Your Family Tree

To best document your family tree, use Microsoft Word or Works to write a family history. Write the names of all your family members, and specify the relationships between all members. Be sure to include the names of children, and verify the spellings of surnames.

You can't assume that your memories or assumptions are always accurate. Your crazy Uncle Zoltan may not actually be a blood uncle; adoptions, sibling remarriages (when a widow or widower marries her/his brother/sister in-law), and intimate friendships are the sorts of surprises that crop up in many, many family trees.

After you have initially mapped your tree, be sure to confirm its accuracy with other relatives. Distribute your notes and tree outline to those relatives who can provide feedback or input on your work. Be sure to explain what you are doing, and encourage and solicit new or revised information. If you have relatives who have e-mail accounts, this is a great time to set up a family mailing list.

Interviewing Family Members

After your family tree sketch is confirmed and revised, consider interviewing older members of your family to see what names and perhaps branches they can add to the tree. If you can interview the person so that you can enter the information on to your PC via

TIP

Outlining your family tree is a good way to get started.

Microsoft Word or Microsoft Works, doing so might save you a lot of time. Be sure to get as much information as you can, and make it as detailed as possible.

Finding Resources on the World Wide Web

Not only does the World Wide Web contain a mountain of material to help you with your genealogical endeavor, it has legions of others pursuing the same goal as well. Many of the people you run into will be well versed in the ways of genealogy, others will be relatively green, but all will be happy to provide pointers.

Find Fellow Seekers on the Microsoft Genealogy Forum If you want to start by getting a feel for how other people are pursuing their research, visit Microsoft's genealogy forum at *http://communities. msn.com/genealogy*. A glimpse of the Welcome to Genealogy newsgroup is shown in Figure 26-1 (news://msnnews.msn. com.msn. forums. genealogy.general).

Take Advantage of Advice on the rootsweb.com Site You'll find a nice piece of research wisdom at *http://www.rootsweb.com/ roots-1/20ways.html* in an article called "The 20 Ways to Avoid Genealogical Grief," the beginning of which appears in Figure 26-2.

This article first appeared in *The British Columbia Genealogist*, vol. 17 #1, March, 1988, and it is every bit as valuable today as it was then.

The aforementioned article, "The 20 Ways to Avoid Genealogical Grief," represents a sliver of what you'll find when you check in at rootsweb.com. Visiting the rootsweb.com site is as inspiring as

Not only does the World Wide Web contain a mountain of material to help you with your genealogical endeavor, it has legions of others pursuing the same goal as well.

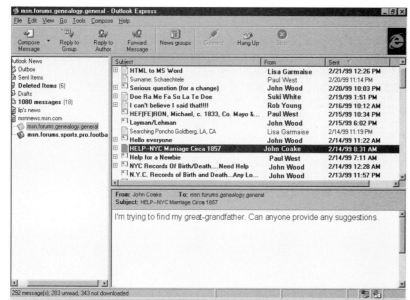

Figure 26-1
You can discuss genealogy with many seekers at the MSN community page

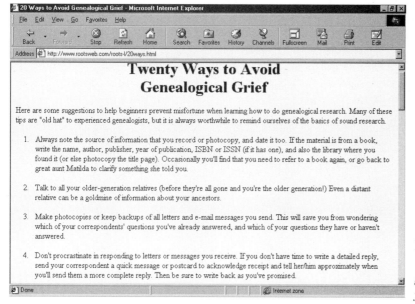

Figure 26-2
The 20 commandments of genealogy—follow these and you'll stay on track

it is staggering in its depth. Shown in Figure 26-3, rootsweb.com offers resources and links to resources that will make you wonder how anyone could map his or her family tree without Web access.

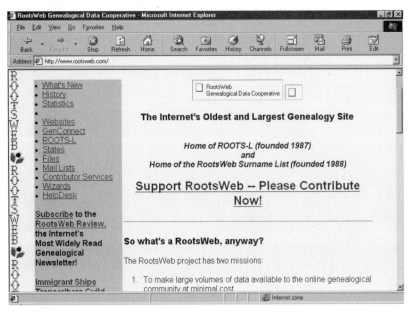

Figure 26-3
Rootsweb.com gives you an appreciation of the work other genealogists have done

Obtain Even More Help on the cyndislist.com Site Another site offering a wealth of information is Cyndislist (*http://www.cyndislist.com*), which is now linked from rootsweb.com. Figure 26-4 shows a fraction of what's available just under surname research referenced under "Military."

Genealogy is about digging. It's about tracing surnames, birth records, and branches you didn't know existed. With rootsweb.com and cyndislist.com, the searchable archives and databases are cross-referenced so that you can follow leads with relative ease.

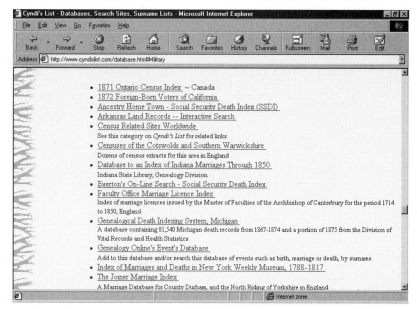

Figure 26-4
If you've got some good leads, you'll be able to track down your ancestors with cyndislist.com

Maximizing the PC Advantage

If you have a scanner, your family tree can take on a marvelous added dimension: photos, images, passports, birth certificates, and marriage licenses can all be nicely preserved and incorporated into your computer-based, family-tree journal. In this way, you can gather memorabilia from everyone in the family, scan it, return it, and have a central repository for all the images and historical extras.

Let the Genealogists Beware Be wary of people and Web wheeler-dealers who promise you shortcuts or a fully researched genealogical tree for a modest fee. Don't believe them. Genealogical research is time consuming, and there's no way around that fact. If

TIP

With a scanner, you can preserve documents related to your family's history. You can also save recorded information.

WARNING

In your research, you may come upon unexpected stories that you didn't want to find. Most of us have at least one horse rustler in our past, so when you happen upon the family bad guy, consider it a (tiny) part of your family's colorful past, and just keep right on researching!

you want to familiarize yourself with some of the scams being played out (not just on the Web), read the list at *ftp://ftp.cac.psu.edu/pub/genealogy/roots-l/faq/faq.scams*.

∼ Chapter Twenty-Seven ∼

Using Business Accounting Software

"I know! Let's put on a show!"

Mickey Rooney and Judy Garland sure made success look easy in the movies, but we all know that it's not that easy. Many of us dream about starting our own successful business, but sometimes starting a business is a dream that can't happen until later in life. Well, now's the time to make it happen.

What You'll Need

- Microsoft Works (or Microsoft Office)
- A business account with your bank—for *this* business
- The entrepreneurial spirit

Recipe for Success: Being Accountable

1. Open Microsoft Works.
2. Select the Business Management Wizard.
3. Create an Accounts Receivable database.
4. Create An Accounts Payable database.
5. Create a Contacts database.
6. Buy Microsoft Corporation and call it your own!

You're the Boss: Starting a Business

The first thing you need to do before you can start your business is to establish an independent business account with your bank. The Internal Revenue Service and your customers will no doubt look upon you suspiciously without this. To do that, you need to register your business' name (with the county). When you do, you can open a business account. Your business account gets you a company checking account and lets the IRS know you are hanging out your shingle. After you take care of the preliminary paperwork, you can get down to business.

Setting Up Your Accounting Department

Your PC can help you immensely with your new endeavor. To create a business, you need to stay organized and on track. To stay on track for the long haul, you need a business plan. Your business plan should act as a road map for where you expect your business to go and how you expect it to grow. A business plan also puts any flaws in your thinking in stark relief, and that's important. To stay in business, you need to stay realistic.

You can't get much more realistic than accounting. For the day-to-day operations, you have a number of accounting tasks that are pivotal to your success and could be especially time consuming if you didn't have a computer and the right software. The easiest and best choice for this job is Microsoft Works. No matter what the nature of your new business is, you must spend a lot of time keeping your accounts in order, but Microsoft Works can help you with many of the time-consuming tasks you will face.

TIP

The first steps to starting your own business are establishing an independent business account and registering your new business' name.

Your business plan should act as a road map for where you expect your business to go and how you expect it to grow.

Microsoft Works is an integrated software program that includes scaled-down versions of the meat and potatoes of business: a spreadsheet program, a database program, a word processing program, and other features.

Accounts Receivable First, set up an accounts receivable database. A "database" is an organized collection of information, such as a recipe box or a phone book. It allows you to track the details of your business's financial transactions and to access those details instantaneously. Here's how to create one for your new business:

1. Open Microsoft Works from the Start menu. The Works Task Launcher appears (see Figure 27-1).

2. Click Business Management to view the available business options, as shown in Figure 27-2.

3. Double-click the Accounts option. When the Task Launcher appears, click Yes to run the Task Wizard. The Accounts Task Wizard appears on-screen.

4. Double-click the Accounts Receivable box, and the seed of your first accounts receivable database appears. Open the File menu, and save this project, giving it your company's name: *"Your Business Accts. Receivable."*

5. You are looking at the first record in your accounts receivable database (see Figure 27-3 on page 298). You can think of a "record" as a recipe card in a recipe box; each record describes a different customer and that customer's account information. Enter the information for one of your customers in the appropriate fields. When you have finished, click the

A *"database" is an organized collection of information, such as a recipe box or a phone book.*

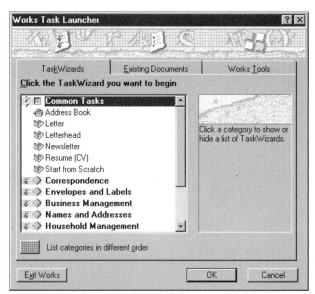

Figure 27-1
*The Works Task Launcher
has categories to fit most
of your needs*

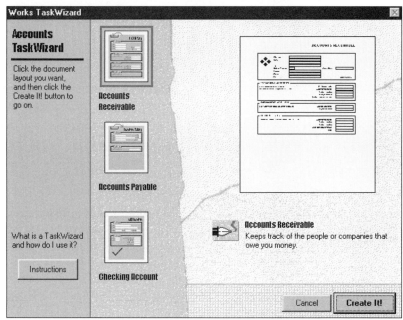

Figure 27-2
*The Works TaskWizard
is ready to walk you through
the process*

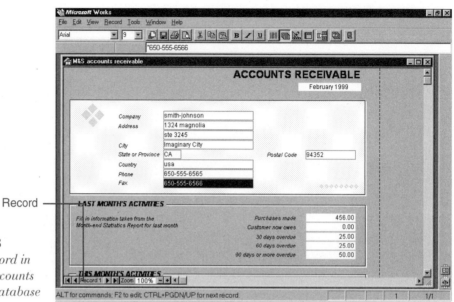

Record ——————

Figure 27-3
The first record in your new accounts receivable database

right-pointing record arrow in the lower left corner to display the next record. Fill in records for all your customers.

Up-to-Date Accounting Here's an important way that Microsoft Works silently and effectively works for you: your database is part spreadsheet, constantly helping you keep your books current. When you scroll to the lower half of your accounts receivable record, as shown in Figure 27-4, the account status information is automatically calculated, based on the account information you have entered for the last and current month.

Accounts Payable To make your bookkeeping complete, you need to create an accounts payable database and a checking account database. To create both (sequentially, not simultaneously), open the File menu and select New. Follow the procedure

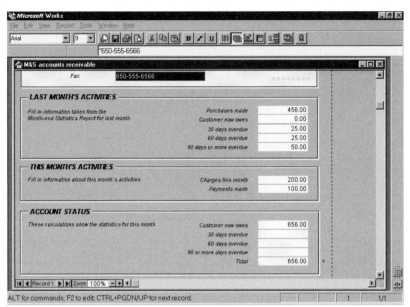

Figure 27-4
Your accounting assistant never sleeps—and never takes a lunch break—if you use Microsoft Works as your assistant

you used to create the accounts receivable database, except change Step 4 so that you select the Accounts Payable option and the Checking Account option, respectively. When you have completed these tasks, save each database, giving it a descriptive title so that you can identify what each contains.

Your Contacts Database Staying in touch with business associates, customers, and potential customers is crucial to maintaining and expanding your business. Keeping track of all those phone numbers, cellular numbers, pager numbers, e-mail addresses, fax numbers, business numbers, home numbers, and company addresses is no trivial task.

Microsoft Works can help in this department as well by assisting you in building a contacts database. A contacts database is like an

A contacts database is like an address book listing all the contact information on the people listed in the database.

address book listing all the contact information on the people listed in the database. Here are the steps to creating a contacts database:

1. Open Microsoft Works and click Business Management.

2. Scroll to the end of the Business Management options, and double-click Suppliers And Vendors. Click Yes to run the TaskWizard.

3. Double-click the Business option (see Figure 27-5). Click the Next button and the Create button, and you have a contact database. Enter the appropriate information by clicking the fields and entering the vital statistics on your business contacts.

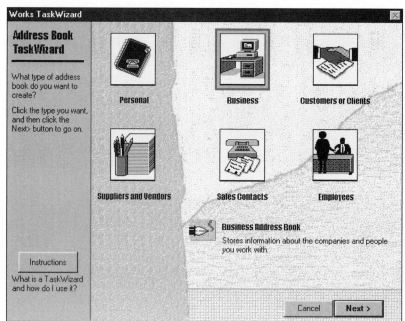

Figure 27-5
You can create an address book to fit your needs

Reopening a Database

Now that you have built a segment of your accounting department, here's how to find and open your databases:

1. Open Microsoft Works and select Open. A list of your Works documents appears.

2. If you are at the Works Task launcher, click the Existing Documents tab, as shown in Figure 27-6, and a list of all your Works documents appears.

TIP

Experiment with the other features that Microsoft Works has to offer so that you can improve the odds of your company's success.

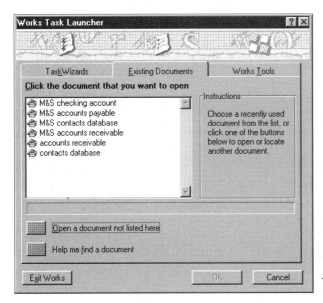

Figure 27-6
You can open any database you've created from the Works Task Launcher

Chapter Twenty-Eight

Getting Computer Help

When things start going wrong, or when you are trying to track down how to do something, it helps to know where to go for help and how to ask for help.

In this recipe, we look at what to do when you need help—on the Internet and off. This recipe points out the gold mine of help resources that are available to you and how you can get access to all of them.

What You'll Need

- A modem
- A browser, preferably Microsoft Internet Explorer 4.0 or higher
- The ability to ask for directions when you're lost
- Some time at the local library or bookstore

Quick Recipe for Getting Help

1. Hit a roadblock.
2. Consider the nature of your problem and who can best help you with it.
3. Be prepared to *answer* questions about your problem.
4. If the solution doesn't work, try again.
5. Got the answer? Write it down (in your notebook).

Sending Out an S.O.S.

Many of us do best when we can find another person to help solve our problem. Because we all have our learning foibles, it's best if you have a family member or members who can help you out on occasion. Friends are a great resource, and if you can, hook into a neighborhood computer club that can prove ideal in overcoming PC problems. In the event you aren't lucky enough to have a couple of well-qualified relatives around, many other alternatives are available.

Determine Whether It's a Software or Hardware Problem

Before trying to find an answer to your problem, you need to isolate the nature of the problem. Distinguishing whether your problem falls within the domain of hardware or software can be tricky; technical support people often identify your problem as being in someone else's domain—other than their own. Classifying a problem is not always easy, but the following sections offer some help.

Hardware Problems

Certain problems clearly fall into the realm of hardware. When your monitor stops working and no programs, not even Windows, show up, well, that's a hardware problem. If your computer fails to start properly and alerts you to some errors, that's hardware again. If your computer starts making horrible noises that it never made before, and you can't pin the problem down to a specific program, again, that's hardware.

Friends are a great resource, and if you can, hook into a neighborhood computer club that can prove ideal in overcoming PC problems.

Classifying a problem is not always easy, but the following sections offer some help.

When you have a problem with hardware, do not hesitate to call the manufacturer or dealer at once. If the machine is under warranty, the problem needs to be corrected, possibly by replacing the bad components.

Software Problems

Software problems can be far more challenging than hardware problems. You can perform a task for months and, suddenly, something changes: something is not responding, or you're receiving an error message.

Other enigmas can come up. Perhaps you just can't get a program installed; you are following the steps listed in the instructions, but you are not having any luck. This is when attention to detail really pays off. You need to transcribe the events that led up to the derailment so that the person you communicate with can completely understand the problem and help you solve it.

Don't Dismiss the Easy Sources of Help

It's nice to have other people who can help you through those computing rough spots, but don't automatically rely on someone else. Many sources of information are available, and your answer man/woman might get miffed if you aren't at least *trying* to answer the basic questions on your own. Following are some basic places where you can go for information.

Readme Files A readme file (pronounced reed-me) comes with many programs and is installed on your hard drive when you install the program. A readme file provides information about the program as well as late-breaking information that was compiled after the documentation was printed. It's a good habit to read the readme files even when you aren't having a problem; they often provide information that will make your computing experience easier.

Documentation Your PC and your computer programs came with volumes of documentation. Although so many manuals may seem forbidding at first, you should always check the documentation when trying to solve a particular problem.

Online Help When you run into a problem while working in a program, opening the online help option is easy. To obtain some immediate help, open the Help menu and select the help option. A table of contents appears to help you find the topic that you need.

Bookstore or Library If you don't like the documentation for a program, locate a supplementary text that you feel comfortable with. Go into any bookstore, and you'll find an ample supply of computer books on every topic. Microsoft Press, for example, publishes books addressing almost every computer topic or subject you might be interested in. Computer books are also categorized based on their level of difficulty, so if you are looking for a beginner's book, be sure that the cover indicates that it is aimed at the level appropriate to your needs. If you want to do a little browsing without leaving home, check out the Microsoft Press Web site (*http://mspress.microsoft.com/*), shown in Figure 28-1.

Magazines offer a similar supplementary option. Magazines have especially timely product information blended with new product reviews and help columns. Magazines also address very different segments of the computer-using community; you can find

TIP

Always check the product documentation if a problem occurs.

TIP

Magazines are expensive on the newsstand. Consider subscribing to one, and you typically save about half over the newsstand price.

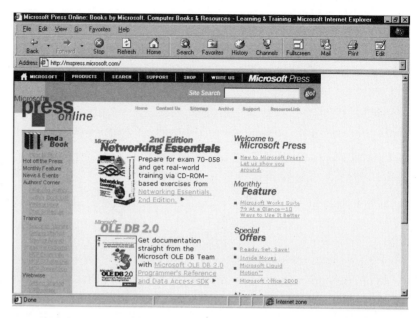

Figure 28-1
The Microsoft Press Web site can help you answer those tough questions

separate publications for Macintosh users, for example. You can also find magazines about games and some aimed at people with different levels of expertise. Be sure to pick one that addresses the right topics and possesses the right tone and level of difficulty for you.

The library is also a good source for books and magazines, although few libraries can offer the range of computer books you find in the bookstore; computer books become outdated very fast, and libraries typically can't keep pace with the changes.

Bring on the Internet Cavalry

You knew we were going to come back to the Internet, didn't you? The Internet is crowded with all sorts of help resources on every topic and every program on the market. Following are some ways to get your problems solved via the Internet.

TIP

Both the library and the Internet offer many sources.

Visit the Product/Vendor Web Page All software makers have a Web page where they hawk their wares. To help support their products, they also serve up plenty of supplemental help information about their products. Some software companies, such as Microsoft, have pages dedicated to each product. Figure 28-2 shows Microsoft's Web page for Microsoft Works (*http://www.microsoft.com/works*).

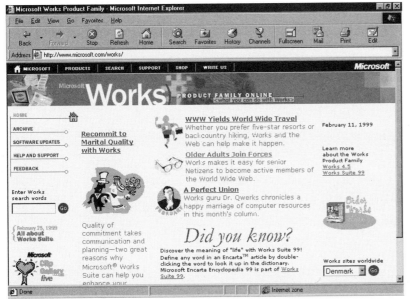

Figure 28-2
Microsoft wants you to get answers to your questions, and it provides Web pages for each product to keep you problem free

Discussions, Forums, Newsgroups Online discussions, newsgroups, or forums are especially helpful; the information comes from users like yourself. Personal experience and seeing other people's problems aired in this setting can be refreshing and helpful. Figure 28-3 shows the Microsoft discussion on Microsoft Works.

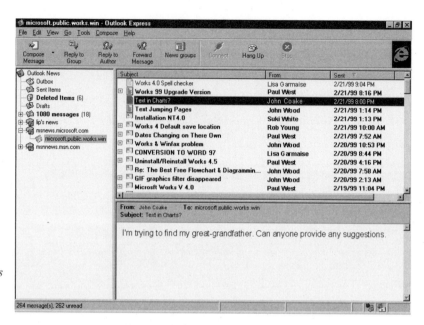

Figure 28-3
If you're having problems with a product, join the discussion or newsgroup

FAQs FAQs, which stands for Frequently Asked Questions, are lists of common questions that are constantly evolving. They are often maintained by Web angels—people who are being helpful and supportive of others without asking for anything in return. An FAQ includes the 10 or 20 most-asked questions. To find an FAQ that might help answer your question, do an Internet search on "Microsoft Works FAQ," substituting "Microsoft Works" with your product or topic of choice.

Use Technical Support as a Last Resort

When all else fails, try calling the company associated with the product you are having problems with. Hardware and software companies will have special support phones set up for people facing issues that can't be resolved without the help of the manufacturer. Depending on the company and the product, technical support might not be toll free *and* might require an additional fee. It might also be very slow. Some tech support lines can get incredibly busy, and your time on hold might be worse than just interminably long; if it's a toll call, it could be very costly.

If you do call technical support, be prepared to answer a set of questions:

1. What kind of a PC do you have? (Pentium, Pentium II or Pentium III, or equivalent? 486? Mac?).

2. How much RAM do you have?

3. What operating system are you running? (Windows?)

4. What version of the operating system are you running?

5. If you received an error message, what *exactly* did it say? (If you didn't write it down, repeat the procedure to duplicate the error and write it down.)

6. If it's a software problem, what version of the software are you running?

7. If it's a software problem, what's the product registration number?

8. Did you refer to your manual first?

WARNING

Technical support is for customers only. Are you having a problem with a program you copied from a friend? If the program isn't a shareware program and if it didn't come on your PC and you didn't purchase it (or download it), you're guilty of software piracy, the illegal duplication of software. The only proper course of action is to delete the illegal version of the software and purchase a copy for which you can be the licensed owner.

Chapter Twenty-Nine

Watching Your Purse Strings: Financial Planning

Personal finance software has become enormously successful and immensely popular because it has proven to be very useful *and* very safe. This recipe illustrates the immense value to be gained from managing your personal finances from your PC.

What You'll Need

- A modem
- A browser—Microsoft Internet Explorer 4.0 or higher, for example
- Microsoft Money 99
- The desire to better track your finances

Quick Recipe for Keeping Track of Your Favorite Sites

1. Open Microsoft Money 99.
2. Listen and watch the introductory tutorial.
3. Set up a checking account ledger.
4. Use a Decision Calculator to help with budgeting.

Microsoft Money 99 as Financial Analyst

If you've ever been to a financial analyst, you'll understand what Microsoft Money 99 is all about. There are tutorials set up from the start to help you through this material. Open Microsoft Money 99 to see how things are set up.

1. Insert the Microsoft Money 99 CD-ROM in the CD-ROM drive.

2. Open the Start menu, and select Microsoft Money from the program list.

3. After you install Microsoft Money 99, the Money Home Screen appears.

NOTE

Money 99 is a complete financial program. If you don't have it, you can order it from http:// www.shop.microsoft.com.

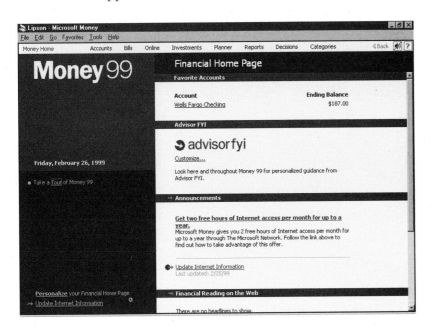

4. Click Take A Tour of Money 99.

5. When the tour ends, open the File menu and select New. Enter your name as the file name and click OK. When you do, you'll be asked to back up your information to floppy disk. You should click the Back Up Now button when you aren't just practicing.

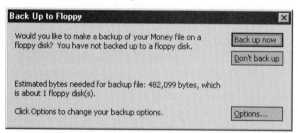

Tracking Your Checking Account

Like a financial analyst, Microsoft Money asks 18 basic questions to create a personal profile for you. When you finish answering the questions, open the Accounts window by clicking Accounts, just below the menu bar. Click the New button at the bottom of the window, and the New Accounts Wizard appears. The New Accounts Wizard walks you through the steps required. Here are some basic steps:

1. Click the Financial Institution button, and choose from the list provided (see Figure 29-1).

2. Complete the other steps the wizard presents. When you have finished, you can investigate what online services your financial institution offers (see Figure 29-2).

3. Click Investigate Offerings, and Money 99 goes out on the Internet and gets you the information regarding the financial institution your account is associated with. In many

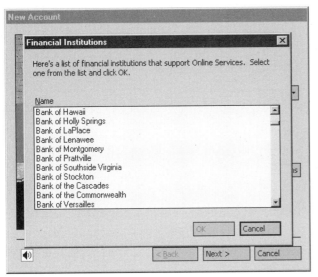

Figure 29-1
Money shows you a list of financial institutions

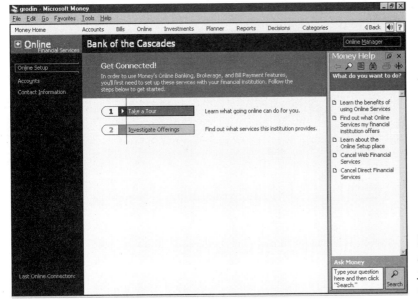

TIP

Using Money 99 gives you an easy-to-follow, centralized system to manage your finances. This is especially important for your children in the event that you meet with any unforeseen circumstances. By opening your Money 99 file, your adult kids will have a summary of all your accounts and account activities.

Figure 29-2
See what online services your financial institution offers

NOTE

Microsoft Money allows you to view your checkbook entries in different ways.

TIP

To exit your checkbook and look at other accounts, double-click Accounts as it appears under the menu bar.

NOTE

Microsoft Money does not replace your checkbook. When you shop, you still need the check ledger that you can carry with you to keep track of your checks.

instances, online services are free with your account when you maintain a specified minimum balance.

4. When the icon for your checkbook appears, double-click it. Click the New button to make new entries, and enter the information in the fields as they appear at the bottom of the screen.

Looking at Your Checkbook in a Whole New Light

It can be time consuming and hard on the eyes when you need to find out about a particular check or group of checks that you have written—with your paper checkbook, that is. With Microsoft Money, it's a breeze; you can look at your entries in whatever way is easiest for you.

Click the View arrow just above the column that displays your check numbers, as shown in Figure 29-3.

Choose a few different views to see how you can sort and review your ledger.

Using the Decisions Calculators

The problem with personal finances is that you have to be a professional financial analyst to keep track of everything—or you can use Microsoft Money's very helpful Decisions Calculators.

To explore what your Decisions Calculator options are, click Decisions and open the Decisions window, as displayed in Figure 29-4.

When you select a calculator (we selected "Figuring Your Retirement Expenses"), you step through an analysis process to

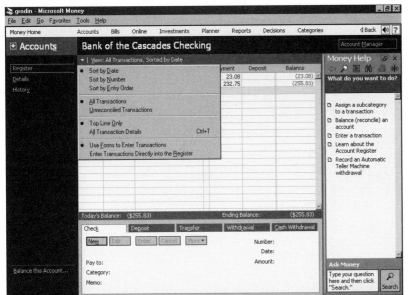

Figure 29-3
The Microsoft Money electronic check ledger offers options that the paper version never will

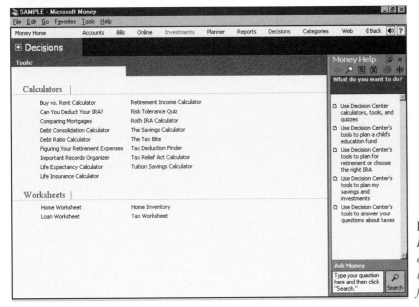

Figure 29-4
Decisions Calculators can give you a toehold when it comes to financial planning

help you obtain answers to your financial questions. Figure 29-5 shows part of the Retirement calculator.

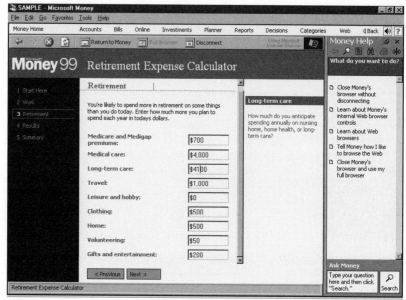

Figure 29-5
The Retirement calculator helps you ask the questions you need to ask to keep your financial picture rosy

Chapter Thirty

Find Sports News and Products on the Internet

Are you a sports nut? Do you go to the basketball game with a radio glued to your ear or a mini-television set in your pocket so that you won't miss the play-by-play from the pro golf tournament? Do you sequester yourself in the back room with your like-minded comrades on Thanksgiving while the (presumably) more civilized family members remain at the dinner table to talk about the moral and spiritual decay eating away at Western civilization?

What You'll Need

- A modem
- A browser, preferably Microsoft Internet Explorer 4.0 or higher
- Your lucky baseball hat
- A love of sports

Recipe for the Armchair Sportsman

1. Open your browser.

2. Cruise to the sports-minded Web sites.

3. Get up-to-the-minute sports information.

4. Check out the souvenir stands—from your den!

The Sporting Life

Don't worry, we can sympathize. It's hard to *not* be running at least a little bit of a sports fever these days. Between home run titans Mark McGwire's and Sammy Sosa's colossal achievements, the ferocious Tiger Woods tearing up the greens, and former Chicago Bulls' legend Michael Jordan's retiring, sports headlines showed up on the front page of the newspaper more often than they did in the sports section.

If you do enjoy the thrill of victory, or at least enjoy watching your favorite team or player savor it, the Web represents a huge conduit through which you can get plenty of news on the sporting life. You don't have to be a rabid sports fan to be a fan of sports on the Web; you can pick and choose how much sports you want and how intense it should or shouldn't be.

Take Me Out to a Web Site

If you don't want to wait until the end of the news for the sportscaster to reveal who won or lost the big game, turn off the tube and turn on the Web. On the Web, nobody is holding back news in order to get you to watch another beer commercial.

One easy site to get the news from *immediately* is *http://www.msnbc.com*, part of which is shown in Figure 30-1.

With MSNBC, you'll find all the sports news you're looking for on one convenient Web site.

Visiting the Big Leagues

All the major sports leagues have their own Web sites that are chock full of team- and league-related news, statistics, and history.

You don't have to be a rabid sports fan to be a fan of sports on the Web.

Figure 30-1
Get the sports news at any time from msnbc.com

To get the low-down on recent trades or the latest on your favorite team or player, be sure to visit one of the following sites and bookmark the ones you really enjoy:

• National Football League	*http://www.nfl.com/*
• Major League Baseball	*http://www.majorleaguebaseball.com/*
• National Basketball Association	*http://www.nba.com*
• National Hockey League	*http://www.nhl.com/*
• Professional Golfers Association	*http://www.pga.com*

Hitting the Campus Scene

For college sports and related news, check out the National
Collegiate Athletic Association at *http://www.ncaa.org*.

Getting Out on the (Hyper) Links

If golf is your game, you'll want to check out *http://www.
golfonline.com* before getting out on the green again. Besides having
everything you could ever imagine that's golf related, the site includes
Golf Magazine's top 100 U.S. courses and its top 100 world courses.
Figure 30-2 shows what you can look forward to at this site.

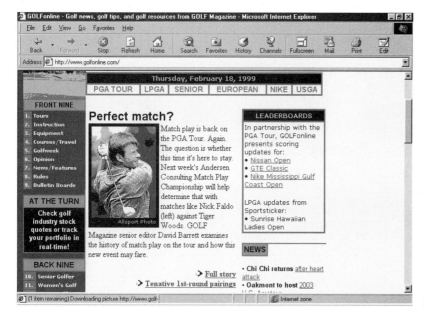

Figure 30-2
*Golfonline.com provides
valuable information for
golf fans*

NOTE

Its URL is case-sensitive. That is, you must enter the letters as indicated.

Going Overboard

You know you're a sports fanatic when you need the sympatico.com site to satisfy your appetite (*http://www1.sympatico.ca/Contents/Sports/*). This list of links, compiled by a group of very dedicated fellows north of the U.S. border, includes every sport popular in the western hemisphere, with a bit of emphasis on the *north*western part: synchronized swimming, rugby, fishing, softball, gymnastics, curling, inline skating, martial arts, and mushing. In case you are unfamiliar with mushing, think of what Eskimos yell at their dogs for more power. Mushing is dogsled racing.

The sympatico.com site offers hundreds of links to major sports sites as well as the more obscure ones. Figure 30-3 shows a slice of the offerings.

TIP

Sports chats and discussions are all over the Web, and you'll find them on the major league Web sites as well.

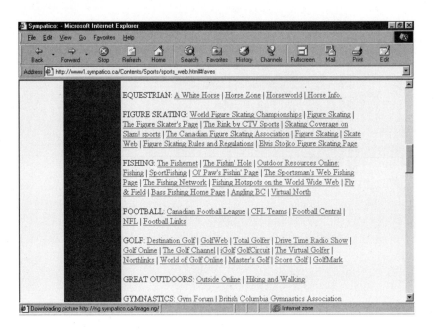

Figure 30-3
You can't get a much more diverse set of links than this!

Less Action and More Talk

At some point, you might tire of nonstop action and look toward comparing notes with others to get some tips on your game or to chat about your favorite sport or player. If you're looking for an online haunt that has the feel of an intimate sports bar, check into the MSN Sports & Recreation Communities (scroll down for the list) at *http://communities.msn.com/home/community.asp*. An example of one of the postings is shown in Figure 30-4.

Getting a Souvenir Without Fighting the Crowds

Need a new sun hat? How about a big sweatshirt with your favorite team's name on it? All the major league sports sites include online

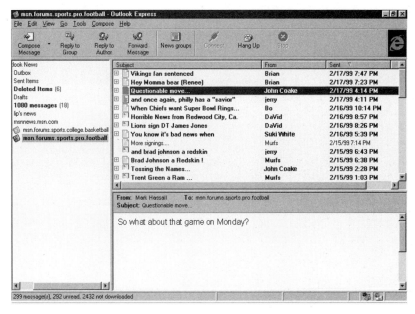

Figure 30-4
MSN Sports & Recreations Community

WARNING

Don't visit the online stores with a grandkid in the room unless you're willing to spend some big bucks. The NBA store, for example, has a portable basketball system that sells for $600, not including shipping.

gift shops; you don't need to fight stadium traffic or stand in those huge lines to get a souvenir. Figure 30-5 shows the NBA's store.

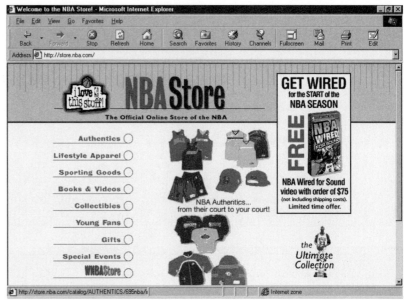

Figure 30-5
Want a souvenir? Make your life easier; get it through the Web

Customizing Your PC Desktop Theme

Turning on the computer and going through a daily PC routine can get pretty boring, at least visually. You turn on your computer, and you always have the same screen saver or the same background or the same icons or the same color scheme. You can give your PC screen and contents a new flair. Whatever you choose to do is reversible at any time, so if you don't like how your changes turn out, you can go back to the original settings or try something else.

What You'll Need

- Microsoft Windows 98
- The spirit to try a new computer "look"
- A flair for the dramatic

Quick Recipe for a PC Makeover

1. Open the Start menu.
2. Select Settings.
3. Select Control Panel.
4. Select Desktop Themes.
5. Pick a theme.
6. Show your friends what a gifted designer you are!

Giving Your Desktop a Facelift

We all have our routines, and some of them, like rituals, are comfortable and help to keep us centered. Others get boring and leave us uninspired. We yearn for something to spice up those dreary parts of our routine, to add a little oomph to an otherwise humdrum state. Your PC makeover comes in the guise of a desktop theme. A "desktop theme" is the PC equivalent of a theme party: the dance hall is made to look like a certain era, and everyone dresses to complement the theme. The Windows desktop theme option allows you to select a motif for your computer, and everything changes to fit the motif, including sounds, color scheme, and icons.

Here's what you do to change your desktop theme:

1. Open the Start menu, and select the Settings option.

2. Open the Control Panel, and double-click Desktop Themes. The Desktop Themes window appears (see Figure 31-1 on the following page).

3. Click the list box next to Theme to open the Themes list box. A scrollable list of desktop themes appears (see Figure 31-2 on the following page).

4. Click one of the themes and a preview of it (and the associated menu bars) appears in the preview window (see Figure 31-3 on page 329).

Previewing Your New Theme

Desktop themes give you more than a designer desktop; they also provide you with aural ambiance: a complementary set of sounds and mouse pointers. Before you select a desktop theme, it's a good

The Windows desktop theme option allows you to select a motif for your computer, and everything changes to fit the motif.

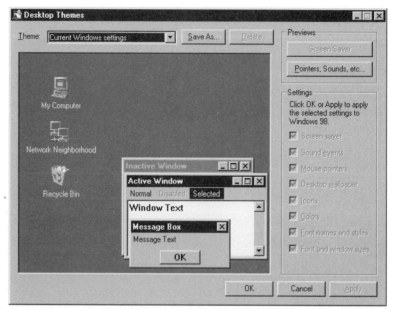

Figure 31-1
You can select a motif for your computer under Desktop Themes

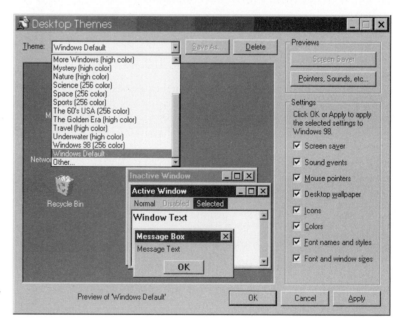

Figure 31-2
You can find a variety of themes here

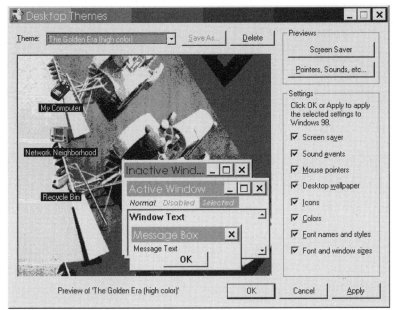

Figure 31-3
Here's a preview of the theme selected in Windows 98

policy to preview the screen saver, pointers, and sounds first. To do so, open the Desktop Themes window and display a preview.

To preview the theme's screen saver, click the Screen Saver button in the Previews area. The screen saver will appear until you move your mouse or press a key, so when the screen saver preview appears, don't touch anything for a few moments so that you can see what the screen saver really looks like. Figure 31-4 shows the screen saver with "The Golden Era" desktop theme.

To preview sounds and pointers, click the Pointers, Sounds, Etc. preview button. The Preview window appears, as shown in Figure 31-5.

To preview any of the elements, click the appropriate tab, and the list of items or icons appears. Click an item in the list, and you can hear the item or see the associated icon.

Chapter Thirty-One Customizing Your PC Desktop Theme

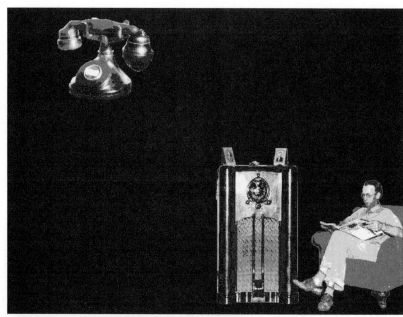

Figure 31-4
Windows 98 Desktop Themes gives you access to an additional list of cool screen savers

Figure 31-5
The Preview button allows you to see and hear what your new theme has to offer

After you find a theme that you like, click to select it and then click the OK button. The installation of your desktop theme takes several moments, but you'll be pleased with the results. Figures 31-6 and 31-7 show examples of themes you can choose.

Figure 31-6
The Jungle desktop, replete with a font that appears to be carved out of bamboo and a Venus flytrap instead of a recycling bin

Each of the themes gives your PC a complete facelift; the system beep and other sounds are replaced, as is the color scheme of the windows so as to match that of the background image. Even the fonts are changed to complement the theme.

TIP

If you want to spice things up with different screen savers and a cornucopia of fonts, you'll find thousands of both—free—online.

Figure 31-7
*Windows 98 lets
you customize with
precision*

Chapter Thirty-Two

Community Outreach with E-Mail

Being community minded can be hard work. Whether your goal is to protest and prevent something from happening or to gather the forces to build something and make it happen, you have to work hard to convince others to jump on the bandwagon. The Internet can't make people get involved, but it can certainly help to get people organized and assist in the arduous task of spreading the word.

What You'll Need

- A modem
- Microsoft Internet Explorer
- Microsoft Outlook
- Community spirit
- A list of like-minded friends and neighbors
- Completion of Chapter 18

Recipe for a Quiet Revolution

1. Learn from the successes and failures of other grass roots movements.
2. Collect a list of community members whom you want to organize.
3. Enter their e-mail addresses into your Microsoft Outlook address book.
4. Establish an e-mail campaign that keeps participants informed of the issue.
5. Create an online petition, and distribute it to community members.
6. Campaign for your cause.

Starting a Grass Roots Movement

Invariably, a grass roots movement derives its momentum from public support and participation, whether it be for a referendum, a PTA initiative, or a neighborhood program.

For people who are less experienced in the ways of organizing a grass roots campaign, the Internet can be a powerful teacher, allowing people in one community to learn from the successes and failures in distant communities.

Learning from Others

If you want to ensure the success of your grass roots movement, take a look at the @grass-roots.org Web site *(http://www.grass-roots.org/)*, shown in Figure 32-1.

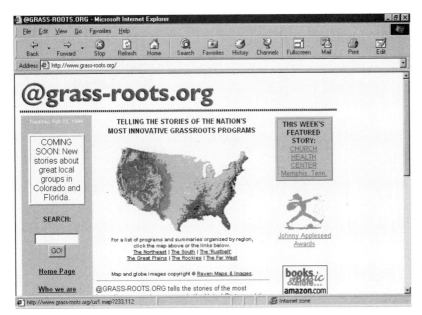

Figure 32-1
@grass-roots.org offers hundreds of homegrown success stories that both inspire and illuminate

The site offers more than 200 grass roots success stories along with contact information and histories. To find other grass roots movements, go to *http://search.msn.com* and type in the words "grass roots." Figure 32-2 shows a partial list of results you might find.

Increasing Support Through E-Mail

Whatever your cause, you need to coordinate with your neighbors and share news and information. Here's a fairly common community scenario (that we just experienced ourselves): a neighborhood development proposal before the city council jeopardizes the quality of life and in turn the property values in your city. The city council meetings are rancorous, and it is difficult for you and your neighbors to organize.

Whatever your cause, you need to coordinate with your neighbors and share news and information.

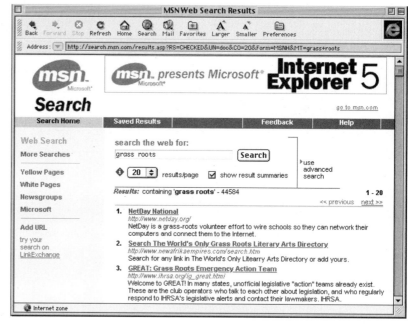

Figure 32-2
Search results for "grass roots" using MSN Search

Here's the Internet way:

1. Attend a meeting at which you know a number of citizens concerned with your issue will be present.

2. Pass a sign-up sheet requesting names and, most important, e-mail addresses.

3. Take the e-mail sheet home, and enter the addresses into your Microsoft Outlook address book. Make a personal distribution list containing the names from your sign-up sheet.

4. Send an e-mail to the group asking members for feedback and whether they want to remain on your mailing list.

5. Continue to send e-mail messages on a regular basis, either to pass along new information or to gather more information. You can also use e-mail to strategize.

6. Be on the lookout for names and addresses to add to your list. Enlist the help of those on the list to assist you in increasing the size of your ranks.

Petitioning Without Ever Leaving Your Home

No matter what their cause, you have to give those door-to-door volunteers credit for braving the elements to garner support from unknown and occasionally unpredictable or angry neighbors.

E-mail provides a much easier way to solicit support. Write a statement of protest or a letter of concern in an e-mail. Send your e-mail to 10 like-minded friends. The petition should instruct them to send an e-mail note of support to a particular destination and to forward copies of the original message on to three or more of their friends who might be interested in what the original message has to say. Figure 32-3 is a fictional example of one such e-mail.

E*-mail provides a much easier way to solicit support.*

TIP

The Internet is ideally suited for helping cultivate a grass roots movement or any community-oriented endeavor. If you are part of a church group, Kiwanis Club, credit union, or other community group, they can all benefit by organizing and communicating via the Internet and e-mail.

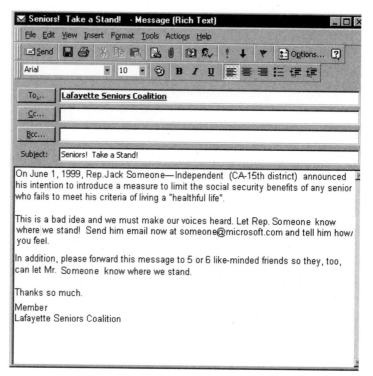

Figure 32-3
One e-mail snowball can cause an avalanche of e-mail in support of your cause

Sustaining the Campaign

Your campaign may be an overwhelming success, or it may be overwhelmed by an even larger opposing campaign. Whether you succeed or not, however, don't abandon the group you have assembled. If the issue that brought you together still exists, keeping your group alive will better guarantee you a long reach the next time the issue—or a variation of it—rears again.

Chapter Thirty-Three

Creating a Web Site

Web page creation can seem mysterious and intimidating, at least before you jump in. This recipe walks you through the steps of creating your own Web page to remove the shroud of mystery. When you finish here, we hope that you won't be intimidated by the page-building process, although you might wish that you had started the process earlier!

What You'll Need

- A modem
- A browser—Microsoft Internet Explorer 4.0 or higher, for example
- Microsoft Publisher
- A personal story and a couple of favorite URLs

Recipe for Cooking Up a Personal Web Site

1. Open Microsoft Publisher.
2. Select a Web Wizard.
3. Follow all the steps to completion.
4. Personalize your Web pages in Publisher.
5. Preview your pages in Internet Explorer.
6. Contact your service provider for Web hosting details.

Making a Web Site You Can Call Your Own

Creating a Web site is a lot like swimming at the local pool on a cold, dreary day: the worst part is getting in! After you're in, though, it starts to feel pretty good.

Using the Web Wizard

To start your Web page(s), follow these steps:

1. Open Microsoft Publisher from the Start menu.

2. Click the Web Sites option in the Wizards window (see Figure 33-1).

NOTE

There are many ways to create Web sites and Web pages. Microsoft Publisher is just an example of one way to go.

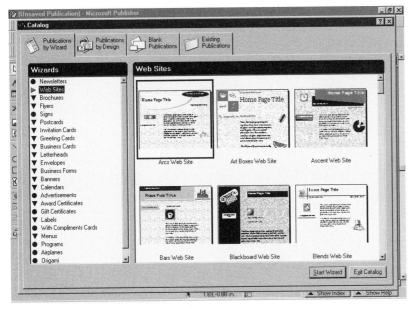

Figure 33-1
Microsoft Publisher offers different options to help you build your site

3. Select the Art Boxes Web Site by double-clicking it.

4. Click the Next button in the Wizards window, select a color scheme, and click Next again.

5. Click Story and Related Links to add additional pages. Click Next (see Figure 33-2).

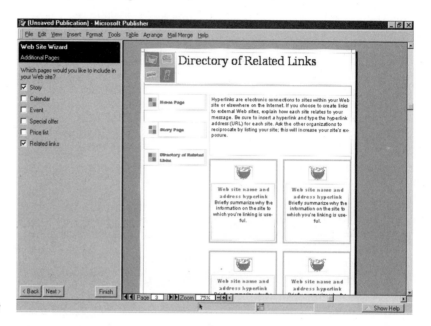

Figure 33-2
Choose the additional pages to add to your site

6. Continue to click Next until the Personal Information Screen appears. Click the Home/Family button and then click Finish.

Congratulations! You have just created a collection of Web pages!

Personalizing Your New Web Site

Now that you've created your pages, you need to make them distinctly yours. Before you do, make the Publisher display easier to read. Open the View menu and click Hide Wizard. When the wizard vanishes, click the + Zoom button at the bottom of the Edit window, and increase your view to 100% of scale.

Now you're ready to personalize:

1. Click the banner that says "Home Page Title," and type your own title to replace it.

2. Click the body text below the banner (it begins with "Your home page gives..."), and replace it with an explanation of what your Web site is all about (don't worry, you can change it later!). See Figure 33-3.

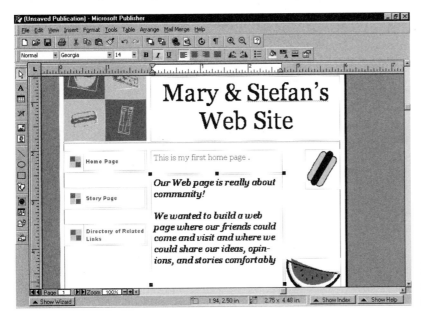

Figure 33-3
Publisher makes it easy to customize your site

3. Click the Forward page arrow at the bottom of the screen to move to Web Page 2. Enter an interesting story here at your leisure. Click the page arrow key again to go to Page 3.

4. Click each Web site name and address, and replace the existing text with a favorite URL.

5. Right-click the mouse, click Add, and then right-click again and select Hyperlink. Specify the URL in the designated field.

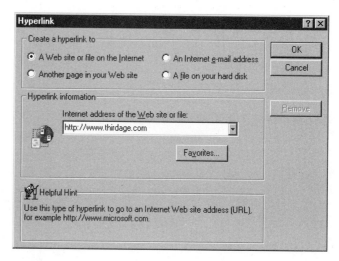

6. Add an explanation of the site replacing the text below the URL.

7. Open the File menu, click Save, name your file, and click OK.

8. Open the File menu again, and this time click Save As HTML.

9. Congratulations! You have your first Web site designed and ready to go.

Viewing Your Masterpiece

To see what your Web pages look like, follow these instructions:

1. Open Internet Explorer.

2. Open the File menu and click Open.

3. Click the Browse button, and navigate to your page file (it should be in the Publish Folder in My Documents).

4. Click the file called Index, and your Web site appears in Internet Explorer. See Figure 33-4.

Figure 33-4
Here's the completed Web page

Getting Your Pages on the Web

Now that you've created the Web pages for your site, you need to get them on the Web. For that, you need to follow the procedure outlined by your Internet service provider. When you follow the service provider's instructions, you will receive a URL for your site, and your Web pages will be accessible by netizens around the world. For more information, see Chapter 13 for how to get connected to the Internet.

☙ Chapter Thirty-Four ❧

Downloading Programs from the Internet

We all grew up knowing that nothing's free. Well, almost nothing. In the world of software and the Internet, some things *are* pretty close to free, or as close an approximation as you'll ever hope to find. This recipe shows you how to find the free or cheap stuff on the World Wide Web and download it for use on your own PC.

What You'll Need

- A modem
- A browser—Microsoft Internet Explorer 4.0 or higher, for example
- A desire for free—and super cheap—software

Recipe for Cheap and Free Software

1. Open your browser.
2. Go to the MSN free download area.
3. Download software: demos, freeware, and shareware.
4. Download WinZip.
5. Install the software.
6. Test-drive the programs.
7. Take a friend out to lunch with the money you've saved!

No Free Lunch?
How About Free Software?

There are a number of programmers out there who see a problem, apply their creativity and ingenuity, and come up with a solution. Or they write a fun computer game just for the fun of writing it. Those same folks decide to make their programs available to others for free, hence the term "freeware."

Other programmers write programs that they want to market independently. These people make their programs available on the Internet with a simple request: if you like the program and want to keep it, send a nominal fee. These programs, called "shareware," are sometimes so good that everybody adopts them.

Free demonstration software is also used as a lure to entice you to buy the full-blown product. The software company gives away a scaled-down version of a program with the hope that you'll like it so much—and need the more advanced features —that you'll pay for the complete product.

Free? Where Do I Sign?

We confess: this recipe is intended to teach you about downloading, but we know the power of the word "free" and how it can grab your attention. We also know that before you can get free software via the Internet, you need to understand downloading. So, when you learn how to download, you'll be able to get free software!

What's Downloading?

Downloading is the act of getting a computer file or files from one computer to your computer via your modem. When you download,

When you learn how to download, you'll be able to get free software.

Downloading is the act of getting a computer file or files from one computer to your computer via your modem.

you are bringing something from one location to your own computer. What could that file be? Anything: a picture, a story, or a video clip. It could also be a software program. You might find many pictures and programs on the Internet that you might like to have on your computer. In fact, you might want to upgrade a program you already have on your PC, and in many instances, you can do this with a simple download.

So, without further ado, go ahead and download a program.

Finding the Freebies

Before you can download some software goodies, you need to find where they are stashed on the Internet. Follow these steps to find one place:

1. Using Internet Explorer, go to the MSN site (*http://www.msn.com*).

2. Click Downloads near the top of the page. The Downloads page appears. See Figure 34-1.

3. Besides the MSN archives that we explore momentarily, the bottom of this page lists links to archives and libraries on other sites. See Figure 34-2.

4. Click the Computer Games Option, and a list of game categories appears. Click the Demos & Games folder, and the real software buffet appears. See Figure 34-3 on page 346.

5. The number after the filename is the size in bytes or Kilobytes of the file. For now, click 3 space (it's small) to download it. The Description screen appears. This page includes when the game was uploaded, what the requirements for the

TIP

There are many places to find free software on the Internet.

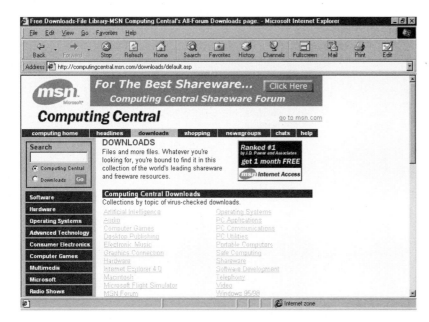

Figure 34-1
The Downloads page can help you find a lot of neat programs

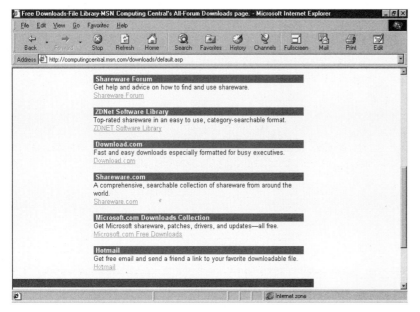

Figure 34-2
Links to archives and libraries on other sites

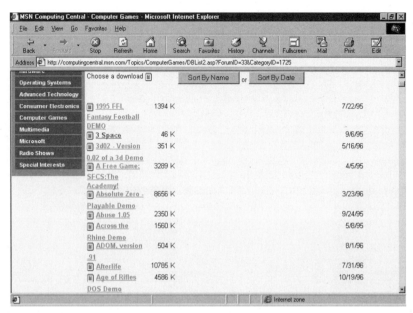

Figure 34-3
Get ready to download

game are, and what kind of computer and version of Windows are needed.

6. Click the Download Now button, and the File Download window appears. See Figure 34-4.

7. Save the file to disk, and click OK. The Save File window appears. Be sure to save the file on your desktop. When you click OK, the file is downloaded and appears on your desktop.

Congratulations! You've just downloaded your first game.

The Zen of Downloading

Downloading files usually requires a bit of patience. After you find the program you want to download, you need to wait while the file transfers, relying on your PC's and modem's speed to get the job

TIP

Download software after you are finished using your computer so that the download doesn't interfere with your computing activities.

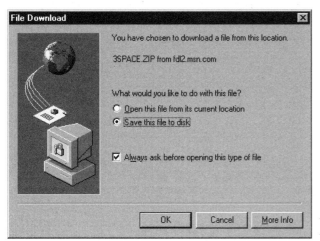

Figure 34-4
*Here's a sample File
Download window*

done. If you download software often, you'll get a feel for just how fast or slow your PC really is. Downloads will also teach you just how *big* a big file is.

PC and modem speed is of the essence. If you have a **14.4** modem, it will take twice as long to download a file as it would with a 28.8 Kbps modem. And a 28.8 Kbps modem will take twice as long as a 56 Kbps modem. Translated, a 10-minute download with a 56 Kbps modem will take 20 minutes on a 28.8 and 40 minutes on a **14.4** modem.

Unzipping Your Software

Programs are big. The bigger the program, the longer it takes to download, and the longer the download, the higher the probability that something will go wrong. To accelerate the download process and avoid problems, programmers found a way to shrink a program for the file transfer process and then unshrink it after it arrives on your PC. The unshrinking (or reconstituting) process

WARNING

If your PC doesn't meet a program's requirements as specified in the program description, don't bother to download the program; it won't work. If you have a PC and you download a Mac program, for example, it won't work. If you have only 3 megabytes of hard disk space left on your computer and the program is 5 megabytes, the download will stop in midstream, and you'll just receive a message that says the download failed.

requires a program called WinZip that is also available online. The next sections tells how and where to get it.

Downloading WinZip

To get WinZip, go to *http://www.winzip.com*. Click the Download Evaluation Version link. The program that you download is a shareware program for evaluation; if you use it for a while and decide to keep it, you are expected to pay for it.

Now you have what it takes to use the programs you download. You'll then be able to open your new game.

Opening Your Downloaded Program

Return to your downloaded program (in our example, 3space), and double-click the icon. The 3space file opens as a WinZip "archive," which is a collection of compressed files (see Figure 34-5).

1. Click the Extract button, and the Extract window appears, as in Figure 34-6. Click the desktop entry to unzip the file on the desktop.

2. Click the new folder button, and create a new folder called "3 space."

3. When the Extract window reappears, click the Extract button.

4. Close all your windows, return to your desktop, and look for your 3 space folder. The game will be inside.

TIP

You can find WinZip at http://www.winzip.com.

TIP

Now that you know how to download and you have WinZip, browse through some of the different download categories available on the MSN site, and try downloading those that seem most interesting.

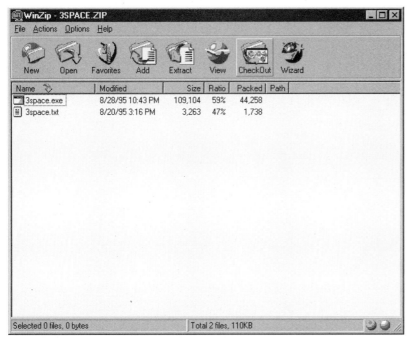

Figure 34-5
*Your WinZip files need
to be reconstituted*

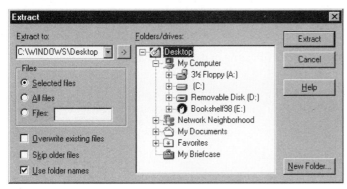

Figure 34-6
*The Extract window
allows you to specify
different options for
the new files*

Chapter Thirty-Five

Gardening on the Web

There's nothing like gardening to nourish the soul. It replenishes the spirit when you can see both renewal and beauty come from your hard work. On the Internet, not only can you learn about gardening, you can commune with others all over the world: share problems, provide answers, and enjoy the company and support of like-minded, international friends.

What You'll Need

- A modem
- A browser—Microsoft Internet Explorer 4.0 or higher for example
- A green thumb

Recipe for a Non-Garden-Variety Garden

1. Open your browser.
2. Tour the World's Botanical Gardens via the Web.
3. Talk with others online about gardening issues and ideas.
4. Plant, prune, enjoy!

The Garden of E-Den

What would you do if you had the fertile crescent as your botanical canvas? Visit the Seven Wonders of the Ancient World Web Site (*http://pharos.bu.edu/Egypt/Wonders/gardens.html*), shown in Figure 35-1, to see what the Babylonians did.

Figure 35-1
The Babylonians had the right gardening stuff

Included with the Colossus of Rhodes and the Great Pyramids as one of the seven wonders of the Ancient World, the Hanging Gardens of Babylon were a masterpiece—if they really existed! When you visit the site, find out what is really known about this legendary garden.

Around the World of Botany

If it's just too miserable outside to garden, or if you're sore from yesterday's weedfest, try doing a Web search on "Botanical Garden." Your listing will have you hopping the continents, from Asia to Europe, Africa to Australia. Figure 35-2 shows you this chapter's first stop at Kew Gardens (*http://www.rbgkew.org.uk/*).

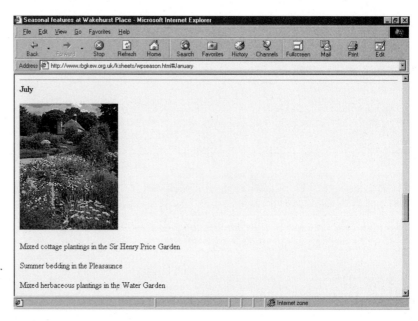

Figure 35-2
You can learn a lot from our horticultural heroes in the United Kingdom

We stop in Hawaii, too, at the Hawaii Tropical Botanical Garden (*http://htbg.com/*), as shown in Figure 35-3. After this, you can choose the rest of the stops.

Tilling the Web

For a good one-stop index of great gardening resources, visit the Botanique site (*http://www.botanique.com*) and select the Links option. As shown in Figure 35-4, the site provides links to a wide range

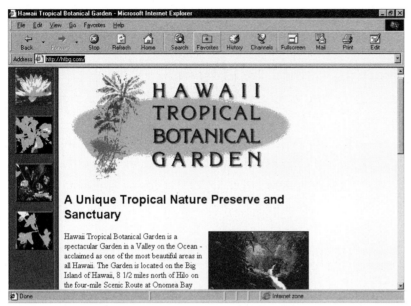

Figure 35-3
Who could resist a Web visit to the Hawaii Tropical Botanical Garden?

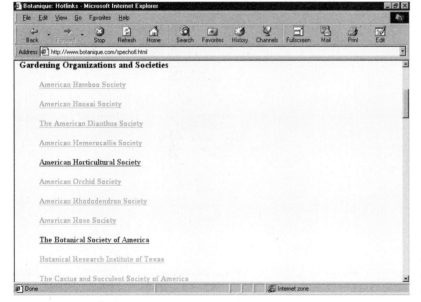

Figure 35-4
Link to one of the many botanical societies listed at the Botanique site

of societies, including the American Horticultural Society, the American Bamboo Society, and the American Bonsai Society.

From Gardener to Gardener

For help or a second opinion, *http://www.gardenweb.com*, shown in Figure 35-5, is a great site. GardenWeb has the *most* extensive collection of discussion topics we've seen, and it's highly active. The site even includes forums in Spanish, French, and Portuguese.

We went to the GardenWeb California forum and found a query on what to grow under a magnolia tree. Suggestions and answers came within 24 hours.

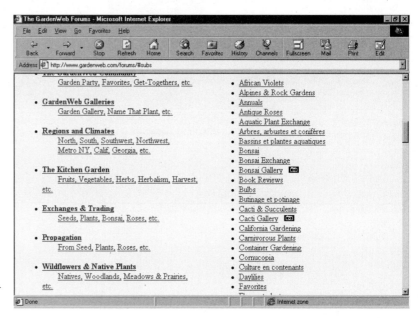

Figure 35-5
A garden of gardeners— and thriving

≈ Chapter Thirty-Six ≈

Navigating into Newsgroups

The Internet lets you subscribe to newsgroups—online discussions—so that you don't have to go surfing every which way to participate in those discussions that get your juices flowing. Subscribing to a newsgroup lets you leisurely breeze through numerous posts with ease.

What You'll Need

- A modem
- A browser—Internet Explorer 4.0 or higher, for example
- Microsoft Outlook Express
- Free reading time

Recipe for Newsgroup Home Delivery

1. Open your browser.
2. Call up Microsoft Outlook Express.
3. Subscribe to several different newsgroups.
4. Sign up for a couple of mailing lists to be delivered to your e-mail account.

Free Subscriptions Delivered to Your PC!

No, you don't have to worry about Ed McMahon coming to your house and pestering you about magazine subscriptions, and no, he won't show up as a screen saver, either.

Considering that the Internet has tens of thousands of newsgroups, it's nice to know you can pick and choose what you want delivered. It's also nice to know that there are numerous mailing lists that you can subscribe to so that daily postings can be delivered to you via e-mail.

Deciphering Newsgroup Titles

Like Internet addresses, newsgroups also have naming conventions to make it easier to identify their theme. Here are some of the most common naming conventions.

Common Newsgroup Labels

Label	Meaning
alt	Alternate (misc)
comp	Computer
humanities	Humanities
k12	Kindergarten through high school
misc	Miscellaneous
msn	Microsoft
rec	Recreation, hobbies, art
sci	Science
soc	Sociology

There are now hundreds of different category labels for newsgroups under which posts fall.

Although these are a few of the most common, there are now hundreds of different category labels for newsgroups under which posts fall. They are, in most cases, a good shorthand for the newsgroup's content. For example, msn.forums.sports.pro.football is a forum on pro football on MSN.

Try subscribing to a few newsgroups. To begin, you need to open Internet Explorer and Microsoft Outlook Newsreader (Express). Here's what to do:

1. Open Internet Explorer and get online.
2. Open the Go menu and select News. The Outlook Express window appears, as shown in Figure 36-1.

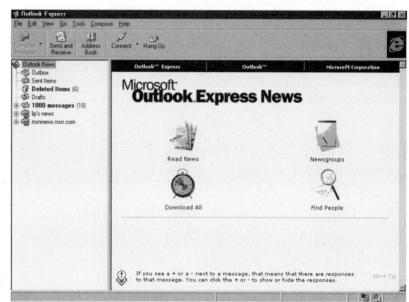

Figure 36-1
The Outlook Express News window

3. Click the Newsgroups icon in the big window, and the Newsgroups Window appears. If the window is blank, click

the All tab. If it's still blank, click the Reset button. You may need to wait while your list of thousands of newsgroups loads (see Figure 36-2).

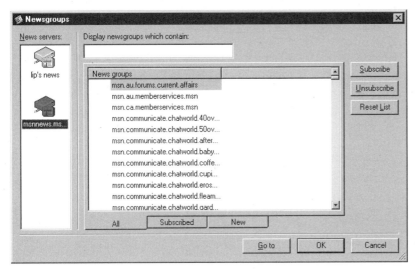

Figure 36-2
A list of the current newsgroups

4. Scroll through the list to get a sense of what is available to you. The list is alphabetized, so be sure to browse at least past the *A*s!

5. Click a newsgroup name that catches your eye, and click the Go To button. The newsgroup appears with the name of the newsgroup in the left window and the newsgroup messages listed in the Information list, and when you click a message, the first lines of it appear in the Preview window, as shown in Figure 36-3.

Deciding Whether You Want to Subscribe

Do a little exploring here, and see whether you like the newsgroup. If you decide you want to have easy access to it, and you want to

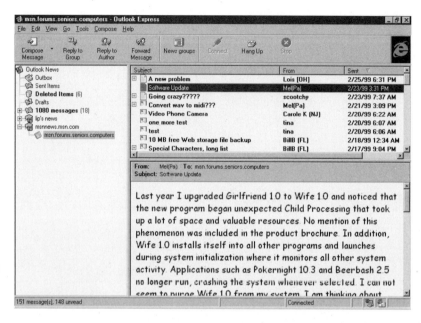

Figure 36-3
You can get a quick look at the first few lines of a message

subscribe, right-click the newsgroup name in the left window, and select Subscribe to this Newsgroup, as shown in Figure 36-4.

Canceling Your Subscription

One advantage of newsgroups is that your participation and subscription is up to you. If you decide that you no longer want to subscribe, cancel your subscription!

1. Right-click the name of the newsgroup as it appears in the Folder list.

2. Click Unsubscribe. That's it. Subscription canceled.

If you decide that you no longer want to subscribe, cancel your subscription!

Getting More Subscriptions

If you want to subscribe to more newsgroups, click the Newsgroups button in the toolbar, and the list of newsgroups reappears.

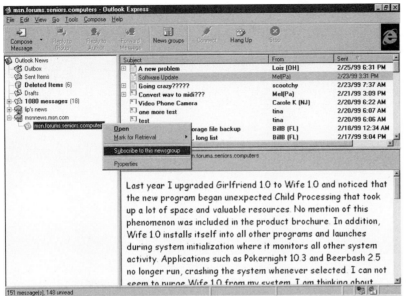

Figure 36-4
You can get all the news from your newsgroups of choice by subscribing to them

You can select a newsgroup and preview it as you just did, or you can double-click it here to automatically subscribe to it. Each newsgroup that you subscribe to appears with a subscription marker in the left margin. Figure 36-5 shows a group of newsgroups that are subscribed to.

Finding Mailing Lists You Want to Be On

Besides newsgroups, you may want to be put on a mailing list so that you receive messages from groups via e-mail. Here's a super place to sign up:

1. From Internet Explorer, go to *http://www.liszt.com*. See Figure 36-6.

2. Scroll down and select a topic of interest. For starters, click the main heading, "Health." Another list of options appears.

WARNING

If you click messages in the Information List, and nothing appears in the Preview window, it means you have lost your connection. To reconnect, click the Connect button in the toolbar to re-establish your connection.

Figure 36-5
You can spend a great deal of time just reading the posts in the newsgroups you subscribe to

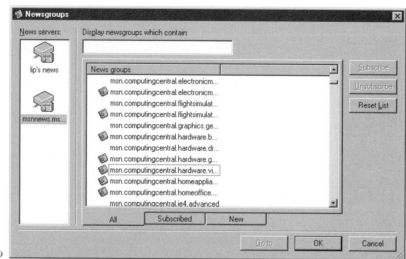

Figure 36-6
An example of a mailing list directory

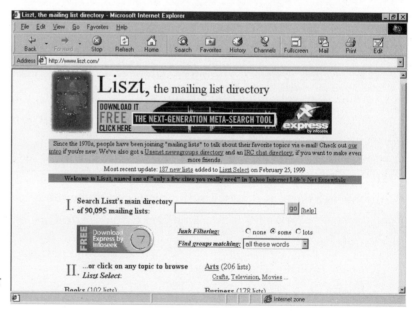

Here we click Arthritis and that offers three different mailing lists. See Figure 36-7 below.

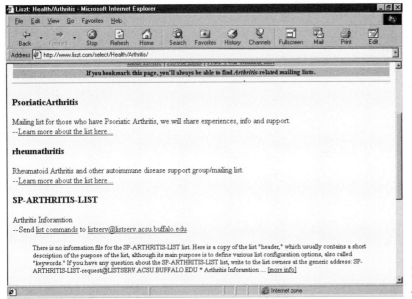

TIP

Each mailing list is slightly different; to subscribe to some, you send an e-mail to the designated address containing just the word "subscribe." Other lists might also require a single word, but it might be subject related. Click "list commands" for the mailing list of interest to get the correct procedure.

Figure 36-7
Mailing lists for "Arthritis"

3. Click "learn more about the list" or "list commands" to learn more about the particular list and to obtain instructions on how to subscribe.

Index

Y

Z

About the Authors

Mary Furlong

Mary Furlong, Ed.D a leading authority on aging and technology, is the C.E.O. and founder of Third Age Media—a full-ranged media company geared toward the more than 70 million aging baby boomers. In her capacity as the vision behind Third Age, Furlong spearheaded the creation of one of the premiere virtual communities on the web.

Recognized as one of the leading expert on aging and technology, Furlong holds a presidential appointment to the National Commission on Libraries and Information Sciences and provides counsel to the U.S. House of Representatives Select Committee on Aging. In 1996, New Choices magazine awarded Furlong, along with Jimmy Carter and Lena Horne, the coveted "New Choices Award" for her commitment to the aging community. Most recently, Upside magazine named Furlong one of its "Elite 100" and Interactive Age deemed her one of the "Twenty-Five Unsung Heroes on the Web."

Also a respected author, Furlong writes a nationally-syndicated column "Web for Grown-Ups" and has published several books Furlong speaks regularly at national and international conferences on topics ranging from "Technology and Aging" to "Community Building in Cyberspace." In l986 she created SeniorNet—a national non-profit organization for older adults and technology.

She lives in Lafayette CA with her husband and two sons.

About the Authors

Stefan B. Lipson

Stefan B. Lipson has been active in the area of computer technology for seniors for several years. He consults for corporate clients on Web publishing and Web community development and has a degree in electrical engineering. He lives with his wife and two kids in Northern California.

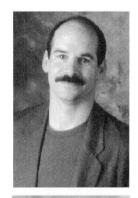

Craig D. Spiezle
Director, Microsoft Senior Initiative
Microsoft Corporation

Craig Spiezle is the director of the Microsoft Senior Initiative, a worldwide program committed to bridging the "digital and generational divides" by bringing communities together through the use of technology. As an advocate on policy issues and the needs of older adults, he focuses on engaging organizations, government agencies, employers and private enterprise, to better understand the needs of the aging populations and their families. As a result Microsoft has developed innovative programs with the US Administration on Aging, Department of Health and Human Services and organizations such as the American Association of Community Colleges, the United Nations, SeniorNet and Green Thumb. As an international speaker and author of several white papers and research studies, he regularly educates audiences about how technology can positively impact the lives of older adults and their families. Craig is also a member of the International Federation of Aging, National Council on Aging, and serves on the Governing Board of the American Society on Aging and the Advisory board of the Community Preservation Development Corporation. Married with two sons who now keep in touch with their grand-parents via email, Craig resides in a suburb of Seattle, Washington.

Colophon

The manuscript for this book was prepared and submitted to Microsoft Press in electronic form. Text files were prepared using Microsoft Word 6.0. Pages were composed using Adobe PageMaker 6.5, with text in Adobe BauerBodoni and Helvetica. Figures were set using Adobe Photoshop and MacroMedia Freehand 8.0. Composed pages were sent to the printer as electronic prepress files.

Cover Design and Illustration
Tom Draper Design

Interior Graphic Designers
Jimmie Young & Sally Slevin
ProImage

Layout Artist
Jimmie Young

Indexer
Sherry Massey

Manuscript Editor
Susan Christophersen

Editorial Assistant
Kristen Weatherby

Illustrator
Ben Long

Technical Editor
James McCarter

Proofreader
Chuck Hutchinson

Optimize
Microsoft Office 2000
with multimedia training!

MICROSOFT® OFFICE 2000 STEP BY STEP INTERACTIVE is a multimedia learning system (in both audio and text versions) that shows you, through 20 to 30 hours of simulated live-in-the application training, how to maximize the productivity potential of the Office 2000 programs: Microsoft Excel 2000, Word 2000, Access 2000, PowerPoint® 2000, Outlook® 2000, Publisher 2000, and Small Business Tools. If you already use Microsoft Office 97, this learning solution will help you make the transition to Office 2000 quickly and easily, and reach an even greater level of productivity.

U.S.A.	**$29.99**
U.K.	$27.99 [V.A.T. included]
Canada	$44.99
ISBN 0-7356-0506-8	

mspress.microsoft.com

See clearly—
now!

Here's the remarkable, *visual* way to quickly find answers about the powerfully integrated features of the Microsoft® Office 2000 applications. Microsoft Press AT A GLANCE books let you focus on particular tasks and show you, with clear, numbered steps, the easiest way to get them done right now. Put Office 2000 to work today with AT A GLANCE learning solutions, made by Microsoft.

- MICROSOFT OFFICE 2000 PROFESSIONAL AT A GLANCE
- MICROSOFT WORD 2000 AT A GLANCE
- MICROSOFT EXCEL 2000 AT A GLANCE
- MICROSOFT POWERPOINT® 2000 AT A GLANCE
- MICROSOFT ACCESS 2000 AT A GLANCE
- MICROSOFT FRONTPAGE® 2000 AT A GLANCE
- MICROSOFT PUBLISHER 2000 AT A GLANCE
- MICROSOFT OFFICE 2000 SMALL BUSINESS AT A GLANCE
- MICROSOFT PHOTODRAW™ 2000 AT A GLANCE
- MICROSOFT INTERNET EXPLORER 5 AT A GLANCE
- MICROSOFT OUTLOOK® 2000 AT A GLANCE

Microsoft®

mspress.microsoft.com

Register Today!

Return this
Grown-Up's Guide to Computing
registration card today

Microsoft®*Press*

mspress.microsoft.com

0-7356-0637-4

Grown-Up's Guide to Computing

_____   _____   _____

FIRST NAME   **MIDDLE INITIAL**   **LAST NAME**

_____

INSTITUTION OR COMPANY NAME

_____

ADDRESS

_____

_____   _____   _____

CITY   **STATE**   **ZIP**

                                                      (   ) _____

_____   **PHONE NUMBER**

E-MAIL ADDRESS

U.S. and Canada addresses only. Fill in information above and mail postage-free.
Please mail only the bottom half of this page.

For information about Microsoft Press®
products, visit our Web site at
mspress.microsoft.com

Microsoft®*Press*